The MICAH MANDATE

The MICAH MANDATE

Balancing the Christian Life

George Grant

Cumberland House
Nashville, Tennessee

A previous edition of this book was published by Moody Press, Chicago, Illinois.

Published by Cumberland House Publishing, Inc., 431 Harding Industrial Drive, Nashville, TN 37211-3160.

Scripture quotations are from THE NEW KING JAMES VERSION. Copyright © 1979, 1980, 1982, Thomas Nelson, Inc., Publishers, except for Micah 6:8, which is the author's own translation.

Cover design: Harriette Bateman
Interior design: Mary Sanford

Library of Congress Cataloging-in-Publication Data
Grant, George, 1954–
      The Micah mandate : balancing the Christian life / George
Grant.
        p.   cm.
    Originally published: Chicago, Ill. : Moody Press, c1995.
    Includes bibliographical references.
    ISBN 1-58182-055-0 (pbk. : alk. paper)
    1. Christian life. 2. Christian life—Biblical teaching. 3. Bible.
O.T. Micah VI, 8—Criticism, interpretation, etc. I. Title.
    BV4501.2 .G7254 1999
    248.4—dc21
                                                                99-30190
                                                                CIP

Printed in the United States of America
1 2 3 4 5 6 7—04 03 02 01 00 99

In Memoriam
William L. Lane

He has shown you, O man, what is good and what the Lord requires of you: to do justice, to love mercy, and to walk humbly with your God.

MICAH 6:8

Contents

Acknowledgments

The greatest part of a writer's time is spent in reading, in order to write: a man will turn over half a library to make one book.

SAMUEL JOHNSON

Those who are in rebellion against memory are the ones who wish to live without knowledge.

RICHARD WEAVER

"The only possible excuse for this book," G. K. Chesterton once wrote in a preface, "is that it is an answer to a challenge. Even a bad shot is dignified when he accepts a duel."[1]

Though written nearly a century ago, Chesterton's remark almost perfectly describes my justification for this project. It grew out of a challenge. That challenge came from many of my dearest and most trusted friends. Together they encouraged me to put into words and into print the thoughts and reflections that have shaped my tandem inner and outer walks over the past twenty years. I can only pray that this "bad shot" may indeed be "dignified" by rising to the occasion.

In his case, Chesterton quipped that such a challenge "was perhaps an incautious suggestion to make to a person only too ready to write books upon the feeblest provocation."[2]

Again, his description is all too apt in my case. Even so, it was only the support and encouragement of those stalwart friends that enabled me to actually *work out* what has taken so long to *work in*.

The first abridged edition of this project was realized through the efforts of Jim Bell at Moody Press when it was little more than a fuzzy notion and a sketchy outline. This unexpurgated edition has come into existence because of the constancy and commitment of Ron Pitkin at Cumberland House. To both, I am grateful.

In addition, my pastors, Scotty Smith, Clyde Godwin, Scott Roley, and Mike Smith, and my circle of confidants and mentors—Don Finto, D. James Kennedy, Stephen Mansfield, David Vaughan, Tom Clark, Lane Adams, Steve Wilkins, Doug Wilson, and Charles Wolfe—inspired me by their lives of balance and reinforced the notion that Biblical balance can indeed be lived out in very practical ways. Gene and Susan Hunt, as well as all the other intrepid members of the PCA Christian Education and Publications Study Tour, tolerated my preoccupation with this book while I was supposed to be showing them the sights. Much of the manuscript was initially outlined in snatches while we were together in Israel and Holland. That they still happily followed me hither and yon is no less evidence of their long-suffering than of God's grace. My former coworkers at Coral Ridge Ministries, the Christian Worldview Institute, Legacy Communications, and the King's Meadow Study Center stood by me through thick and thin—even when there was a lot less thick than thin. And my students at the Franklin Classical School and Bannockburn College patiently endured earlier incarnations of these ideas and helped to shape them into their present form.

Snippets of this material and earlier versions of these ideas made their way into innumerable sermons, lectures, and speeches—in local churches, at Crisis Pregnancy Center banquets, and in schools, colleges, and universities across the nation. My attentive audiences helped me reshape the work through both their constructive criticism and their willingness to let me think out loud.

The soundtrack for this project was provided by J. S. Bach, W. A. Mozart, and Johann Strauss with backup vocals by Steve Green, Susan Ashton, and Out of the Grey. Meanwhile the midnight musings were provided by Mel Bradford, Andrew Lytle, Colin Thubron, Ellis Peters, Tom Clancy, Hilaire Belloc, and P. D. James.

Phil and Sally Bartels gave me the run of their marvelous Victorian "castle" in New Hampshire during the final few days of intensive writing on the first draft. In addition, the good people of Tri-City Covenant Church and Auburn Avenue Presbyterian Church offered me every benefit of their gracious hospitality— among them I have found homes away from home. Meanwhile back at the ranch, Pete Volpitta helped to craft for me a home right at home.

To all these I offer my deepest and profoundest thanks.

As always though, it was my family—my wife, Karen, and our beloved children, Joel, Joanna, and Jesse—that most enabled me to write this very personal exploration of the balanced Christian life. With nary a complaint, they sacrificed many a weekend as I struggled to squeeze some writing into an already too-hectic schedule:

> I thank my God upon every remembrance of you, always in
> every prayer of mine making request for you all with joy, for
> your fellowship in the gospel from the first day until now,
> being confident of this very thing, that He who has begun a
> good work in you will complete it until the day of Jesus Christ.
> (Philippians 1:3–6)

In the end, that is perhaps the only justification that matters for any work, on any subject, in any discipline.

Eastertide 1999
King's Meadow

Introduction: A Fractured World

In political as well as natural disorders, the great error of those who commonly undertake either cure or preservation, is, that they rest in second causes, without extending their search to the remote and original sources of evil.

SAMUEL JOHNSON

The sin of egotism always takes the form of withdrawal. When personal advantage becomes paramount, the individual passes out of the community.

RICHARD WEAVER

By almost any standard, it appears that our culture is now coming apart at the seams. Despite all our prosperity, pomp, and power, the vaunted American experiment in liberty seems to be disintegrating before our very eyes.

According to historian Hilaire Belloc: "It is often so with institutions already undermined: they are at their most splendid external phase when they are ripe for downfall."[1]

How true. According to *The Index of Leading Cultural Indicators*, amid all our comfort and affluence we have become a nation of mayhem and woe.[2] Crime is up. Educational standards are down. Families are crumbling. Basic virtues are disappearing. Government is less reliable. Scandal is more common. Our communities are sundered by antagonistic interests and competing factions. We are divided racially. We are divided economically. We are divided politically. We are divided culturally.[3]

And things are getting worse with every passing day.

We are witnessing what Arthur Schlessinger calls the "disuniting of America."[4] Or worse, we are in the midst of what Daniel Patrick Moynihan pointedly calls "social and geo-political pandaemonium."[5]

Pundits and prognosticators, critics and commentators, gadflies and curmudgeons, prophets and seers alike agree.

According to George Will we are suffering from "a kind of slow-motion barbarization."[6] Aleksandr Solzhenitsyn says our "spiritual axis of life has grown dim."[7] Os Guinness states that we have already entered the "time of reckoning."[8] Zbigniew Brzezinski says we are simply "out of control."[9] And Paul Johnson asserts we are ensnared by "a moral and ethical folly" that we appear to be "helpless to correct."[10]

As Chuck Colson has noted, "The times seem to smell of sunset."[11]

Despite our obvious distress at such disconcerting notions, the fact that we live in a fractured culture actually comes as no great surprise to most of us. Ours is a fallen world after all.

Instead, what often surprises us—or at least what most often grieves us—is the fact that we live in a fractured church as well. The disuniting of America would not be so frightening if it were not accompanied by a disuniting of the faith.

But it is.

We are more divided today than at any time since the Reformation. We are divided over what is right and what is wrong.[12] We are divided over what is good and what is bad.[13] We are divided over what we should do and what we should not do.[14] And as a result, "absolute confusion" is now our most apt epithet according to demographer George Barna.[15]

Certainly we have always had our squabbles. Substantial theological differences have "enlivened" relations between Christians since the earliest days. But more often than not, our contemporary divisions have little or nothing to do with dogmatic formulations or creedal disputations—as has always been the case before. The fact is, we hardly know enough doctrine to fight over it—as David

Wells has asserted, the modern church has "cheerfully plunged into astounding theological illiteracy."[16]

Instead our divisions tend to be much less substantial—usually along experiential, methodological, or pragmatic lines.[17] We fight over styles and approaches. We part company over techniques and appearances. We are far less concerned with axiomatic first principles than we are with generic public poses. We are far less concerned with what we say or do than with *how* we say or do it.

Perhaps the most glaring example of this is the stark division between activism and piety in the modern church—the dichotomy between pro-lifers on the one hand and prayer warriors on the other, between those involved in politics and culture and those involved in church growth and evangelism, between those concerned about the issues of our time and those concerned about the matters of eternity. Nearly every church in America has felt the tension of this breach.

The real trouble with the dichotomy though, is that it is a false dichotomy.

Activism without deep spiritual resources inevitably draws from shallow wells that soon run dry—it cannot long be sustained. Thus it ceases to be active.

Similarly, piety without a forthright cultural agenda inevitably capitulates to the prevailing pressures of the world—it cannot exist in a vacuum. Thus it ceases to be pious.

We cannot be authentically Christian but so heavenly minded that we're no earthly good any more than we can be so earthly minded that we're no heavenly good. The only possibility for us is to be so heavenly minded that we do the earth good. And that demands a substantive lifestyle balance where both faith and work are operative, where both holiness and service motivate, where both Word and deed dominate, where the Gospel is proclaimed both in doctrine and in life.

Nevertheless, in this day of magpie logic and bumptious rhetoric, aggravatingly false dichotomies continue to fracture the faith. Thus the battle lines in the spiritual and cultural wars of our time remain unclear and the trumpets sound uncertainly.

In the midst of such circumstances, the incomparable Francis Schaeffer once asked, "How should we then live?"[18]

This book is an attempt at a partial answer. It is a Biblical and historical reflection on how the supposed tensions between activism and piety can and should ultimately be resolved in our lives, in our vocations, and in our callings. It is an exploration of how to bring authentic balance to the Christian life.

Growing out of an understanding of the covenant lawsuit sequence in the prophecy of Micah, the book revolves around a kind of shorthand triad of mandates found there: justice, mercy, and humility. The first two chapters introduce these mandates, then the succeeding chapters take up each of them in turn—in two chapters apiece. Thus, Chapter One focuses on the "Micah Mandate" itself. Chapter Two deals with the thorny problem of worldliness and how our faith fits in the context of the earth. Chapter Three examines the concept of justice through the twin lenses of law and grace while Chapter Four looks at it in light of the inevitable offense of the Gospel. Chapter Five begins the discussion of mercy with a study of the connection between service and priesthood and Chapter Six concludes it with an examination of the peculiarity of the Christian calling. The discussion of humility before God begins in Chapter Seven with a study of worship and sovereignty and it concludes in Chapter Eight with a profile of the basic devotional disciplines. Chapter Nine returns to the subject of balance via the great Reformation doctrine of the priesthood of believers. Chapter Ten attempts to illustrate how the mandates of justice, mercy, and humility can provoke in us a commitment to genuine obedience. Finally, throughout the text, historical sidebars and application exercises are supplied to provide practical anchors for any elusively theoretical principles.

Opening each new section are epigrams from the works of

Samuel Johnson and Richard Weaver. Johnson was a brilliant eighteenth-century essayist, lexicographer, and literary critic. Noted for his iconoclastic wit and unbending conservatism, Johnson is an apt reminder of the philosophical root of Christian balance. Weaver was a renowned twentieth-century philosopher, professor, and bestselling author. Noted for his thoughtful regionalism and unshakable traditionalism, Weaver is an apt reminder that the philosophy of balance has not yet entirely vanished.

Umberto Eco, the noted Italian semioticist and novelist, has written that "there is nothing more wonderful than a list, instrument of wondrous hypotyposis."[19] Even a cursory glance at my writing reveals that I am an adherent of that time-honored medieval convention: Throughout this monograph you'll find lists of historical figures, lists of Biblical texts, lists of practical applications, lists of authors and their ideas, lists of movements and trends, and even lists of lists. Though this is not necessarily a popular form of communication in these abbreviated, get-to-the-point, cut-to-the-chase, modern times, it is nevertheless a critical aspect of my own approach to the question at hand. And so, I have let them stand.

This little book was never intended to provide a comprehensive new approach to social theory in the way that the works of Henry Van Til[20] or Phillip Schaff[21] once did. Neither is it intended to point the way to a profound new insight into the devotional disciplines in the way that the works of Charles Hodge[22] or Gardiner Spring[23] once did. Indeed, I have self-consciously drawn from these earlier masterpieces—as I have from the works of Calvin, Beza, Knox, Chalmers, Machen, Warfield, Thornwell, McLeod, Spurgeon, Kuyper, and many others—to merely restate their conception of the balanced Christian life in the context of our present perilous situation.

I have simply tried to serve as an observer, a reporter. I dared not attempt to suggest twelve innovative steps toward cultural recovery or seven new management habits for highly effective churches. The best that I can offer you is the tried and true, the old and familiar, the well-trod sod. But then, as J. C. Ryle said long ago:

> All heaven and earth resound with that subtle and delicately balanced truth that the old paths are the best paths after all."[24]

Indeed, they do. Because, they are.

PART ONE
An Imbalancing Act

The prevailing spirit of the present age seems to be the spirit of skepticism and captiousness, of suspicion and distrust in private judgment; a dislike of all established forms, merely because they are established, and of old paths, because they are old.

SAMUEL JOHNSON

Modernism is in essence a provincialism, since it declines to look beyond the horizon of the moment.

RICHARD WEAVER

From Pillar to Post

*Some men please themselves with a constant regularity of life,
and decency of behavior. Some are punctual in attendance on
public worship, and perhaps in the performance of private devotion. Such men are not hypocrites; the virtues which they practice arise from their principles. Their religion is sincere; what is
reprehensible is, that it is partial.*

SAMUEL JOHNSON

*Those who have not discovered that worldview is the most
important thing about a man, as about the men composing a
culture, should consider the train of circumstances which have
with perfect logic proceeded from this. The denial of universals
carries with it the denial of everything transcending experience.*

RICHARD WEAVER

I have always been fascinated by high-wire acts. I can still recall
with vivid clarity the very first time I craned my neck up toward
the pinnacle of the Big Top to witness the astonishing spectacle of
a beautiful woman prancing across the wide span of the tent with
nothing beneath her but a thin cable. I was transfixed.

I was probably about five years old and my father—finally giving in to my relentless begging—had taken me to the circus to see
"the lions and tigers and bears, oh my." The pungent closeness of
the sawdust-covered arena floor, the wafting aromas of popcorn
and cotton candy, the dazzling sights of clowns on motorcycles,

3

acrobats on horseback, and daredevils in cages with roaring beasts captivated my imagination to be sure. I was wide-eyed with wonder. But the moment the high-wire act began, nothing else seemed to matter. Though there were three rings of furious and fabulous activity before me, I only had eyes for the daring woman balanced a hundred feet above me.

I was hooked.

For the next several years I learned everything I could about high-wire acts. I followed the amazing careers of the Flying Wallendas—a single family that somehow produced three generations of the greatest performers the circus world has ever known. I collected their stats, figures, and memorabilia as relentlessly as any baseball fan.

As I look back on it now, I'm not entirely sure what it was that so gripped my imagination. I'd always been just a tad afraid of heights—so it wasn't as if I ever wanted to do what the Wallendas did. Certainly I did not relish the thought of living the life of a circus performer—even as a youngster I was a committed homebody. Perhaps it was simply a recognition of the phenomenal sense of balance the acts demanded—the ability to avoid the extremes of either left or right, forward or backward. It seemed as if I was always striving for balance—whether I was learning to ride my bike, or climbing to the highest branches of a tree, or seesawing with friends on the playground. A sense of balance lends grace and agility to almost any activity—and I'd always desired that. Maybe that is why the Wallendas and their high-wire kith and kin were always so attractive to me. Maybe that is why they made such an indelible impression on me.

I don't know about you but as an adult I have often had to realize how much like a high-wire act my daily life tends to be. Again and again I find myself dangerously shuffling a hundred urgent tasks, precariously perched high above my circumstances, hanging by what seems to be just a thread—and all without a net.

I feel as if I really ought to have the balance of a Flying Wallenda. And that is no mean feat—especially since this is no circus act. What I'm trying to balance is my life.

❖ FINDING BALANCE

Chuck Swindoll has said: "The longer I live the more I realize the ease with which we can slip into extremes. I see it all around me and sometimes, to my own embarrassment, I find it in myself."[1]

All of us struggle with the competing concerns of life. How do we juggle our obligations at work with our responsibilities at home? How do we give proportionate weight to the things that we know we need to do and the things that we just want to do? How do we keep our priorities at the forefront of our daily agenda even in the face of the tyranny of the urgent? How do we maintain a clearheaded perspective in our fast-paced, willy-nilly, fly-by-the-seat-of-our-pants world?

Like a high-wire act, we need balance. As Swindoll surmised:

> We need balance between kindness and firmness, between waiting and praying, working and obeying, between saving and spending, between taking in and giving out, between wanting too much and expecting too little, between warm acceptance and keen discernment, between grace and truth. For many folks, the struggle with imbalance is not an annual conflict— it's a daily grind.[2]

Recognized as a cardinal human virtue since the earliest days of antiquity, balance has been lauded in fable, legend, myth, logic, rhetoric, discourse, and law throughout all of history.[3] Though called by any number of different names—"moderation" by Aristotle, "soberness" by Cicero, "equilibrium" by Seneca, "deliberation" by Plato, "temperance" by Tacitus, "self-control" by Apuleius, and "poise" by Plutarch—balance was universally thought to be an essential character trait of the successful and happy life.[4] According to historian James Brewster: "In the ancient world, balance was particularly valued—above even knowledge, power, or beauty. It was the practical equivalent of wisdom and it pervaded nearly every philosophy, nearly every law system, and nearly every religion."[5]

The importance of maintaining a life of balance figures prominently in much of the best literature of the ages as well. From Shakespeare's *Merchant of Venice* to Milton's *Areopagitica*, from Ascham's *Schoolmaster* to Chaucer's *Canterbury Tales*, from Defoe's *Robinson Crusoe* to Moore's *Utopia*, from Johnson's *Rasselas* to Bacon's *Essays*, balance is portrayed as a kind of saving grace.[6] By it heroes overcame tremendous obstacles, the innocent recompensed the guilty, the weak rose above their oppressors, while the unloved and unlovely found everlasting romance. "Balance was the organizing ethic of the most prized character traits that men used in the building of western civilization," says literary critic A. N. Wilson. "It was the virtue that essentially enlivened all the noble aspirations and ideals of men and nations: chivalry, integrity, discretion, valor, energy, and simplicity."[7]

The Bible, too, commends a life of balance. We are to speak the truth; but we are to speak it in love (Ephesians 4:15). We are to desire neither poverty nor riches; we're to embrace neither fullness nor want (Proverbs 30:7–9). We are to bear one another's burdens; we are to bear our own (Galatians 6:2–5). Salvation is a free gift; good deeds must necessarily accompany it (Ephesians 2:8–10). The eternal Gospel is good news; but it is news of fear and judgment (Revelation 14:6–7). We are to hate the sin; we are to love the sinner (Jude 21–23). We are in the world; we are not of the world (John 17:15–16). Faith is not of works; but without works, faith is dead (James 2:26).

Interestingly though, for the Greeks, balance was often little more than a compromised life—a surly detante of pragmatic resignation. For the Romans it was simply the conservative suppression of wilder urges—a kind of taming of residual barbarian impulses. For many medieval troubadours and mystics it was an awful and indecipherable paradox—a metaphysical fulcrum upon which hinged duty.[8]

But Biblical balance is altogether different—not just in degree, but in kind. It entails far more than a happy medium between virtue and vice. It is not just a dialectical synthesis of two extremes or a New Age centering of mind, will, and emotions. It is instead a well-rounded, wholehearted, fully integrated life rooted in an unswervingly Scriptural worldview. It is the singular fruit of incarnational faith.

Unlike the kind of balance lauded in the ancient catalog of common virtues, Biblical balance is not dependent upon the rigors of self-imposed discipline. Neither is it monolithic or one-dimensional in its scope. It is an animated lifestyle of symmetry and stability, of equilibrium and equanimity, of imperturbability and unflappability. It is a fruitful harvest of "love, joy, peace, long-suffering, kindness, goodness, faithfulness, gentleness, self-control" (Galatians 5:22–23).

The reason is simple. Biblical balance is a happy melding of devotion and action, being and doing, patience and passion. It manifests word and deed, faith and works, forgiveness and discipline. It is a careful integration of the inner life and the outer life. It makes quiet conviction the natural companion of strident confession. It enables the head to coincide with the heart. Without compromising God's grace, it reveres God's decrees. Without suppressing spiritual liberty, it upholds spiritual responsibility.

In other words, it is mature.

And in a day marked by its notable revolt against maturity, Biblical balance is a rare commodity indeed. Extremes dominate. One-dimensional obsessions control our churches, our discussions, and our lives. A thousand competing programs, projects, or paradigms lay exclusive claim on our limited time, attention, and resources. A kind of spiritual balkanization process has thus blurred our sharpest focus and muffled our best efforts.

But it need not be so.

Biblical balance is more practical than pragmatism. It is more thoughtful than rationalism. It is more experienced than existentialism and more romantic than sentimentalism. It is more stable than conservatism and more progressive than liberalism.

A faithful return to that kind of balance could very well be the harbinger of hope, the clarion cry for revival, that we so desperately long for in these dire days.

❖ A SHORTHAND STATEMENT

Descriptions of Biblical balance take various forms throughout the Scriptures—in terms of duties to God and man (Luke 10:27), in terms of purity and charity (James 1:27), in terms of behavior and civility (Matthew 7:12), in terms of mission and witness (Mark 16:15), in terms of vocation and discipleship (John 13:34–35), and in terms of fellowship and worship (Acts 2:42).

Each of these is a shorthand statement—an abbreviated version of a deeply profound truth. None of them were ever intended to be comprehensive in scope. Rather, they capture in very plain terms different aspects of the multifaceted beauty of spiritual maturity. Each has its own emphasis. Each has its own perspective. But each points to the same spiritual fundamental—the very practical, nuts-and-bolts, rubber-meets-the road conception of Biblical balance.

Arguably, one of the most complete of these partial descriptions is found in the Old Testament prophetic book of Micah: "He has shown you, O man, what is good and what the Lord requires of you: to do justice, to love mercy, and to walk humbly with your God." (6:8)

In 1917, when American troops were preparing to sail across the seas in order to take to the battlefields of France and Belgium in the First World War, the New York Bible Society asked former president Theodore Roosevelt to inscribe a message in the pocket New Testaments that each of the soldiers would be given. The great man happily complied. And he began by quoting Micah's striking triune call for Biblical balance—what he called the "Micah Mandate."[9]

Why this particular passage? Because he said, "The whole teaching of the New Testament" is actually "foreshadowed in Micah's verse."[10]

In his brief message to the soldiers, he explained:

> Do justice; and therefore fight valiantly against those that stand for the reign of Moloch and Beelzebub on this earth. Love mercy; treat your enemies well; succor the afflicted; treat every woman as if she were your sister; care for the little children; and be tender with the old and helpless. Walk humbly; you will do so if you study the life and teachings of the Savior, walking in His steps.[11]

He concluded, saying:

> Remember: the most perfect machinery of government will not keep us as a nation from destruction if there is not within us a soul. No abounding of material prosperity shall avail us if our spiritual senses atrophy. The foes of our own household will surely prevail against us unless there be in our people an inner life which finds its outward expression in a morality like unto that preached by the seers and prophets of God when the grandeur that was Greece and the glory that was Rome still lay in the future.[12]

Roosevelt believed that the ultimate security of men and nations depended on a faithful adherence to Micah's threefold demonstration of true Biblical balance: a strident commitment to justice, a practical concern for mercy, and a reverent humility before almighty God. He was certain that even with the deployment of superior forces in superior numbers with superior armaments, the American armies would ultimately be defeated during the war—if they took to the field bereft of this kind of spiritual integrity. And he was convinced that if we as individuals and families take only our limited material resources into the conflagration of our daily warfare, we, too, will be defeated and destroyed.

Several generations earlier, George Washington also recognized the unique applicability of the "Micah Mandate" to America's corporate life. In one of his final statements to the young nation that he had taken such a pivotal role in establishing, he said:

> I now make it my earnest prayer, that God would most graciously be pleased to dispose us all, to do justice, to love mercy, and to demean ourselves with that charity, humility, and pacific temper of mind, which were the characteristics of the Divine Author of our blessed religion, for without an humble imitation and example in these things, we can never hope to be a happy nation.[13]

Likewise, a half-dozen other presidents laid their hands upon Bibles opened to the page of the "Micah Mandate" as they were sworn into office.[14] Two more quoted it in their inaugurations.[15] At least three others cited the passage in speeches during their terms of office. It is found engraved upon at least three prominent monuments or buildings in the nation's capital. And it has figured prominently in innumerable public lives—from Patrick Henry and Samuel Adams to Claire Booth Luce and Jacob Riis.[16]

Through the ages theologians and preachers as varied as Ambrose, Chrysostom, Tertullian, Origen, Calvin, Whitefield, and Cranfield emphasized its central importance in comprehending the full dimensions of the balanced Christian life.[17]

Charles Haddon Spurgeon, the great Victorian voice of orthodoxy, asserted that the verse "beautifully expounded" the "lavish excellencies" of spiritual maturity—by "testing the authenticity of salvation," divining the "symptoms of spiritual health," and provoking the "deepest conceivable pleasures" in a Christian's walk.[18]

Pastors, presidents, and patriots alike recognized that within this single nugget of truth was a world of wisdom. It was for them a lodestone of authenticity. It was a benchmark of balance.

❖ A COVENANT LAWSUIT

The often-quoted, highly touted Micah Mandate is actually the conclusion of an emotionally charged narrative near the end of the prophecy:

> Hear now what the Lord says: "Arise, plead your case before the mountains, and let the hills hear your voice. Hear, O you mountains, the Lord's complaint, and you strong foundations of the earth; for the Lord has a complaint against His people, and He will contend with Israel. O My people, what have I done to you? And how have I wearied you? Testify against Me. For I brought you up from the land of Egypt, I redeemed you from the house of bondage; and I sent before you Moses, Aaron, and Miriam. O My people, remember now what Balak king of Moab counseled, and what Balaam the son of Beor answered him, from Acacia Grove to Gilgal, that you may know the righteousness of the Lord." With what shall I come before the Lord, and bow myself before the High God? Shall I come before Him with burnt offerings, with calves a year old? Will the Lord be pleased with thousands of rams, ten thousand rivers of oil? Shall I give my firstborn for my transgression, the fruit of my body for the sin of my soul? He has shown you, O man, what is good; and what does the Lord require of you but to do justly, to love mercy, and to walk humbly with your God? (Micah 6:1–8)

With all the elements of a dramatic courtroom scene, the prophet here describes a kind of covenant lawsuit—brought by the Lord against His chosen people. The case is called from the very throne room of heaven (v. 1). All of the teeming creation—from the mountains and hills to the very foundations of the earth—is summoned to hear the evidence and to bear witness to the proceedings (v. 2). The prosecutor then presents His evidence (vv. 3–5) and the defendant explores the possibility of a plea bargain (vv. 6–7).

Apparently, Israel had "wearied" of the Lord (v. 3). This charge against her was a very serious one: infidelity. The indictment rested on four incidents from the people's redemption history. The first was their dramatic rescue from slavery in Egypt (v. 4). The second was the raising up of Godly leadership—Moses, Aaron, and Miriam—during the wilderness wanderings (v. 4). The third was the reversal of Balaam's curses just as they were about to make their way into the promised land flowing with milk and honey (v. 5). And the fourth was the long-awaited crossing over the Jordan—Shittim was the last east bank encampment, Gilgal was the first west bank encampment (v. 5).

In each case, God had demonstrated His covenant faithfulness. In His good providence He had brought the people through every danger and supplied their every need. But Israel had failed to respond in kind. Her love had grown cold.

Notice that the defendant readily accepts her guilt, but then wonders how reparations might be made. Perhaps burnt offerings? Maybe yearling calves? Or thousands of rams? Or ten thousand rivers of oil? Or even the firstborn among her children (vv. 6–7)?

No, the King, Judge, and Lawgiver answers by saying that He requires something far greater, far more precious than any of these things. He does not require a gift. Instead, He requires the giver: "He has shown you, O man, what is good, and what the Lord requires of you: to do justice, to love mercy, and to walk humbly with your God" (Micah 6:8). The mandate for Israel was clear.

In thus addressing His fickle covenant people—as opposed to the lost nations at large—the Lord outlined a basic standard for discipleship. Though obviously not a requirement for salvation or a prerequisite for redemption, it appears that the Micah Mandate was intended to be a hallmark of fealty in the kingdom.

In other words, the Micah Mandate was a precise shorthand description of the mature life of faith. It was a snapshot of Biblical balance.

And it still is.

As theologian C. E. B. Cranfield asserted, the Micah Mandate is "one of those great Biblical definitions of true religion" that "utterly transcend dispositions or dispensations."[19] In fact, Jesus summed up "the weightier matters of the law" by repeating the prophet's triad of virtues (Matthew 23:23), securing them as central paradigms for the balanced Christian life ever after.

Thus, the Micah Mandate intrudes as a truth not a tradition, as an innovation in the affairs of men not as an inversion amid the swarm of lies and libels in our time. Composed as it is of the three essential virtues of justice, mercy, and humility, the prophet's mandate sunders the howling jingoism, the topsy-turvy tests, and the tail-foremost arguments that pass for facts, in a flurry of spiritual precision.

❖ JUSTICE

The word Micah uses for "justice" is the Hebrew *mishpat*. It literally means "the way prescribed, the rightful action, or the appropriate mode of life." But the definition of the word only tells half the story.

Throughout the Bible *mishpat* is inextricably linked with the principle of righteousness. They are inseparable concepts. In more than sixty different passages all across the wide span of the Old and New Testaments, the Scriptures make it plain that any attempt to secure life, liberty, and the pursuit of happiness—whether at home, in the community, or among the nations—any attempt apart from the clearly revealed ethical parameters of goodness, truth, purity, faithfulness, and holiness is utter folly. On the other hand, any people that diligently seek to do right—to do righteousness—will inevitably pursue justice as well.

The two simply go together. One cannot be had without the other.

Again and again the refrain sounds:

- "Thus says the Lord: 'Keep justice, and do righteousness, for My salvation is about to come, and My righteousness to be revealed'" (Isaiah 56:1).

- "Righteousness and justice are the foundation of Your throne; mercy and truth go before Your face" (Psalms 89:14).
- "Let justice run down like water, and righteousness like a mighty stream" (Amos 5:24).

Jesus emphasized this same unity between moral purity and juridical integrity throughout His earthly ministry. He made it plain that if we are to be His disciples in spirit and in truth then we have a God-ordained duty to uphold—to be salt and light in the midst of this poor fallen world (Matthew 5:13–16). We have a mandate to redeem our culture (Genesis 1:28) and a commission to disciple all the nations (Matthew 28:19–20).

We must not make the mistake of imagining a sharp division between the "spiritual" and the "earthly." The Bible asserts that we are to think hard about the nature of Christian civilization (1 Peter 1:13), to try to develop Biblical alternatives to the inhuman humanism in our society (Matthew 18:15–20), to prophesy Biblically to the cultural problems of our age (Isaiah 6:8), and to pursue justice in tandem with righteousness (1 Kings 10:9).

There can be no outward life if there is no inward life. But, there can be no inward life if there is no outward one, either. Justice and righteousness are inseparable.

Gouverneur Morris, the great merchant, lawyer, and planter from Pennsylvania who actually drafted the final version of the Constitution, believed with Alexander Hamilton, Patrick Henry, George Washington, and many of the other framers that in order for the American experiment in liberty to succeed, justice and righteousness had to be "welded together as one in the hearts and minds of the citizenry." He yearned that America ever be steadfast in what he called its "Christian consensus." He said:

> Liberty and justice simply cannot be had apart from the gracious influences of a righteous people. A righteous people simply cannot exist apart from the aspiration to liberty and justice. The Christian religion and its incumbent morality is

tied to the cause of freedom with a Gordian knot; loose one from the other and both are sent asunder."[20]

According to the Micah Mandate, true discipleship tolerates no distinction between the inward and outward, the heart and the hand, the soul and the body. That is Biblical balance.

May we thus ever be able to say with Job, "I put on righteousness, and it clothed me; my justice was like a robe and a turban" (Job 29:14).

❖ MERCY

The word Micah used for "mercy" is the Hebrew *chesed*. It literally means "goodness, kindness, loyal deeds, or faithfulness." Once again though, there is more here than meets the eye.

In the same way that *mishpat*—or justice—is linked with the practice of righteousness throughout the Bible, *chesed* is linked with the exercise of authority. They too are inseparable concepts in the Scriptural scheme of things. Authority cannot be had apart from mercy—and vice versa.

The Bible is unflinching in its declaration: If we are ever to influence our families or our culture to stand for goodness, faithfulness, and kindness, then we must graciously serve the hurts, wants, and needs all around us. Just as God has shown us mercy we must demonstrate mercy to others (2 Corinthians 1:3–7).

In 1929, the Council of Religious Affairs in the Soviet Union was instructed by Joseph Stalin and the Central Committee of the Communist Party to enforce a comprehensive "ban on charitable or cultural activities by churches."[21] According to Vladimir Kharchev, a spokesman for the Kremlin at the time, "The State cannot tolerate any challenge to its claim on the heartstrings of the Russian people."[22]

Stalin, Kharchev, and the Soviet leadership apparently understood only too well the connection between authority and merciful service. They understood the very Biblical notion that whoever becomes the "benefactor" of a people will ultimately be able to wield all manner of authority with them (Luke 22:25).

This is one of the most basic principles of the Christian worldview: The ability to lead a society is earned, not inherited. And it is earned through faithful, compassionate, and merciful service.

Unfortunately, this is not a principle that has been widely understood by the modern church—even by those of us actively involved in the cultural arena.

Servanthood—the ministry of exercising mercy—is a much neglected, largely forgotten Christian vocation today. It has been a coalition of humanists that has claimed the moral high ground by championing the causes of the hurting, the poor, and the outcast. It has been a motley band of bureaucrats, social reactionaries, and judicial activists that have won the hearts of the people—despite the impotence and inadequacy of their programs—because they have at least made a *pretense* of mercy.

What a terrible irony. Jesus made it plain that if the Christian community wants to have the authority to speak truth into the lives of the people around us, to give moral vision to our culture, and to ultimately shape civil justice we must not grasp at the reins of power and prominence. We must serve. We must live lives marked by mercy.

Money, manpower, and mailing lists—as fine and as important as those things may be—are not the keys to cultural transformation. Expansive user-friendly church facilities and services, high-tech growth management seminars, and demographically precise niche targeting are not the means to reach this generation. Mercy is.

Jesus was a servant (Luke 22:27). He came to serve, not to be served (Matthew 20:20). He came offering mercy at every turn (Mark 5:19; Matthew 9:13).

Not surprisingly, He called His disciples to a similar life of selfless giving (Luke 22:26). He called us to be servants (Matthew 19:30). He said:

- "Whoever desired to be first among you, let him be your slave" (Matthew 20:27).
- "Be merciful, just as your Father also is merciful" (Luke 6:36).

The attitude of all aspiring leaders should be that "which was also in Christ Jesus, who, being in the form of God, did not consider it robbery to be equal with God, but made Himself of no reputation, taking the form of a bondservant" (Philippians 2:5–7).

The fact is, modern men are looking for proof. They want evidence.

Genuine mercy is that evidence. It verifies the remarkable claims of Scripture. It tells men that there is indeed a sovereign and gracious God who raises up a faithful people. It tells men that God then blesses those people and gives them workable solutions to the most difficult dilemmas in life.

Clearly, it is not enough for us to merely believe the Bible. It is not enough to simply assert an innate trust in Scriptural problem solving. It is not enough for us to blithely assert that Jesus is Lord. We must authenticate and validate our claims. In short, we must serve, backing up Word with deed (James 2:14–17).

This is, after all, our Christian legacy. It was the faithful followers of Christ that launched the first hospitals, orphanages, almshouses, soup kitchens, charitable societies, relief agencies, rescue missions, hostels, and shelters. And as a result, it was the faithful followers of Christ who led Western civilization to new heights of freedom and prosperity for nearly two millennia.

Charles Haddon Spurgeon once charged:

> Those who are quick to promise are generally slow to perform. They promise mountains and perform molehills. He who gives you fair words and nothing more feeds you with an empty spoon. People don't think much of a man's piety when his promises are like pie crust: made to be broken.[23]

Stalin, Kharchev, and the Soviet leadership understood that basic truth only too well. That is why they went to such great efforts to stymie Christian service in their vast land—to make it like broken pie crust.

Are we for real? Are we authentic? Then we must prove it to a watching world: "He has shown you, O man, what is good and what the Lord requires of you: to do justice, to love mercy, and to walk humbly with your God" (Micah 6:8).

We must fully grasp the monumental significance of Christ's assertion: "Blessed are the merciful, for they shall obtain mercy" (Matthew 5:7).

❖ HUMILITY

The word Micah uses for "humility" is the Hebrew *tsana*. It literally means "a modest approach, to come appropriate with decorum, or to bring wisely." But like *mishpat* and *chesed* its normal use is perhaps even more telling than its dictionary definition.

Again and again in the Bible, *tsana* is used to describe the proper attitude toward the person of God Himself.

The Christian approach to any issue, or any problem, or any situation, or any circumstance—in fact, the Christian approach to the whole of life—must always be *theocentric*. In other words, it must begin and end with—and ultimately be centered in—the Lord. He is, after all, the Alpha and the Omega of all things in reality (Revelation 1:8). To attempt any approach to reality without this in view is to invite frustration and failure. God is sovereign (Psalm 115:3). This is the fundamental truth that underlies the Christian worldview. Thus, our lives must be suffused with a holy fear and reverence of Him—to the point that everything is thereby affected.

The Bible is prolific in its vehement assertion of this truth:

- "The fear of the Lord is the beginning of knowledge, but fools despise wisdom and instruction" (Proverbs 1:7).

- "In the fear of the Lord there is strong confidence, and His children will have a place of refuge. The fear of the Lord is a fountain of life, to turn away from the snares of death" (Proverbs 14:26–27).

- "Be clothed with humility, for 'God resists the proud, but gives grace to the humble.' Therefore humble yourselves under the mighty hand of God, that He may exalt you in due time, casting all your care upon Him, for He cares for you" (1 Peter 5:5–7).

Humility is not exactly a popular concept these days. Fernanda Eberstadt, in her brilliant coming-of-age novel *Isaac and His Devils*, captured this sentiment: "Humility has a dank and shameful smell to the worldly, the scent of failure, lowliness, and obscurity."[24]

How different is the Biblical perspective. A nation whose leaders are humbled in fear before God will suffer no want (Psalm 34:9). It will ever be blessed (Psalm 115:13). It will be set high above all the nations of the earth (Deuteronomy 28:1).

Similarly, families—and even individuals—that walk in humility will be exalted and lifted up in due time (Proverbs 3:34; James 4:6).

Thomas Jefferson once asked: "Can the liberties of anyone or any people or any nation be secure, when we have removed the conviction that those liberties are the gift of God?"[25]

The answer from Holy Writ is clearly no. Thus, the *Shorter Catechism of the Westminster Confession* properly begins by asserting that, "the chief end of man is to glorify God and to enjoy Him forever."[26] The English reformers that composed that venerable tome recognized that the beginning of any serious endeavor must necessarily be rooted in a humble and holy fear of our gracious and almighty God—that worship of Him, fellowship with Him, service to Him, and communion in Him, must be the vortex of any and all other activities. The Biblical faith is a circumspect fear of the living God. That is its essence.

Applying this most fundamental truth to the arena of national and cultural integrity, George Washington asserted: "It is the first duty of all nations to acknowledge the providence of Almighty God, to obey His will, to be grateful for His benefits, and to humbly implore His protection and favor in holy fear."[27]

Likewise, it is the first duty of all men and women: "He has shown you, O man, what is good and what the Lord requires of you: to do justice, to love mercy, and to walk humbly with your God" (Micah 6:8).

❖ TIPPING THE BALANCE

In both our individual lives and our culture at large, the profound necessity for justice, mercy, and humility before God—and not just one or two of those virtues, but all three—is everywhere apparent. You don't have to look too far to see how desperately the world needs the kind of balance the Micah Mandate portrays. Even the greatest gifts, the best advantages, and the finest opportunities are quickly squandered without it.

Thomas Chatterton, for example, was among the brightest orbs in the starry English literary constellation. Byron praised him as "a master of the poetic craft." Coleridge, Shelley, and Keats each acknowledged his "stunning evocative abilities." Walpole ranked him "above Dryden" and perhaps "only second to Shakespeare." Wordsworth dubbed him "the marvelous boy." And Wise inscribed his name "among the brightest of the sons of genius."[28]

Nevertheless, he was unable to maintain even a modicum of balance in his life, and his great promise was squandered.

Early on, Chatterton evidenced extraordinary gifts. He began to compose songs, ballads, satires, and verses at twelve. When his mother, an impoverished widow, secured his apprenticeship with a Bristol scrivener three years later, he turned his hand to political essays, elegies, criticism, and social commentary.

In 1768, when he was just sixteen, he startled editors, antiquaries, and critics by publishing a brilliant eyewitness memoir of the dedication of an old bridge by ancient Benedictine friars—vividly detailing the pomp and ceremonies of the long-forgotten event. The beautiful account—he told the public—was merely translated from a brittle old manuscript found, with others of like character, in a muniment room over the chapel of a local rural parish house.

In short succession he published a whole series of the papers—historical, theological, and poetical—each exciting the interest of experts and common readers alike. Chatterton maintained they were written by a fifteenth-century monk, Thomas Rowley. Though most of the medieval academics of the day questioned the authenticity of the manuscripts, the undeniable beauty and the stunning maturity of the pastoral eclogues made them doubt that a neophyte like Chatterton could have manufactured such an elaborate ruse much less have written such magnificent literature.

So despite their clinging and persistent misgivings, several publishers began accepting the precocious young writer's purported translations for their journals and magazines—paying him liberal fees. In Colonial America, where attachments to tradition were often even more profound than in Europe, he created a sensation and became quite the celebrity. It soon appeared that he had made both his fame and his fortune.

Chatterton quickly plunged into the rough and tumble literary world of the eighteenth century. He frequented the theaters, dressed fashionably, and drank profligately. He boldly rejected the faith of his childhood and embraced a life of defiant worldliness.

He continued to write prodigiously as well—often in dissipated all-night binges. And, though he managed to create an authentic medieval style from a unique conflation of his reading and his own invention, his now obviously false insistence that his texts were truly ancient began to cast a shadow over his character.

Eventually he carried his ruse a bit too far. Scholars began to attack Chatterton as a fraud, perhaps even a plagiarist. Reluctantly, publishers began to reject his submissions.

Commissions disappeared. And the fickle public rushed on to other, newer fascinations.

As quickly as his star had risen, it suddenly fell.

The city of London was anything but hospitable to the virtues of justice, mercy, and humility before God in those days. Though it had been almost entirely rebuilt a century earlier—following the Great Fire of 1660—and had not yet suffered the Dickensian horrors of the Industrial Revolution, the city was dingy, dirty, and crowded. Though the skyline was dominated by the majestic spires of Christopher Wren and the royal residences at St. James, Westminster, and Buckingham, the warren of narrow streets, alleyways, and tenement lanes were grim, dismal, and claustrophobic. Many of the historic buildings were in shameful disrepair. The Thames was an open sewer. And the pitifully impoverished and dispossessed seemed to haunt every corner. Combined with the perpetually damp and foggy climate, the city was a distressing sight—as so many visitors attested at the time.

Some of the most gifted orators and statesmen ever to lead the kingdom were then in Parliament including Burke, Pitt, and Walpole. Nevertheless, the nation was in the throes of turmoil. The foundations of the Indian Empire had hardly been laid. The Australian possessions were a part of the world only just discovered. The colonies in America were in open rebellion against the Crown. There was still a strong and rebellious contingent of support for the Stuart pretenders to the throne.

The entire city shook with the cataclysms of dissent, discontent, and distress.

Worst of all though, London was gripped by a moral crisis. According to J. C. Ryle, the city was actually "deluged with infidelity and skepticism."[29] In fact, he said:

> Dueling, adultery, fornication, gambling, swearing, Sabbath-breaking, and drunkenness were hardly regarded as vices at all. They were the fashionable practices of people in the highest

ranks of society, and no one was thought the worse of for indulging in them.[30]

Wilberforce had not yet undertaken the abolition of slavery. Howard had not yet begun to reform the prisons. Raikes had not yet established Sunday schools. And the great eighteenth-century revivalists—Whitefield, Wesley, Grimshaw, Romaine, Rowlands, Berridge, Venn, and Herby—had not yet had their full effect.

Meanwhile, the churches were awash with modern new philosophies and methodologies that seemed to have little correlation whatsoever with the Gospel. The famed barrister William Blackstone undertook "to go from church to church and hear every clergyman of note" in the city. He reported that he "did not hear a single discourse which had more Christianity in it than the writings of Cicero."[31] In fact, he said that it would have been impossible for him to discover, from what he heard, "whether the preacher was a follower of Confucius, of Mahomet, or of Christ."[32]

It was hardly an environment conducive to Biblical balance.

As Chatterton accommodated himself to the intemperance of the city, his excesses became even more pronounced. Though his advances and royalties were quickly squandered, he actually intensified his dissolute lifestyle. Going without food or sleep for days on end, he wrote ceaselessly with a tortured passion unequaled in English letters. Then he would indulge in drinking sprees, carousings, and fierce street brawls.

Such a sad public spectacle made editors even more reluctant to publish his work—even though its beauty and originality continued to be unimpeachably brilliant. Chatterton simply had exhausted his welcome. Tragically he had exhausted his body as well. His prolific energy could only last so long. He never seemed to do anything halfheartedly—whether in work or in play. His brilliant imbalance drove him from one extreme to another.

Early one summer morning in 1770, finally weighed down and worn out by circumstances of his own making, the poetic genius took his own life.

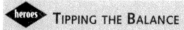 TIPPING THE BALANCE

He has shown you, O man, what is good and what the Lord requires of you: to do justice, to love mercy, and to walk humbly with your God (Micah 6:8).

Since the earliest days of the church, the kind of balance between justice, mercy, and spiritual humility highlighted in the Micah Mandate has been a distinguishing characteristic of the lives of virtually all the heroes of the church. Examples abound:

Basil of Caesarea (330–379) was renowned in his day as a man of encyclopedic learning. He left a promising legal practice at the imperial court to establish a Christian community in Annesi committed to the care of the sick and needy. It was not long before his reputation for justice, mercy, and humility before God reached the farthest edges of the Roman Empire: He was a quick-witted adversary to the heretical Arians, he was a valiant defender of Biblical orthodoxy, he had a productive theological pen, and he was a man who combined a deep and sincere piety with a tough and realistic practicality. He was responsible for the establishment of the world's first nonambulatory care hospitals, for the criminalization of abortion and infanticide throughout the realm, and for liturgical reforms that revitalized the worship of the church for generations. When he died at the age of fifty, he was mourned by believers and unbelievers alike.

As a young woman, *Bathild of Chelles* (631–680) was carried away from her English home by pirates and indentured to the court of Clovis II, ruler of the Frankish kingdom. Her great beauty and piety attracted the attentions of the king, and he made her his wife in 649. Some years later, upon the king's death, Bathild became regent for their eldest son, Chlotar III. Utilizing the powers of her position, she stridently opposed the profligate slave trade and the practices of infanticide, exposure, abandonment, and abortion. She encouraged evangelism among the barbaric Celts, she supported local ministries to the needy, and she helped to bring reform to the old Roman legal code. Her patronage of the arts and her commitment to the sciences were notable as was her devotion to the disciplines of the Christian life. Her life of balance served as an inspiration to the emerging French nation—who emphasized justice, mercy, and humility before God long before they embraced liberty, equality, and fraternity.

A devoted son of the Scottish Reformation, *Andrew Geddes* (1518–1586), was a sterling example of compassion, integrity, and truth during the fierce religious conflicts that wracked his tiny nation throughout the sixteenth century. Converted under the preaching of John Knox, he served as a deacon in that great Reformer's church. Taking his cue from the Biblical injunction to faithfully demonstrate justice, mercy, and humility before God, he utilized his office as a force for righteous change: He helped to organize the famed "seasons of prayer" in cottages all across Scotland that so profoundly shaped the character of the times, he pioneered a ministry to abandoned and orphaned children, and he consulted with local magistrates in an effort to bring the standards of jurisprudence in line with Scriptural principles of justice. A Latin translation of the widely read book *On the Help of the Poor,* by Jean Louis Vives, left a deep impression on Geddes—so much so that he used the book as a model for his various pro-life and charitable activities. Emphasizing Micah's balanced triad of virtues, Geddes left a mark on his land that is still felt to this day.

Dozens of others could be cited throughout the wide span of history: George of Diospolis (d. 304), Cuthbert of Lindisfarne (d. 687), Giles Aegidius (d. 796), Edward the Confessor (d. 1066), Otto Blumhardt (d. 1632), James Ramsay (d. 1789), J. Hudson Taylor (d. 1905). Each portrayed the comprehensive claim of Christ on the totality of their lives by daily seeking to illumine the Gospel with justice, mercy, and humility before God. And each played a significant role in laying the foundations for the most glorious flowering of civilization that the world has ever known.

When the door of his small attic room was broken open the next day, hundreds of small sheaves of paper—covered with his florid handwriting—were scattered across the floor. At his small writing desk was an unfinished lament entitled *Balance*:

Stepe by stepe, through lyturgy of deathe in life
He hast besought sweete release somme-where;
Tottering ere the brynk of devastation and fyre:
O, to attayne to such an balance: as to but stande.[33]

It was obvious to all who witnessed the tragic scene that Chatterton had been desperately searching for balance. He yearned for the ability to find a place of stability, security, and stillness where he could stand and not be shaken by his own raging passions. Sadly, he never found that elusive balance—the balance to merely stand—that he so movingly craved. He was just eighteen when the parish sextons buried him in an unmarked pauper's grave.

❖ WE LIKE HE

The more things change the more they stay the same.

At first glance, Chatterton's desperate experience may seem more than a little remote from our own—rather like the sad sagas of rock musicians or Hollywood starlets. In his tragic search for balance he was driven to extremes.

In fact though, balance seems as out of reach for many of us more sober and conservative moderns as it was to young impulsive Chatterton. And we, like he, are all too often driven to extremes, even if our extremes are extremely conventional.

Actually, we face many of the same obstacles that Chatterton did. All about us is the clear testimony of an entire culture fascinated by the bizarre spectacle of an imbalancing act. So, when we try to make it on our gifts and abilities alone, we are destined to stumble and fall. Like Chatterton, we discover that in this poor fallen world an overreliance on our most obvious strengths often leaves us vulnerable to our most profound weaknesses. The tragic result, now as then, is the blind destruction of life and hope.

All the more reason to take up the challenge of the Micah Mandate. All the more reason to visibly authenticate the work of grace within us by a faithful witness without us—demonstrating to all the world the possibility of actually living well-rounded lives of integrity and balance.

In writing to the young Ephesian church, the apostle Paul underscored the importance of that kind of resolve:

> For by grace you have been saved through faith and that not of yourselves; it is the gift of God, not of works, lest anyone should boast. For we are His workmanship, created in Christ Jesus for good works, which God prepared beforehand that we should walk in them" (Ephesians 2:8–10).

Paul's message comes through loud and clear: God saves us by grace. There is nothing we can do to merit His favor. We stand condemned under His judgment. His bequest of salvation is completely unearned and undeserved.

But we are not saved capriciously, for no reason and no purpose. On the contrary, "we are His workmanship, created in Christ Jesus for good works." We are "His own possession," set apart and purified to be "zealous for good deeds." We are to demonstrate the reality of God's grace before a watching world. We are to authenticate God's good providence in our lives.

And that is precisely what the balance of the Micah Mandate enables us to do.

Developing a Sense of Balance

He has shown you, O man, what is good and what the Lord requires of you: to do justice, to love mercy, and to walk humbly with your God (Micah 6:8).

❖ Compare the lists of character traits in Galatians 5—the fruit of the Spirit and the work of the flesh. Notice how, in each case, the virtues and vices cross the boundaries of the internal and the external life. How do these then apply to Micah's triad of virtues?

❖ Study Christ's allusion to the Micah Mandate in Matthew 23:23. In what ways do justice, mercy, and humble faith portray the "weightier matters" of the law?

❖ Read through the biographies of several of the great heroes of the faith throughout the ages, noting how thoroughly they integrated the virtues of justice, mercy, and spiritual humility into their daily lives. You might even want to keep a small journal record of stories that illustrate each virtue or of quotations that highlight their importance. Discipleship is in many ways an art of imitation, so this kind of exercise is more than just an academic accumulation of historical vignettes, it is part and parcel of our maturation in Christ.

❖ Next, do a serious spiritual inventory of your life. Make a chart: *pro* and *con*. But don't simply compare and contrast yourself with the saints of yore—none of us stack up very well in that light. Instead, take note of the ways that you've successfully implemented certain virtues in your Christian walk. Then look for a couple of specific areas where the balanced life still seems to elude you. Seek to apply the lessons you've learned from your victories to your defeats.

❖ Finally, seek out some practical opportunities to bring more wholesome balance to your walk and witness. If you're involved in all kinds of activism, you might want to look for some new ways to strengthen your inner life: a prayer partner, a discipleship group, or a serious Bible study. If you've tipped the scales in the other direction, why not seek to volunteer once a week at the local crisis pregnancy center, or serve meals at a homeless shelter, or stuff envelopes and answer phones for a ministry aimed at stemming the tide of pornography in your town. Round out the expression of your faith and exercise your calling beyond the narrow, normal confines of your comfort zone.

2

In, Out, or Of

Indifference in questions of importance is no amiable quality.

SAMUEL JOHNSON

All the evils in our now extensive catalogue flow from a falsified picture of the world which, for our immediate concern, results in an inability to interpret current happenings.

RICHARD WEAVER

Adjacent to Lambeth Palace just across the Thames from Westminster is one of London's most delightful gardens. There, within the tiny churchyard of the St. Mary Parish, is a carefully tended walled plot bursting with color and fragrance. A narrow brick-lined pathway winds through lush beds of forget-me-nots, polyanthus, and crown imperial fritillaries. What appear to be haphazard clumps of lilac, viburnum, and philadelphus are linked integrally to one another by a wide, wavy border planted with alchemilla, nepeta, and several other sturdy herbaceous plants that I've never quite been able to identify. There are assorted blooming primroses, lilies, and canterbury bells in spring and snapdragons, hardy geraniums, and lavender in summer. Along one wall, in front of a magnificent wisteria, is a bed redolent with herbs—basil, thyme, oregano, and cilantro. There is parsley among the hollyhocks, honeysuckle twisted round the roses, and tiger lilies peaking through the shrubby euphorbias. It is a hard-won taste of paradise planted in the midst of a hustle-bustle urban sprawl.

Though the celebrated English gardens of Hever Castle, of Sissinghurst, or of Glyndebourne are certainly more spectacular, it is this little parish vicar's garden that epitomizes for me all that a garden ought to be. Its personal scale, its wide-ranging palette, and its orderly conception portray a distinctly practical vision of both the possibilities and the limitations of this poor fallen world.

As if to underscore this truth, a little bronze plaque adorning one corner of the garden declares: "A good theology will invariably produce a good garden." The first time I read that I chuckled and quickly dismissed it as just another bit of gardener's hyperbole. But then, the more I thought about it the more I began to realize that the plaque's epigram actually conveys a uniquely Scriptural worldview.

A good theology is more than the sum of its parts. While it is composed of certain essential dogmas and doctrines, each of those essentials must also be carefully related to all the others. It sees all too clearly the crucial connection between the profound and the mundane. While it wisely attends to the minutest of details, it also remains fully cognizant of how those details affect the bigger picture. It places as much significance on the bits and pieces as it does on the totals.

A good theology is good for the soul. But it is also good for the world. Its spiritual vision gives vitality to all that it touches—from flower gardens and herbiaries to nation states and cultures—simply because the integrity of that vision ultimately depends as much on a balanced Biblical worldview as on a solid Scriptural soteriology. Its attention to heavenly concerns is integrally bound to its fulfillment of earthly responsibilities.

Of course, actually making that connection between heavenly concerns and earthly responsibilities is never easy. We are all constantly tugged between piety and practicality, between devotion and duty, between communion with God and calling in the world. Like tending a well-groomed garden, honing a balanced Biblical worldview involves both the drudgery of daily labor and the high ideals of faith, hope, and love. But the results are always worth the extra effort.

A good theology—with its comprehensive worldview—inevitably affects the world for good. While a bad theology—with its fragmented worldview—sows only tares. In our day, that basic fact has been borne out again and again.

❖ WORLDLINESS

In his landmark book *A Christian Manifesto*, Francis Schaeffer asserted that "the basic problem with Christians in this country" over the last two generations or more has been that "they have seen things in bits and pieces instead of totals."[1] The result has been a kind of hesitant hit-or-miss approach to the dire dilemmas of our day:

> They have very gradually become disturbed over permissive-ness, pornography, the public schools, the breakdown of the family, and finally abortion. But they have not seen this as a totality—each thing being a part, a symptom, of a much larger problem.[2]

He said that part of the reason for this was:

> They failed to see that all of this has come about due to a shift in worldview—that is, through a fundamental change in the overall way people think and view the world and life as a whole.[3]

When the subject of worldview comes up, we generally think of philosophy. We think of intellectual niggling. We think of the brief and blinding oblivion of ivory tower speculation, of thickly obscure tomes, and of inscrutable logical complexities.

In fact, a worldview is as practical as potatoes. It is less metaphysical than understanding marginal market buying at the stock exchange or legislative initiatives in congress. It is less esoteric than typing a book into a laptop computer or sending a fax across the continent. It is instead as down to earth as tilling the soil for a bed of petunias.

The word itself is a poor English attempt at translating the German *weltanshauung*. It literally means a "life perspective" or "a way of seeing."[4] It is simply the way we look at the world.

You have a worldview. I have a worldview. Everyone does. It is our perspective. It is our frame of reference. It is the means by which we interpret the situations and circumstances around us. It is what enables us to integrate all the different aspects of our faith, and life, and experience.

Alvin Toffler, in his book *Future Shock*, says: "Every person carries in his head a mental model of the world, a subjective representation of external reality."[5]

This mental model is, he says, like a giant filing cabinet. It contains a slot for every item of information coming to us. It organizes our knowledge and gives us a grid from which to think. Our mind is not as Pelagius, Locke, Voltaire, or Rousseau would have had us suppose—a tabula rasa, a blank and impartial slate. None of us are completely open-minded or genuinely objective. "When we think," said economic philosopher E. F. Schumacher, "we can only do so because our mind is already filled with all sorts of ideas with which to think."[6] These more or less fixed notions make up our mental model of the world, our frame of reference, our presuppositions—in other words, our worldview.

In his marvelous book *How to Read Slowly*, James Sire writes:

> A worldview is a map of reality; and like any map, it may fit what is actually there, or it may be grossly misleading. The map is not the world itself of course, only an image of it, more or less accurate in some places, distorted in others. Still, all of us carry around such a map in our mental makeup and we act upon it. All our thinking presupposes it. Most of our experience fits into it.[7]

A worldview is simply a way of viewing the world.

And the Christian view of the world and all the things of the world is fraught with a sort of gardener's paradox—an appreciation for both the potentialities and the liabilities of fallen creation.

We know for instance, that the world is only a temporary dwelling place. It is "passing away" (1 John 2:17) and we are here but for a little while as aliens and sojourners (Acts 7:6). Because we are a part of "the household of God" (Ephesians 2:19), our true "citizenship is in heaven" (Philippians 3:20). Our affections are naturally set "on things above" (Colossians 3:2).

In addition, the world is filled with dangers, toils, and "hidden snares" (Jeremiah 18:22). In tandem with the flesh and the devil, it makes war on the saints (John 15:18). "All that is in the world—the lust of the flesh, the lust of the eyes, and the pride of life—is not of the Father" (1 John 2:16). The world "cannot receive the Spirit of Truth" because "the cares of this world and the deceitfulness of riches choke the word," and it becomes unfruitful (Matthew 8:22).

Thankfully, Christ overcame the world (John 16:33) and then "chose [us] out of the world" (John 15:19). Thus, we are not to be "conformed to this world" (Romans 12:2), neither are we to "love the world" (1 John 2:15) because Christ "gave Himself for our sins, that He might deliver us from this present evil age" (Galatians 1:4). Though we once "walked according to the course of this world" (Ephesians 2:2) now we are to keep ourselves "unspotted from the world" (James 1:27). Indeed, "friendship with the world is enmity with God" so that whoever is "a friend of the world makes himself an enemy of God" (James 4:4).

Thus, warnings against worldliness, carnal-mindedness, and earthly attachments dominate Biblical ethics. As Oswald Chambers has said: "The counsel of the Spirit of God to the Saints is that they must allow nothing worldly in themselves while living among the worldly in the world."[8]

But then, that is the problem, isn't it? We must continue to live in the world. We must be "in" it but not "of" it. And that is no easy feat. As John Calvin wrote in his helpful little *Golden*

Booklet of the True Christian Life: "Nothing is more difficult than to forsake all carnal thoughts, to subdue and renounce our false appetites, and to devote ourselves to God and our brethren, and to live the life of angels in a world of corruption."[9]

And to make matters even more complex, we not only have to live in this dangerous, fallen world, but we have to work in it (1 Thessalonians 4:11), serve in it (Luke 22:6), and minister in it (2 Timothy 4:5). We have been appointed ambassadors to it (2 Corinthians 5:20), priests for it (1 Peter 2:9), and witnesses in it (Matthew 24:14). We even have to go to "the end" of it (Acts 1:8), offering a good confession of the eternal life to which we were called (1 Timothy 6:12).

The reason for this seemingly contradictory state of affairs—enmity with the world on the one hand, responsibility to it on the other—is simply that "God so loved the world that He gave His only begotten Son" (John 3:16). Though the world is "under the sway of the wicked one" (1 John 5:19) and "knows not God" (1 Corinthians 1:21), God is "in Christ reconciling the world to Himself" (2 Corinthians 5:19). Jesus is "the light of the world" (John 8:12). He is the "Savior of the world" (John 4:42). He is the "Lamb of God who takes away the sin of the world" (John 1:29). Indeed, He was made "the propitiation for our sins, and not for ours only but also for the whole world" (1 John 2:2). Through Christ all things are reconciled to the Father (Colossians 1:19–20) so that finally "the kingdoms of this world [shall] become the kingdoms of our Lord and of His Christ" (Revelation 11:15).

A genuinely integrated Christian worldview must be cognizant of both perspectives of the world—and treat them with equal weight. It must be engaged in the world. It must be unengaged in worldliness. It must somehow correlate spiritual concerns with temporal concerns. It must coalesce heavenly hope and landed life. It must coordinate heartfelt faith and down-to-earth practice.

And that is just what the Micah Mandate does. A vision of life and faith that integrates justice, mercy, and humility before

God will cover the whole wide spectrum of heaven and earth. By vitally connecting the head with the hand with the heart; by placing emphasis on hard-hitting issues, gentle human compassion, and unflinching holiness; and by establishing the priorities of cultural, interpersonal, and devotional integrity, the high ideals of a Biblical worldview are happily instituted by the grace of God.

❖ BACK TO THE GARDEN

This kind of balanced perspective of the created realm in which we live is highlighted and reinforced all throughout the Biblical story of redemption. Whenever and wherever God reveals His providential purposes for us, He makes clear the connection between the things of heaven and the things of earth. And He does it by illustrating profound spiritual matters in very mundane physical terms.

When Adam and Eve were banished from the paradise of Eden, for example, they were not only cut off spiritually from God's presence, they were physically locked out of their garden home as well (Genesis 3:17–24). Their tilling became toiling. Their innocence became ingenuousness. Their sin not only ravaged their hearts and souls, it ravaged their situations and circumstances. The metaphysical was made manifest in the physical. The supernatural was revealed in the natural. Apparently obscure spiritual realities were expressed in painfully obvious practical experiences.

And the story of Adam and Eve is by no means unique in this regard. Incarnational truth—the spiritual revealed and made manifest in the physical—is the very nature and essence of Biblical revelation.

An integral aspect of the covenant God made with Abraham, for instance, was the promise of a gardenlike inheritance. Abraham was promised land. Though "he waited for the city which has foundations, whose builder and maker is God"

(Hebrews 11:10), he was given a glimpse of that heavenly hope in the very earthly realms of the Canaanites, Amorites, and Jebusites (Genesis 15:18–21).

When Moses and the children of Israel came up out of the bondage of Egypt, they, too, sought that which "is invisible" (Hebrews 11:27). But the invisible rewards of a world yet to come were illustrated for them by the visible blessings of a world already here. Thus, they went forth to claim a promised land—a bounteous garden flowing with milk and honey.

Jeremiah, even when he knew judgment was imminent and his own fate was grim, bought a garden plot as an inheritance for his family (Jeremiah 32:6–15). The hope of divine deliverance in the future was vividly and objectively portrayed in a real estate transaction.

Even the proclamation of the Gospel is described in very earthly terms: It is seed sown upon the soils, it is wheat amid the tares, it is a tract white unto harvest, it is a ripened vineyard, it is a treasure in a field.

A balanced Biblical worldview takes all this into account. It recognizes that though this world is fallen, corrupted, and defiled it is to be cared for as a garden. Until God takes us out of this world, our lives—physical and spiritual—are inescapably tied to it. Thus, the just society of a righteous people is invariably portrayed in the Bible as a "watered garden" (Isaiah 58:11). Though it is not yet the "better country" of our eternal hope, it is nevertheless to be responsibly tended (Hebrews 11:16).

It is only as we understand this redemptive link between heaven and earth that we can ever hope to comprehend the glorious provisions and purposes of grace. It is only as we forge a Biblical worldview that we can fathom the intentions of God's good providence in His creation.

❖ THE GREAT COMMISSION

"The earth is the Lord's" (Psalm 24:1). God has not limited the jurisdiction of His sovereignty to heaven. Despite the disruption of the Fall, He continues to execute His authority over the world with "an everlasting kingdom" (Daniel 4:3). He rules it from His "throne in heaven" (Psalm 11:4). That is clear enough. At the same time though, He graciously apportions it out to His people. He commissions us to exercise stewardship over it. We are to be more than just salt: preserving. We are to be light: reclaiming (Matthew 5:13–16). Justice, mercy, and humility before God are to be tandem virtues in our lives as we reach out to a lost and dying world.

This is the crux of a balanced Biblical worldview. And it is dramatically underscored in Christ's final instructions to His disciples—in the Great Commission. He said:

> All authority has been given to Me in heaven and on earth. Go therefore, and make disciples of all the nations, baptizing them in the name of the Father and of the Son and of the Holy Spirit, teaching them to observe all things that I have commanded you; and lo, I am with you always, even to the end of the age. (Matthew 28:18–20)

All authority in heaven is His, of course. The heights and the depths, the angels and the principalities are all under His sovereign rule. But all authority on earth is His as well. Man and creature, as well as every invention and institution, are under His sovereign rule. There are no neutral areas in all of the cosmos that escape the authority of the Lord Jesus Christ (Colossians 1:17).

Therefore, on this basis, the Great Commission states that believers are to extend Christ's kingdom, making disciples in all nations by going, baptizing, and teaching. This mandate is the essence of the new covenant, which is but an extension of the old covenant: Go and begin the process of reclaiming everything in heaven and on earth for His name's sake (Genesis 1:28). We are called to be a part of that which will, in the fullness of time, "gather together in one all things in Christ, both which are in heaven and which are on earth in Him" (Ephesians 1:10).

The emphasis is inescapable: We are not to stop with simply telling the nations that Jesus is Lord; we are to demonstrate His lordship in our families, in our churches, in our work, in our communities, and in our culture. We are to make disciples who will obey everything that He has commanded, not just in a hazy zone of piety, but in the totality of life.

This is the thrust of the Great Commission. It is the spiritual, emotional, and cultural mandate to win the world for Jesus. And though we know that only Christ Himself can fulfill that mandate in its entirety at the close of human history, our duty is but to trust and obey. We are to "do business" until He comes (Luke 19:13).

The tendency of many modern Christians to sidestep all the implications of the Great Commission except soul-saving has, in stark contrast, paved the way for inhuman humanism's program to afflict the helpless, crush our liberties, and despoil our culture. When the Christian's task is limited to merely snatching brands from the flickering flames of perdition, then virtually all Christian influence is removed from the world. There is little or nothing to restrain the ambitions of evil men and movements. There are no checks, no balances, no standards, and no limitations. God's counsel goes unheard and unheeded.

Commenting on this tragic tendency, Charles Haddon Spurgeon said:

> There are certain pious moderns who will not allow the preacher to speak upon anything but those doctrinal statements concerning the way of salvation which are known as "the Gospel." We do not stand in awe of such criticism, for we clearly perceive that our Lord Jesus Christ himself would very frequently have come under it. Read the Sermon on the Mount and judge whether certain among the pious would be content to hear the like of it preached to them. Indeed, they

would condemn it as containing very little Gospel and too
much good works. They would condemn it as containing all
too much of the legal. But we must never let be forgotten
Christ's emphasis: the law must be preached, for what the law
demands of us, the Gospel produces in us, else ours is no
Gospel at all.[10]

A Biblical worldview, as Spurgeon asserts, embraces the comprehensive implications of the Great Commission. It applies
Scripture to every area of life and godliness. The fact is, the salvation of souls is the immediate aim of the Great Commission. But
the more ultimate aim is the promotion of the glory of the triune
God (Romans 16:25–27). We must have a passion for souls
(2 Corinthians 5:11). We must take every opportunity
(Colossians 4:5), expend every energy (2 Corinthians 6:4–10),
and risk every expense (Acts 4:29), beseeching men to be reconciled to God (2 Corinthians 5:20). But individualistic redemption
is not the do-all and end-all of the Great Commission.

Thus, our evangelism must include sociology as well as salvation; it must include a new social order as well as a new birth; it
must include reform and redemption, culture and conversion, a
reformation as well as a regeneration. Read the sermons of the
great evangelists through the ages and you will immediately see
that kind of balance—they invariably begin by addressing the
grave injustices of the day, proceed to tender examples of human
need, and conclude with a vital appeal to reconcile with Christ.
Regardless of the text, the outline is simple: justice, mercy, and
humility before God.

Any other kind of evangelism is shortsighted and woefully
impotent. Any other kind of evangelism fails to live up to the
comprehensive high call of the Great Commission. Our monolithic humanistic culture attests all too well that all our niche
group, church growth, twelve-step recovery, and least common
denominator strategies are simply not sufficient in and of themselves for the task of satisfying that kind of world vision. It is

therefore high time to release our evangelism from the restraints of a partial and passive Christianity in order to mount a full-scale assault on the evil and privation of the dominions of darkness. It is high time we set our evangelistic visions by the broad-spectrum Scriptural pattern. It is high time evangelism becomes the invasion of heart and soul, of life and liberty, and of land and faith it was intended from the start to be.

❖ BOTH/AND—NOT EITHER/OR

The prophecy of Micah—as was the case with so many of the Old Testament prophecies—was delivered to a people who seemed to drift to one of two extremes. Either they were terribly spiritual to the neglect of their earthly responsibilities (Micah 3:5–7) or they were terribly worldly to the neglect of their faith (Micah 3:8–11). Either way, the people were prone to see things in "bits and pieces" rather than in "totals" (Micah 3:12). They decried the prophet's clear message of faithful balance, integration, and *worldviewishness*, saying, "Do not prattle" (Micah 2:6).

The tragic result was that their culture was completely awash in disarray, confusion, and debauchery (Micah 2:8–11). They were at risk of losing their covenantal inheritance—and their promised land (Micah 1:9).

The whole point of the Micah Mandate was to shatter their "either/or" mindset with a fully integrated "both/and" worldview. It was to bring solid Biblical balance to their lives.

Admittedly, as pastor and author Fred Lybrand has pointed out: "Balance, as a popular word in Christian circles, is also a very unbiblical concept when it means compromise—especially the compromise of truth."[11] Indeed, he says: "There is no balance between Heaven and earth. No balance between the kingdom of light and the kingdom of darkness. No balance between the wisdom from above and earthly wisdom."[12]

But then, that is precisely what the Micah Mandate guards

FROM WASTELAND TO GARDEN

He has shown you, O man, what is good and what the Lord requires of you: to do justice, to love mercy, and to walk humbly with your God (Micah 6:8).

Through the ages, Christian heroes were invariably able to recognize that though they were not to be of the world, neither were they to be out of it. Time after time, they clearly portrayed a distinctively balanced Biblical worldview. They approached the wasteland of this world with all the intensity of determined gardeners. Examples abound:

Boniface of Crediton (675–754) spent the first forty years of his life in quiet service to the church near his home in Exeter. He discipled young converts, cared for the sick, and administered relief for the poor. He was a competent scholar as well, expounding Bible doctrine in a small theological center and compiling the first Latin grammar in England. But in 718, Boniface left the comfort and security of this life to become a missionary to the savage Teutonic tribes along the Germanic frontier. When he was well past seventy, he and his companions were set upon by heathen Frieslanders and put to the sword. But while they were able to snuff out his life, they could do nothing to stifle his influence. He affected virtually every aspect of life in medieval Germany—from educational institutions and political structures to worship services and evangelistic outreaches. His carefully thought out worldview was all-encompassing and as a result his influence was all-embracing.

The beautiful and beguiling Elizabeth of Bratislava (1207–1231) was the daughter of the Hungarian king, Andrew II. Her marriage at the age of fourteen to Ludwig of Thuringia, though arranged for political reasons, was a happy one and the couple had three children. In 1227, Ludwig died suddenly after joining a band of crusaders bound for the Holy Land. Grief stricken for some months, the young Elizabeth finally vowed to give the rest of her life in service to the needy. She helped to establish one of the first foundling hospitals in Europe, as well as several orphanages and almshouses. Justice and mercy were the hallmarks of her worldview, but they were defined by the parameters of humility and faith. Though her life was short, her legacy was enduring both in heaven and on earth.

Charles Haddon Spurgeon (1834–1892) is commonly heralded as the greatest preacher to grace the Christian pulpit since the apostle Paul. His Metropolitan Tabernacle was undoubtedly a dynamic force for righteousness in Victorian England. But his many years of ministry were marked not only by his masterful pulpiteering, but by his many social and cultural labors as well. In 1861, he erected an almshouse for the elderly. In 1864, he established a school for the needy children of London. In 1866, he founded the Stockwell Orphanages, and to these many enterprises he added still another, a private hospital. In all he was responsible for some sixty different institutions—schools, seminaries, colportage societies, missionary agencies, and mercy ministries. His commitment to fulfilling the Great Commission led him to a fully integrated and dynamically engaged worldview—and ultimately established him as a paragon of balanced and effective evangelical leadership.

Dozens of others could be cited throughout the wide span of history: Giles of Aegidius (d. 796), Clement Slovensky (d. 916), Edburga of Winchester (d. 960), Louis of France (d. 1270), Benedict the Black (d. 1657), Edward Ridley (d. 1699), and Charles Wesley (d. 1788). Each sought to develop a Biblical worldview distinguished by a commitment to justice, mercy, and humility before God. And thus each tended the garden of this world with perspicacity and discernment.

against. It affords us balance, not through compromise, but through a righteous commitment to walk in accord with God's providential working in the world. It focuses our attentions on incarnational truth. It equips and enables us to be "in" the world but not "of" it.

This principle runs all through the Bible. God's redemptive work involves more than saving souls. It involves more than preserving the status quo. It involves making "all things . . . new" (2 Corinthians 5:17). As Francis Schaeffer once said: "If Christ is indeed Lord, He must be Lord of all of life—in spiritual matters, of course, but just as much across the whole spectrum of life, including intellectual matters and the areas of culture, law, and government."[13]

And again: "Evangelism is primary, but it is not the end of our work and indeed cannot be separated from the rest of the Christian life. We must acknowledge and then act upon the fact that if Christ is our Savior, He is also our Lord in all of life. He is our Lord not just in the religious things and not just in cultural things such as the arts and music, but in our intellectual lives, and in business, and in our relation to society, and in our attitude toward the moral breakdown of our culture."[14]

❖ A Balanced Worldview

Forging a genuine Christian worldview—one that integrates a proper concern for this poor fallen world and simultaneously maintains true spirituality—is no easy bill to fill. But then neither is it impossible. In fact, the annals of history are filled with the inspiring stories of men and women who faithfully and diligently hammered out that kind of balance in the context of their lives and work.

Patrick Henry, for instance, was not only a great American patriot, he was a man of profound faith who took seriously the call to view all things through the lens of Scripture. There can be little doubt that he strove to maintain the balance that only a Biblical worldview can afford. He was an exemplar of the Micah Mandate.

It was on the fourth day of the Second Virginia Convention that Henry kindled the fires of the American Revolution with blazing words that would forever alter the course of this continent: "Is life so dear, or peace so sweet, as to be purchased at the price of chains and slavery? Forbid it, Almighty God. I know not what course others may take, but as for me, give me liberty or give me death."[15]

As he spoke, he was in the presence of all the greatest luminaries of the day—Washington, Jefferson, Randolph, Harrison, Wythe, Braxton, and Lee—but he would later say that there was only one witness to his oratory that he was actually concerned to please: "It was my foremost occupation to please the Master of the House. For with His approval, I could not help but to accomplish goodly ends."[16]

Because the Colonial legislative assembly had been dissolved by order of the royal governor, Lord Dunmore, the leaders of the Burgesses had abandoned Williamsburg, then capital of the Dominion, and had gathered some miles inland, just above the James River shoals on Church Hill in the city of Richmond. A local pastor, Miles Seldon, offered to open his small chapel to the convention—an offer the men gratefully accepted. And so it was that Patrick Henry's famous speech was delivered on March 23, 1775, in the makeshift accommodations of St. John's, the Henrico Parish Church. The "Master of the House" that he so desired to please was thus, the Lord Himself.

Henry later said:

> Of all the honors that have befallen me in this life, the chief is that Providence afforded me the privilege of delivering such an address in such a place. Before the very presence of God Almighty, I made appeal for right. The affairs that followed have indeed vindicated our cause and wed our destiny with the cause of Heaven."[17]

That insight helps to explain how and why Henry devoted himself to public affairs throughout his life. He was, after all, a devout Christian—and thus was under no illusions about the relative significance of temporal affairs in the light of eternity. He was a committed family man—and thus was keenly aware of the intrusion of public concerns into private duties. And he was a southern agrarian—and thus was decidedly diffident about the cosmopolitan diversions of civic involvement.

Like so many of the other revolutionary leaders of his day the most notable aspect of Patrick Henry's character was that he was not particularly revolutionary. Thus, like those other protagonists in America's epic conflict—from Samuel Adams and John Hancock to James Iredell and Henry Laurens—he was a profoundly conservative man in both manner and resolve. He was loathe to indulge in any kind of radicalism that had the potential to erupt into violence—rhetorical, political, or martial. He was a faithful son of the Colonial gentry. He was devoted to the time-honored conventions of Whig representative covenantalism: the rule of law, noblesse oblige, unswerving honor, squirey superintendence, and the maintenance of corporate order. He believed in a tranquil and settled society free of the raucous upsets and tumults of agitation, activism, and unrest.

In short, Patrick Henry was very much a man of his time and place.

He was second of eleven children—descended from solid Scottish Presbyterian stock. He worked hard—as a planter, a shopkeeper, and a country lawyer. In addition he was the primary educator of his children—teaching them Greek, Latin, logic, rhetoric, history, and classical literature. And as if that weren't enough, he kept himself busy in his work as a vestryman at church, as the sponsor of several missions to the frontier, as a sometime delegate to the House of Burgesses, and as an informal rotating instructor at a local Presbyterian meetinghouse.

He was too busy with the ordinary responsibilities of life to involve himself in radical politics. His Christian faith was too deeply engrained to dislodge his attentions from what he called "those essential permanent things."[18]

In that regard, he was not alone of course. The reticence of virtually all the notable Colonials to squabble with the Crown or to dally in political petulance was obvious to even the most casual observer. They exhausted every recourse to law before they even thought to resort to armed resistance. For more than a decade they sent innumerable appeals, suits, and petitions to both parliament and king. Even after American blood had been spilled, they refrained from impulsive insurrection.

It took more than the Boston Massacre, more than Lexington and Concord, more than Bunker Hill, more than Falmouth, and more than Ticonderoga to provoke the patriots to commit themselves to forceful secession. Even as late as the first week of July 1776, there was no solid consensus among the members of the Continental Congress that "such an extreme as full-scale revolt," as John Dickinson dubbed it, was necessary. That week, the "Declaration of Independence," drafted by a committee composed of Benjamin Franklin, Roger Sherman, Robert Livingston, John Adams, and the young Thomas Jefferson, was defeated twice before it was diffidently adopted—and even then the cautious delegates managed to keep its pronouncements secret for four more days. And though Patrick Henry was an early advocate of independence, he did not arrive at that conviction easily or casually.

Like virtually all his fellow patriots he was, at best, a reluctant revolutionary.

Why then did he rebel? What could possibly have so overcome his native conservatism? Why would such a naturally taciturn man seek to rouse his comrades to insurrection—however valiant the cause?

It was his abiding Christian worldview—his commitment to those lasting things, both in heaven and on earth, that transcend the ever-shifting tides of situation and circumstance—that finally drove him to action. He resolved to challenge king and motherland in order to preserve all that which king and motherland had always represented before: justice, mercy, and humility before God.

Henry actually abhorred worldly affairs but he was thrust into the affairs of the world. His ultimate concern was the world into which he would someday go but he devoted much of his career to the world into which he had already come. He forged a practical balance between the temporal and eternal as the best expression of authentic Christian faithfulness.

Patrick Henry had his priorities straight. His worldview was sound. His passion for justice—which made him an oratorical firebrand—was carefully balanced by an equal passion for mercy and spiritual humility—which made him a statesman rather than just a politician.

All too often we fall into the trap of focusing on one virtue to the exclusion of all the others. The sad result is that our virtues practically become vices. Thus, when we emphasize justice without mercy, we develop hard heads and even harder hearts. When we emphasize mercy without justice, we develop soft heads and even softer hearts. When we emphasize either one without humility, we develop a kind of spiritual megalomania—thinking that our project, or our focus, or our methodology is the best and only way. We're either so heavenly minded that we're no earthly good, or so earthly minded that we're no heavenly good.

Patrick Henry avoided that trap. He apparently understood that while he was a citizen of one kingdom, he was an ambassador to another. Each role was important. In fact, the roles were essentially inseparable in his mind—the flip sides of a single coin—though he knew that the former determined the latter. It was clear to him that he was to be "in the world" but not "of it." Thus his allegiance to Christ was made manifest just as much in his earthly responsibilities—first to his kinsmen in Virginia, then to his comrades in America, and finally, to the uttermost parts of the earth—as in his heavenly ones. For him, the integration of justice, mercy, and humility before God was simply a matter of course—it was woven into the very fabric of his life and faith. It was the warp and woof of his worldview.

❖ MICAH'S WORLDVIEW

The modern church is sundered by activists who want to save the world on the one hand and by pietists who want to ignore it on the other. Both perspectives are tragically out of sync with the kind of balanced Biblical worldview Patrick Henry and a myriad of other faithful Christians in the past attempted to live by.

Our protests, letter writing campaigns, legal initiatives, and moral crusades will never save the world. Our struggle for political legitimacy, our attempts at media savvy, and our cultural trench warfare will never "take America back." As Michael Scott Horton has aptly asserted: "We are going to have to realize that America is a mission field, not a battlefield."[19] The church is not just another interest group or political action committee. Our goals must never be set by the standards of this fallen world—either positively or negatively. Our ultimate purpose must never be to "change the culture" but to honor the living God. That we all too often lose sight of that fact is shameful.

But God is not honored by either detachment or irrelevance. An etherial and pious disassociation from the great questions of our day is not Christian single-mindedness, it is Gnostic absent-mindedness. To be so heavenly minded that we are no earthly good is not only a poor witness to the transforming power of the Gospel before a watching world, it is a dreadful neglect of the pattern of discipleship before the hosts of heaven. The abhorence of the Gospel by those who control the cultural apparatus in our day is not nearly so frightening as the abhorence of responsibility by those who inhabit the vast Evangelical ghetto. The former is simply evidence of the fallen estate, while the latter bespeaks indifference in the face of grace. That, too, is shameful.

We are not to be of the world. But neither are we to be out of it. Both extremes malign God's intentions for us and those that God has placed around us. Both obscure the divine imperitive to simultaneously live justly, love mercy, and walk humbly with our God. Both obliterate a Biblical worldview. Both impede us from tending the garden of this world and yield it up to the ravages of a howling wilderness.

Our present challenge is therefore as abundantly clear as was the challenge that faced Patrick Henry so very long ago—and indeed that has faced every generation of believers since the day of Pentecost: "How long will you falter between two opinions? If the Lord is God, follow Him" (1 Kings 18:21).

Living Worldviewishly

He has shown you, O man, what is good and what the Lord requires of you: to do justice, to love mercy, and to walk humbly with your God (Micah 6:8).

❖ Read the apostle Paul's very practical instructions in Romans 12. Notice the comprehensive nature of these guidelines for a full-orbed Christian lifestyle—covering everything from societal issues and interpersonal relationships to care for the brethren and solace for the soul. How might the Micah Mandate induce this kind of balanced worldview perspective?

❖ Discernment is one of the weakest links in the modern church. So why not hone your discerning powers? Play a little game of "Identify the Worldview" with a friend. Here's how it works: Start naming some of today's hottest trends, ideas, books, movies, songs, or fashions and then see if you can identify the worldview orientation that each one represents. What about television programs? Or ads and commercials? How do they differ from a Christian worldview? Why?

❖ Now read a couple of the classics from Christendom's past: Chaucer, Shakespeare, Milton, Johnson, or Scott. How do the worldviews of these works differ from the current crop of cultural expressions? How might these differences affect us all— even in subtle, unconscious ways?

❖ There is an old computer programming adage that asserts "garbage in, garbage out." If our only cultural input is utterly and completely contrary to the worldview that we wish to inculcate, there is little chance that we will reflect anything other than contrarian views. Thus, we all ought to try to develop a conscious program of alternative cultural stimuli. Read the classics. Listen to fine and uplifting music. Turn off the television—or better yet, put it out in the garage. Rebuild your worldview from the foundation up.

PART TWO
Justice: To Do Right

He that is warm for truth, and fearless in its defense, performs one of the duties of a good man; he strengthens his own conviction, and guards others from delusion; but steadiness of belief, and boldness of profession, are yet only part of the form of godliness.

SAMUEL JOHNSON

Only the sheerest relativism insists that passing time renders unattainable one ideal while forcing upon us another.

RICHARD WEAVER

3

Legal Entanglements

*Nothing is more common than for men to make partial and
absurd distinctions between vices of equal enormity, and to
observe some of the divine commands with great scrupulousness,
while they violate others, equally important, without any concern, or the least apparent consciousness of guilt.*

SAMUEL JOHNSON

*To establish the fact of decadence is the most pressing duty of
our time.*

RICHARD WEAVER

We arranged to meet in a bookstore. Naturally. Tom Gilmore and
I had been corresponding for more than eighteen months—ever
since he had seen a book review I had written in a literary maga-
zine. He had read the book—a blatantly liberal and humanistic
analysis of recent conservative political frustrations, foibles, and
failures—and was taken aback by my rather positive critique.

"How could you?" he had complained.

I wrote back explaining how I could. And thus began a very
unlikely friendship.

I rode one of the famous cable cars down Market Street and
then crossed through Chinatown on foot. The sights and sounds
and smells of San Francisco in the spring are nearly indescribable.
The rugged hills and glistening bay combine with the sophisti-
cated bustle of street life and the aromas of some of the world's

best cuisine to create an incongruously delightful texture to a supremely urban setting. The variety was eye-popping. It was a carnival of human diversity and cultural heterogeneity.

I was headed toward one of my favorite places in the city, the City Lights bookstore. Since the fifties it has been the city's premier literary meeting place for artists, writers, students, radicals, bibliophiles, and tourists. Over the years it has played host successively to the Beatniks, the Peaceniks, the Hippies, the Yippies, and the Yuppies. It is colorful, eccentric, bombastic, and raucous.

It is also a great bookstore. Its selection of poetry is unparalleled. Its wide array of fiction is remarkable for its breadth and depth. Though a little slanted toward leftist revisionism, its history section is quite vast. And its modern philosophy department is as complete as any I have seen. But it is its section devoted to the subjects of law, justice, and politics that most amazes me.

When Tom caught up with me, that is where I was.

The selections before us ran the ideological gamut—from unrepentant communism to wild-eyed anarchism. There were books advocating everything from a revived Fascism to a refurbished Stalinism. Even the "mainstream" treatises on American legal theory seemed to cover the whole judicial waterfront: Positivism, Determinism, Deconstructivism, Rationalism, Reductionism, Strict Constructionism, Loose Constructionism, Progressive Constructionism, and Organic Constructionism were all well represented.

"I don't know how anyone could ever sort all this out," Tom commented. His mind was a bit agog at the vast disparity of views arrayed before him. "I always thought that there were just two varieties of politics: liberal and conservative. But it appears that justice can mean almost anything to anybody."

"In some ways, error is infinite in its variety," I replied. "While truth is always uniquely singular. At the same time though, all of these ideological formulas seem to gravitate toward either extreme legalism or extreme lawlessness. In the end, all the high sounding rhetoric and the noble political sloganeering boil down to this: We either tend to believe that a strict adherence to some system of law will save us or we believe that no system of law really matters or is binding upon us. They are polar opposites that are nevertheless identical in their ideological rigidity."

For months now I had been challenging Tom to rethink his adamant ideological bent. He had gone from one extreme to another since his conversion a couple of years earlier—from hardcore liberalism to reactionary conservatism. I tried to show him that the two positions were just flip sides of the same coin—that both depended upon an inherently imbalanced view of the law.

"Non-Christian systems of law and justice invariably fall into this twin trap of legalism and lawlessness," I said, sweeping my hand across the shelves in front of us. "The only possible alternative to this Babel-like confusion is a return to Biblical fidelity."

"And that's neither exclusively conservative nor liberal," he surmised.

"That's right," I said. "It's neither. It's entirely nonideological. The rarest of all notions in these difficult days in which we live."

❖ FAITH, HOPE, AND POLITICS

And now abide faith, hope, and politics, these three; but the greatest of these is politics. Or so it seems.

In the twentieth century, the smothering influence of partisan ideology is everywhere evident. It has all too evidently wrested control of every academic discipline, of every cultural trend, of every intellectual impulse, even of every religious revival in our time. From Nazism and Stalinism to Pluralism and Multiculturalism, from Liberalism and Conservatism to Monopolism and Socialism, ours has been an epoch of movements beguiled by the temporal seductions of ideological politics.

In a nutshell, that is what Tom and I had witnessed in that bookstore in San Francisco.

Nearly every question, every issue, every social dilemma has been and continues to be translated into legal, juridical, or mechanical terms. They are supplied with bureaucratic, mathematical, or systemic solutions. If there is something wrong with the economy then government must fix it. If family values are absent then government must supply them. If health care provision is inefficient then government must rectify the situation. If education is in disarray then government must reorder the system. Whatever the problem, it seems that government is the solution.

Virtually all social historians agree that this is indeed the most distinctive aspect of our age: the subsuming of all other concerns to the rise of political mass movements based upon comprehensive, secular, closed-universe, and millenarian intellectual systems. Thus, at one time or another, Henry David Aiken, Karl Dietrich Bracher, Isaac Kraminick, Frederick Watkins, Barbara Tuchman, Antonia Fraser, Paul Johnson, Russell Kirk, and Murray Rothbard have all dubbed this the "Age of Ideology."[1]

The name of the ideological game is power. With all the cool detachment of wintry witchery every other consideration is relegated to a piratical humbug. G. K. Chesterton observes:

> There is, as a ruling element in modern life, a blind and asinine appetite for mere power. There is a spirit abroad among the nations of the earth which drives men incessantly on to destroy what they cannot understand, and to capture what they cannot enjoy.[2]

That power may be obtained by imposing the strict standards of law over the totality of life or it may be obtained by the obliteration of all legal obligations. But either way, the object is power.

According to philosopher Eric Vogelin, this awful tendency is essentially "the politics of spiritual revolt."[3] It is, he says, a kind of "psychic disorientation," a "metastatic faith," a "modern promethianism," a "secular parousianism," or, perhaps most accurately, a "dominion of pneumapathological consciousness."[4]

Elaborating on those notions, political scientist Michael Franz has said:

> Ideological consciousness is typified by a turning-away from the transcendent ground in revolt against the tension of contingent existence. In the modern era this revolt has taken many forms, all of which are expressive of dissatisfaction with the degree of certainty afforded by faith, trust, and hope as sources of knowledge and existential orientation. The great ideologists seek to displace Christian revelation by misplacing the transcendent ground within an immanent hierarchy of being, identifying the essence of human existence as productive relations, historical progress, racial compensation, libidinous drives, scientific rationality, or the will to power. Within the intellectual systems constructed around these misplacements of the ground, humanity appears as an autonomous, self-created species capable of assuming control of its destiny through the self-conscious application of new forms of knowledge.[9]

In short, an ideological approach to law and justice is little more than a revived gnosticism, an abiding humanism rooted in the naked politicization of every detail of life. It is a worldview as thorough and as dominating in our time as was the Faith during the epoch of Christendom. And it plunges us into the maelstrom of the twin perils of legalism and lawlessness with a hearty abandon.

Thus Jane Addams—the radical urban social reformer during the uproarious teens and twenties—was hardly exaggerating when she said:

> Ideology is the modern ecology. It is the landscape we see, the sound we hear, the food we eat, the air we breathe. It is the incarnation of truth for us and the emblem and impress of earthly harmony. It is the essence of modern beauty.[6]

As a result, any discussion of justice is apt to become bogged down in the mechanical details of legal management, regulation, and enforcement. Talk about justice and people naturally expect political partisanship, policy pronouncements, administrative agendas, and strategic systems. It has been reduced to one or another of a myriad of laws to pass, cases to adjudicate, or sentences to impose.

But this modern notion is a far cry from the kind of Biblical vision of justice that the American founders and pioneers maintained. They shared a profound distrust of simplistic legal systems to either positively or negatively solve the grave problems that afflicted individuals, communities, and societies. Certainly they believed in strong and active civil constructs for justice—but only in their proper place. Thus every brand of ideology was abhorred by them.

Thomas Jefferson warned against the danger of "reducing the society to the law or the law to society."[7] Patrick Henry argued that the contention that the systemic legal structures should at their own option intrude into and exercise control over the family and the household was a "great and pernicious error."[8] Gouverneur Morris insisted that the everyday affairs of society should be designed to avoid what he called the "interference of the law beyond its competence,"[9] while Henry Cabot Lodge insisted that law was but a tool:

> If ever we come to the place where our tools determine what
> jobs we can or cannot do, and by what means, then nary a
> fortnight shall pass in which new freedoms shall be wrested
> from us straightaway. Societal problems are solved by families
> and communities as they carefully and discriminantly use a
> variety of tools in obedience to God.[10]

The problem is, even Christians are prone to fall into the twin traps of ideology. We either overemphasize the importance of law and justice or we ignore it altogether. We either become obsessed with systemic legalism or we flirt with a kind of licentious liberty. We fail to see that we can be faithful or that we can be full of faith.

As a result, authentic justice is altogether absent from our lives and our world.

Tom Gilmore and I stepped back out onto the streets of San Francisco and we saw that only too well. The deleterious effects of both legalism and lawlessness were all about us. Our trip to the bookstore had been quite an object lesson.

❖ LEGALISM

With an obvious sense of sober grief, the apostle Paul wrote to the small community of believers in Galatia:

> I marvel that you are turning away so soon from Him who called you in the grace of Christ, to a different gospel, which is not another; but there are some who trouble you and want to pervert the gospel of Christ. But even if we, or an angel from heaven, preach any other gospel to you than what we have preached to you, let him be accursed. As we have said before, so now I say again, if anyone preaches any other gospel to you than what you have received, let him be accursed. (Galatians 1:6–9)

Somehow the Christians in the Galatian church had been "bewitched" (Galatians 3:1). They had fallen into the grips of that most ancient of all heresies: salvation by law.

Galatia was a huge Roman province in the central mountainous region of Asia Minor. On his first missionary journey, the apostle Paul had founded a number of churches there: in Antioch (Acts 14:13–52), in Iconium (Acts 14:1–7), in Lystra (Acts 14:8–18), and in Derbe (Acts 14:19–20). Later he would make at least two follow-up visits (Acts 16:6; 18:23) so that the entire region was evangelized (Acts 19:10) and "the word of the Lord grew mightily and prevailed" (Acts 19:20).

Shortly after Paul's departure, however, a number of Jewish teachers arrived in Galatia. Whereas Paul had taught salvation "by grace through faith" and this alone, these men insisted that non-Jewish converts must also be circumcised and observe all the minutiae of the law in order to be saved. They contradicted Paul and the message of the Gospel, saying that faith is not enough; there are things we must do to merit God's grace.

The Galatians believed this twisted doctrine despite the fact that the whole of the Bible—from Genesis to Revelation—is diametrically opposed to it. Legalism is heresy. It is an Old Testament heresy and a New Testament heresy. It was repudiated by Abraham (Genesis 15:6; Romans 4:3; Galatians 3:6). It was denied by Moses (Deuteronomy 27:26). It was condemned by Isaiah (Isaiah 1:10–18), and Jeremiah (Jeremiah 4:1–9), and Amos (Amos 5:1–7), and Habakkuk (Habakkuk 2:4). David exposed the futility of salvation by works (Psalm 32:1–2; Psalm 51:1–17) no less vehemently than did Paul (Romans 9:32; Galatians 3:10; Ephesians 2:9), Matthew (Matthew 8:22), Luke (Luke 9:60; 15:24, 32), John (John 5:25; 15:4–6), Jude (Jude 4–16), or Peter (2 Peter 1:3–4; 2:1–22).

Legalism abolishes the significance of the Cross (Galatians 5:11). It makes light of Christ's sacrifice (Galatians 2:21). It nullifies the work of the Holy Spirit (Galatians 3:3–5). It abrogates the necessity of grace (Romans 4:4). "Faith is made void and the promise made of no effect" (Romans 4:14) because it makes man and man's ability the measure of all things rather than the rule of God (Matthew 15:6–9).

Salvation according to the Bible is a work of grace. There is nothing we can do to merit God's favor:

> But God, who is rich in mercy, because of His great love with which He loved us, even when we were dead in trespasses, made us alive together with Christ (by grace you have been saved), and raised us up together, and made us sit together in the heavenly places in Christ Jesus, that in the ages to come He might show the exceeding riches of His grace in His kindness toward us in Christ Jesus. For by grace you have been saved through faith, and that not of yourselves; it is the gift of God, not of works, lest anyone should boast. (Ephesians 2:4–9)

He saved us, through the washing of regeneration and renewing of the Holy Spirit, whom He poured out on us abundantly through Jesus Christ our Savior, that having been justified by His grace we should become heirs according to the hope of eternal life. (Titus 3:5–7)

Men from all walks of life, in every age, on every continent have attempted to avoid the implications of salvation by grace alone. We cannot stand the thought of being at the mercy of God. None of us can. And so we are constantly dreaming up new versions of the same old heresy: salvation by works, salvation by law, salvation by education, salvation by legislation.

The Galatians had fallen under the sway of this heresy and thus were preaching another Gospel contrary to that which they had received (Galatians 1:9). They had turned the Biblical notion of justice into something that it was never intended to be.

❖ LAWLESSNESS

But there is an equal and opposite error. It is what Francis Schaeffer called "latitudinarianism,"[11] what John Calvin called "antinomianism,"[12] what Martin Luther called "libertinism,"[13] and what Charles Spurgeon called "permissive and dismissive immorality."[14] It is what the Bible calls "evil desire" (Romans 7:8), "lewdness" (Ephesians 4:19), and "carnal" (1 Corinthians 3:3).

Like legalism, lawless disobedience is heresy. It is an attribute of rank ideological paganism (2 Peter 2:8) and of the Antichrist (2 Thessalonians 2:8). While God loves righteousness, He hates lawlessness (Hebrews 1:9).

Jesus said:

Not everyone who says to Me, "Lord, Lord," shall enter the kingdom of heaven, but he who does the will of My Father in heaven. Many will say to Me in that day, "Lord, Lord, have we not prophesied in Your name, cast out demons in Your name, and done many wonders in Your name?" And then I will declare to them, "I never knew you; depart from Me, you who practice lawlessness!" (Matthew 7:21–23)

Again, He said to His disciples:

> If anyone loves Me, he will keep My word; and My Father will love him, and We will come to him and make Our home with him. He who does not love Me does not keep my word. (John 14:23–24)

This is, as John MacArthur has asserted, "the Gospel according to Jesus."[15] It is, he says, "a call to discipleship, a call to follow Him in submissive obedience, not just a plea to make a decision or say a prayer."[16] It is a life of faith, righteousness, holiness, and consecration demonstrable in both word and deed.

"As obedient children," we are not to conform "to the former lusts" we had when we lived in "ignorance" (1 Peter 1:14). We must "put to death [our] members which are on the earth" (Colossians 3:5). We must "lay aside . . . the sin which so easily ensnares" (Hebrews 12:1) and "make no provision for the flesh" (Romans 13:14). We must not be "conformed to this world" (Romans 12:2) or "walk as the rest of the Gentiles walk, in the futility of their mind" (Ephesians 4:17). Instead, the apostle Peter says, "As He who called you is holy, you also be holy in all your conduct, because it is written, 'Be holy, for I am holy'" (1 Peter 1:15–16).

Any other message is, like legalism, "another" Gospel, a "different" Gospel, a "perverted" Gospel, an "accursed" Gospel (Galatians 1:6–9).

J. C. Ryle stated the case plainly: "I doubt indeed, whether we have any warrant for saying that a man can possibly be converted without being consecrated to God."[17]

George Whitefield similarly asserted:

> Though good works, which are the fruits of faith, cannot put away our sins, or endure the severity of God's judgment—that is, cannot justify us—yet they follow after justification, and do

spring necessarily of a true and lively faith, insomuch that by them a lively faith may be as evidently known as a tree discerned by the fruit.[18]

His friend Jonathan Edwards—perhaps the greatest theological mind America has ever produced—wholeheartedly agreed:

That religion which God requires, and will accept, does not consist in weak, dull, and lifeless wishes, raising us but a little above a state of indifference. God in His Word, greatly insists upon it, that we be in good earnest, fervent in spirit, and our hearts vigorously engaged in religion. . . . Those who thus insist on persons' living by faith, when they have no experience, and are in very bad frames, are also very absurd in their notions of faith.[19]

❖ THE PURPOSE OF THE WORD

Christopher Morely once wrote that "the enemies of the truth are always awfully nice."[20] To that we might add Mark Twain's quip that "the streets of hell are paved with good intentions."[21] The problem with both legalism and lawlessness is that they seem so nice, so well intentioned—at least, at first glance. One brand or another of ideology seems to be as natural as breathing for us.

That is why we so desperately need an objective standard—one that stands above even our experience. We need an absolute against which no encroachment of prejudice or preference may interfere. There must be a foundation that the winds of change and the waters of circumstance cannot erode. There must be a basis for truth and justice that can be depended upon at all times, in all places, and in every situation.

The Bible is that standard, that absolute, and that foundation. All those who have gone before us in faith—fathers, forefathers, patriarchs, prophets, apostles, preachers, evangelists, martyrs, confessors, ascetics, and every righteous spirit made pure in Christ—have known that only too well.

The Bible is the Word of God. It is His revelation of wisdom, knowledge, understanding, and truth. It is not simply a splendid collection of inspiring sayings and stories. It is God's message to man. It is God's instruction. It is God's direction. It is God's guideline, His plumb line, and His bottom line.

From Genesis to Revelation the Bible is God's own Word. Nearly five thousand times throughout, the narrative is punctuated with phrases such as "thus says the Lord," "thus the Lord commanded His people," or "thus came the Word of the Almighty."

Ultimately, it is only this "sure word" in the Bible—with all its uncomfortable offense—that enables us to steer clear of the twin dangers of legalism and lawlessness.

Understand: The Bible is something that we obey because we have been justified. We do not obey it in order to be justified. Obedience to the Word is the effect of salvation, not the cause of salvation. In other words, daily submission to the statutes of God is a means of sanctification and transformation, not the means of justification and redemption. It is a way of life, not a way of salvation.

Jesus constantly upheld the validity of God's Word as a guide for living and an expression of the unchanging standards of His sovereign rule:

- "Man shall not live by bread alone, but by every word that proceeds from the mouth of God" (Matthew 4:4).
- "It is easier for heaven and earth to pass away than for one title of the law to fail" (Luke 16:17).
- "Whoever therefore breaks one of the least of these commandments, and teaches men so, shall be called least in the kingdom of heaven; but whoever does and teaches them, he shall be called great in the kingdom of heaven" (Matthew 5:19).

Again and again He affirmed the truth that "all Scripture is given by inspiration of God" (2 Timothy 3:16), and that it "cannot be broken" (John 10:35). He did not come to do away with the commands of God—to abolish or abrogate them. On the contrary, He came to fulfill them—to confirm and uphold them (Matthew 5:17). He reiterated the fact that every one of His "righteous judgments endures forever" (Psalm 119:160) and that "the Word of our God stands forever" (Isaiah 40:8).

Jesus was affirming that unlike human lawmakers, God does not change His mind or alter His standards: "My covenant I will not break, nor alter the word that has gone out of My lips" (Psalm 89:34). When the Lord speaks, His Word stands firm forever. His assessments of right and wrong do not change from age to age: "All His precepts are sure. They stand fast forever and ever, and are done in truth and uprightness" (Psalm 111:7–8).

Jesus appealed to God's eternal statutes to bolster His teaching (John 8:17). He used them to vindicate His behavior (Matthew 12:5). He used them to answer His questioners (Luke 10:26), to indict His opponents (John 7:19), to identify God's will (Matthew 19:17), to establish kingdom citizenship (Matthew 7:24), to confront Satan (Matthew 4:1–11), and to confirm Christian love (John 14:21). He was, in short, a champion of the Word.

But He also put the juridical aspects of the revelation of Scripture in its place. He showed us that obedience to the Word is not designed to effect salvation for men. Instead, it is designed to effect holiness for men. It is designed to enable men to submit to and evidence the good providence of God in their lives.

This is what the apostle Paul meant when he said that we are no longer "under the law" (Romans 6:14–15), that in fact we are "dead to the law" (Romans 7:4; Galatians 2:19). Instead, we are under the sacrificial covering of Christ's blood fulfilling the death sentence of the commandments against us (Romans 8:1–2). But the Word is not thereby made void; rather, its curse is (Galatians 3:13). In fact, when the commandments are put in their proper grace perspective, they are established (Romans 3:31).

The everlasting Word is thus divinely confirmed to accomplish several tasks in the realms of both heaven and earth:

First, the Word reveals the moral standards of God's sovereign rule. This is what the patriarchs and the Reformers called *usus politicus*: the civil or cultural application of God's commands:

> How can a young man cleanse his way?
> By taking heed according to Your word.
> With my whole heart I have sought You;
> oh, let me not wander from Your commandments!
> Your Word I have hidden in my heart,
> that I might not sin against You.
> Blessed are You, O Lord!
> Teach me Your statutes. (Psalm 119:9–12)

> And all these blessings shall come upon you and overtake you, because you obey the voice of the Lord your God: Blessed shall you be in the city, and blessed shall you be in the country. Blessed shall be the fruit of your body, and the produce of your ground and the increase of your herds, the increase of your cattle and the offspring of your flocks. Blessed shall be your basket and your kneading bowl. Blessed shall you be when you come in, and blessed shall you be when you go out. The Lord will cause your enemies who rise against you to be defeated before your face; they shall come out against you one way and flee before you seven ways. . . . But it shall come to pass, if you do not obey the voice of the Lord your God, to observe carefully all His commandments and His statutes which I command you today, that all these curses will come upon you and overtake you: Cursed shall you be in the city, and cursed shall you be in the country. Cursed shall be your basket and your kneading bowl, cursed shall be the fruit of your body and the produce of your land, the increase of your cattle and the offspring of your flocks. Cursed shall you be when you come in, and cursed shall you be when you go out. (Deuteronomy 28:2–7, 15–19)

Second, the Word convicts us of sin and leads us to Christ. This is what the patriarchs and the Reformers called *usus pedagogus*: the tutorial application of God's commands:

> Therefore the law was our tutor to bring us to Christ, that we might be justified by faith. (Galatians 3:24)

> What shall we say then? Is the law sin? Certainly not! On the contrary, I would not have known sin except through the law. For I would not have known covetousness unless the law had said, "You shall not covet." But sin, taking opportunity by the commandment, produced in me all manner of evil desire. For apart from the law sin was dead. I was alive once without the law, but when the commandment came, sin revived and I died. And the commandment, which was to bring life, I found to bring death. For sin, taking occasion by the commandment, deceived me, and by it killed me. Therefore the law is holy, and the commandment holy and just and good. Has then what is good become death to me? Certainly not! But sin, that it might appear sin, was producing death in me through what is good, so that sin through the commandment might become exceedingly sinful. For we know that the law is spiritual, but I am carnal, sold under sin. For what I am doing, I do not understand. For what I will to do, that I do not practice; but what I hate, that I do. If, then, I do what I will not to do, I agree with the law that it is good. (Romans 7:7–16).

Third, the Word is a testimony to the nations, calling them to repentance. This is what the patriarchs and the reformers called *usus motivatus*: the motivational application of God's commands:

> Surely I have taught you statutes and judgments, just as the Lord my God commanded me, that you should act according to them in the land which you go to possess. Therefore be careful to observe them; for this is your wisdom and your understanding in the sight of the peoples who will hear all these statutes, and say, "Surely this great nation is a wise and understanding people." For what great nation is there that has God so near to it, as the Lord our God is to us, for whatever

reason we may call upon Him? And what great nation is there that has such statutes and righteous judgments as are in all this law which I set before you this day? (Deuteronomy 4:5–8)

I, the Lord, have called You in righteousness, and will hold Your hand; I will keep You and give You as a covenant to the people, as a light to the Gentiles, to open blind eyes, to bring out prisoners from the prison, those who sit in darkness from the prison house. (Isaiah 42:6–7)

Today the Lord has proclaimed you to be His special people, just as He promised you, that you should keep all His commandments, and that He will set you high above all nations which He has made, in praise, in name, and in honor, and that you may be a holy people to the Lord your God, just as He has spoken. (Deuteronomy 26:18–19)

Fourth, the Word is a kind of blueprint for living, a means for attaining our promised walk of victory in the ordinary details of life. This is what the patriarchs and the reformers called *usus normativus*: the practical and normative application of God's commands:

All Scripture is given by inspiration of God, and is profitable for doctrine, for reproof, for correction, for instruction in righteousness, that the man of God may be complete, thoroughly equipped for every good work. (2 Timothy 3:16–17)

His divine power has given to us all things that pertain to life and godliness, through the knowledge of Him who called us by glory and virtue, by which have been given to us exceedingly great and precious promises, that through these you may be partakers of the divine nature, having escaped the corruption that is in the world through lust. (2 Peter 1:3–4)

Only be strong and very courageous, that you may observe to do according to all the law which Moses My servant commanded you; do not turn from it to the right hand or to the left, that you may prosper wherever you go. This Book of the

Law shall not depart from your mouth, but you shall meditate in it day and night, that you may observe to do according to all that is written in it. For then you will make your way prosperous, and then you will have good success. (Joshua 1:7–8)

So, far from being a replacement for grace, or being opposed to grace, the Bible teaches that the commandments and statutes are provisions of grace. "Is the law then against the promises of God? Certainly not!" (Galatians 3:21)

❖ MANIPULATING GOD

The primary difference between Biblical faith and heresy is that true religion is a response to truth and false religion is an attempt to manipulate God. True faith aims at God's satisfaction, while heresy aims at self-satisfaction.

Throughout the ages, men like Cain have used religion to get what they wanted (Genesis 4:3–8; Hebrews 11:4; 1 John 3:12). Men like Balaam have used religion to control circumstances (Numbers 31:16; 2 Peter 2:15; Revelation 2:14). Men like Korah have used religion to enhance their position (Numbers 16:1–3, 31–35). Cain, Balaam, and Korah all believed in the universal power of magic—either the magic of law or the magic of lawlessness. They believed that not only could they manipulate human society and natural elements with their peculiar approach to moral and ethical standards, but that God would also be forced to conform Himself to the desires and demands of men who acted in terms of certain legal strictures: that if they said certain things, did certain things, believed certain things, or acted out certain things, God would have to respond. In essence, they believed that man controlled his own destiny, using either the rituals and formulas of legalism or the license and autonomy of lawlessness like magical talismans to save mankind, to shape history, to govern society, and even to manipulate God.

It seems that men are forever rejecting the grace of God, that they have "gone in the way of Cain, have run greedily in the error of Balaam for profit, and perished in the rebellion of Korah" (Jude 11).

That is the reason why various forms of tyranny—from statism to anarchism—are so predominant among rebellious men and nations. By contrast, the great liberties that have been enjoyed in America for more than two hundred years were secured against the arbitrary and fickle whims of men and movements by the rule of law. American culture has not depended upon the benevolence of the magistrates, or the altruism of the wealthy, or the condescension of the powerful. Every citizen, rich or poor, man or woman, native-born or immigrant, hale or handicapped, young or old, has been considered equal under the standard of unchanging, immutable, and impartial justice.

As Thomas Paine wrote in *Common Sense*, the powerful booklet that helped spark the War for Independence, "In America, the law is king."[22]

If left to the mere discretion of human authorities, all statutes, edicts, and ordinances inevitably devolve into tyranny. There must be a dependable and unchanging basis for justice—and in America that basis has been Biblical righteousness.

Apart from this uniquely Christian innovation in the affairs of men there can be no hope of freedom or justice. There never has been, and there never will be. Many of our republic's Founding Fathers knew that only too well.

The opening refrain of the Declaration of Independence, for instance, affirms the necessity of an absolute standard upon which justice is derived:

> We hold these truths to be self-evident, that all men are created equal; that they are endowed by their Creator with certain inalienable rights; that among these are life, liberty, and the pursuit of happiness. That, to secure these rights, governments are instituted among men, deriving their just powers from the consent of the governed.[23]

Appealing to the "Supreme Judge of the World" for guidance,

and relying on His "Divine Providence" for wisdom, the framers committed themselves and their posterity to the absolute standard of "the laws of nature and nature's God."[24] And the essence of that standard, they said, were certain "inalienable," "universal," "God-given," and sovereignly "endowed" rights.[25] "A just government exists," they argued, solely and completely to "provide guards" for the "future security" of that essence.[26] Take it away, and no standard of justice is any longer possible.

Sadly, this has been thrown into very real jeopardy in our day—in all our human relations, in and out of the church. No one is absolutely secure, because absoluteness has been thrown out of our operational vocabularies. All the liberties and all the protections of all the men are at risk because suddenly arbitrariness, relativism, and randomness have entered the legal, cultural, and spiritual equations. The checks against petty partiality and blatant bias have been forcibly disabled.

Just as they were in Christ's time by the Pharisees and Herodians.

❖ STRANGE BEDFELLOWS

The Pharisees in ancient Israel were a party of religious legalists. The Herodians were a party of lawless secularists. The Pharisees' name literally meant "the separatists," because they were so concerned to remain unstained by the world. The Herodians' name implied a close connection with one of the most worldly, vile, and xenophobic men in all history. The Pharisees withdrew from occupations of power and influence in order to focus on "spiritual things." The Herodians grasped for such occupations with undeterred zeal in order to focus on "earthly things."

And yet these two parties, so diametrically opposed in every other way, became partners by their opposition to Jesus (Mark 3:6; 12:13; Matthew 22:16). Paganism makes for strange bedfellows: The Pharisaic sons of Jacob became the unwitting cultural accomplices of the Herodian sons of Esau (Mark 3:8).

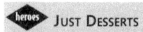 JUST DESSERTS

He has shown you, O man, what is good and what the Lord requires of you: to do justice, to love mercy, and to walk humbly with your God (Micah 6:8).

True justice, being a faithful adherence to God's Word as opposed to some worldly ideological system, has always been a passion for the heroes of the faith through the ages. Despite the conspiratorial scorn of both legalists and antinomians, they stood their ground and leavened their every deed with the undiluted Gospel. Examples abound:

Thomas of Villanueva (1488–1535) grew up in the region of Don Quixote's La Mancha in a devout Christian home where virtuous living and gracious charity were constantly modeled for him by his parents. It was no surprise then when he committed himself to a life of Christian service after graduating from the new university at Alcala. In 1518, at the age of thirty, he was ordained and began a brilliant career as an anointed and effective preacher. His ministry was most distinguished not by his very evident pulpit skills, however, but rather by his care and concern for the poor and needy. He was especially involved in providing relief for abused children and orphans—securing new homes for them as well as meeting their immediate material needs. He was involved in other pro-life activities as well: Once, when he discovered an abortion cabal operating illicitly in a nearby city, he flew into a frenzy of righteous indignation—provoking a criminal investigation and eliciting stronger laws for the protection of children. Relying on neither legalism or lawlessness, he raised once again the standard of justice in the land.

A sudden and glorious conversion transformed *Camillus de Lellis* (1555–1589) from a gruff soldier of fortune into a meek and compassionate servant of Christ. Because he himself had suffered from a chronic affliction, shortly after his decision to trust the Lord he offered himself to the hospital of San Giacomo in Rome, of which he quickly became bursar. This experience opened his eyes to the shocking brutalities of Renaissance life. He began to train and supervise teams of Christian workers to not only care for the sick but to deal with some of the entrenched problems of the poor, the homeless, and the abandoned that lead to disease and contagion. Before the end of the sixteenth century, he had established several hospitals and hospices in Naples to handle the second and third order consequences of both legalism and lawlessness, becoming a champion of justice for thousands.

Education was the privilege of the very few and the very rich until *Jean Baptist De La Salle* (1621–1688) began his great work midway through the seventeenth century. After giving up a life of ease, he dedicated himself to teaching the children of the very poor. He opened day schools, Sunday schools, vocational training schools, teachers colleges, and continuing education centers—actually pioneering many modern techniques and concepts—in more than fourteen cities throughout Europe. He fought hard against the insipid humanistic tendencies within the scholastic community and he deplored the corresponding decline in Christian morality. He believed that if youngsters could be educated in accordance with Gospel principles, the barbarities of both legalism and lawlessness would disappear; but if they were not given the opportunity to advance, such wickedness would eventually prevail—because, as he often quipped, evil desires nothing better than hopelessness and ignorance.

Dozens of others could be cited throughout the wide span of history: Gregory the Great (d. 604), Margaret of Scotland (d. 1093), Sava of Trnova (d. 1235), Bonaventure of Bagnorea (d.1286), Seriphim of Sarov (d. 1833), William Carey (d. 1834), and Jai Ishii of Okayama (d. 1899). Each took the Scriptures as their byword for everything in life. And thus, they left us a legacy of justice unparalleled in all of human history.

The Pharisees opposed Jesus because they felt He had polluted the spiritual realm with earthly cares—such as caring for the poor. The Herodians opposed Jesus because they felt He had polluted the earthly realm with spiritual cares—such as bringing every area of life publicly under the province of God's rule.

So the two parties—the legalistic escapists and the lawless materialists—became co-belligerents. They joined forces to assert a separation of faith and culture, of religion and activism, of righteousness and justice. They joined together in opposition to the Gospel of Christ and its Biblical balance of *usus politicus, usus pedagogus, usus motivatus,* and *usus normativus.*

The party of the Pharisees emphasized a separatist view of piety wherein a sharp division is made between the "spiritual" and the "material." They considered the spiritual realm to be superior to the material. All things physical, all things temporal, all things earthly were spurned. The cultural apparatus was thus left in the hands of evil-doers.

Meanwhile, the party of the Herodians was busy with its work of oppression and repression. The Herodians held seats of cultural power: in government, in education, in the judiciary, and in the financial world. They cared nothing for the morality of the Pharisees. They abhorred their puritanical legalism. They chafed against their piety. They despised their nonconformity.

But they applauded their irrelevancy. They appreciated their distraction from the things of this world. They knew that as long as they maintained a clear separation of justice and righteousness, they would continue to have a free reign. They would be able to perpetuate their defamation of all things holy, all things sacred, and all things pure. They would be able to do "what was right in [their] own eyes" (Judges 21:25).

In this paradoxical fashion, the Herodians counted the irrelevant, isolationist Pharisees as their most trusted allies. And vice versa.

The subversion of true justice is thus a tandem affair induced by equal and opposite extremes that can only unite in this one endeavor.

❖ BETWIXT AND BETWEEN

He was America's first celebrity. Though just twenty-five years old when he began touring the sparsely settled colonies in 1738, George Whitefield was an immediate sensation. And he remained so for the rest of his life. Over the next thirty years, amid some seven visits from his native England, he would leave his mark on the lives of virtually every English-speaking soul living on this side of the Atlantic—from the cosmopolitan businessmen of Philadelphia and the seasoned traders of Boston to the yeomen farmers of Virginia and the frontier adventurers of Canada.

He literally took America by storm. "When he arrived in the colonies," says historian Mark Noll, "he was simply an event."[27] Wherever he went, vast crowds gathered to hear him. Commerce would cease. Shops would close. Farmers would leave their plows mid-furrow. And affairs of the greatest import would be postponed. One of his sermons in the Boston Common actually drew more listeners than the city's entire population. Another in Philadelphia spilled over onto more than a dozen city blocks. Still another in Savannah recorded the largest single crowd ever to gather anywhere in the colonies—despite the scant local population.

Some said he blazed across the public firmament like a "heavenly comet."[28] Some said he was a "magnificent fascination of the like heretofore unknown."[29] Others said he "startled the world awake like a bolt from the blue."[30] There can be little doubt that he lived up to his reputation as the "marvel of the age."[31] As historian Harry Stout has written:

> He was a preacher capable of commanding mass audiences—
> and offerings—across two continents, without any institu-
> tional support, through the sheer power of his personality.
> Whitefield wrote best-selling journals and drew audiences
> totaling in the millions. White and black, male and female,
> friends and enemies—all flocked in unprecedented numbers to
> hear the Grand Itinerant. Whenever he visited, people could
> do anything, it seemed, but stay away.[32]

By all accounts, he was the "father of modern evangelism."[33] He sparked a revival of portentous proportions—the Great Awakening.[34] He pioneered one of the most enduring church reform movements—Methodism.[35] And he laid the foundations for perhaps the greatest experiment in liberty the world has yet known—the American Republic.[36]

All the greatest men of the day were in unabashed awe of his oratorical prowess. Shakespearean actor David Garrick said, "I would give a hundred guineas if I could say *oh* like Mr.

Whitefield."[37] Benjamin Franklin once quipped, "He can bring men to tears merely by pronouncing the word *Mesopotamia*."[38] And Sarah Edwards—the astute and unaffected wife of the dean of American theologians, Jonathan Edwards—remarked, "He is a born orator."[39]

But he was equally beloved for his righteous character. George Washington said, "Upon his lips the Gospel appears even to the coarsest of men as sweet and as true as, in fact, it is."[40] Patrick Henry mused, "Would that every bearer of God's glad tidings be as fit a vessel of grace as Mr. Whitefield."[41] And the poet John Greenleaf Whittier wrote of him:

That life of pure intent,
That voice of warning, yet eloquent,
Of one on the errands of angels sent."[42]

Yet despite his wide acclaim and popularity, Whitefield was often ridiculed, scorned, and persecuted for his faith. Hecklers blew trumpets and shouted obscenities at him as he preached. Enraged mobs often attacked his meetings, robbing, beating, and humiliating his followers. Men were maimed. Women were stripped and occasionally raped. Whitefield himself was subjected to unimaginable brutality—he was clubbed twice, stoned once, whipped at least half a dozen times, and beaten half a dozen more. And he lived constantly under the pall of death threats. Once he recorded in his journal: "I was honored with having a few stones, dirt, rotten eggs, and pieces of dead cats thrown at me. Nevertheless, the Lord was gracious, and a great number were awakened unto life."[43]

Amazingly, it was not just the profane who condemned Whitefield's work. He was also opposed by the religious establishment. Accused of being a "fanatic," of being "intolerant," and of "fanning the flames" of "vile bigotry," he was often in "more danger of attack from the clergy than he was from the worldly."[44]

As a result, biographer Arnold Dallimore says, "Whitefield's entire evangelistic life was an evidence of his physical courage."[45] He fearlessly faced his opposition and continued his work. Though often stung by the vehemence of the opposition he faced, he refused to take it personally, attributing it rather to the "offense of the Gospel."[46]

According to J. I. Packer, most of the English-speaking Christians in Whitefield's day "had taken up with a moralistic, indeed legalistic, recasting of justification by faith."[47] In fact, he says:

> Faith had ceased to be self-despairing trust in the person,
> work, promises, and love of Jesus Christ. It had become, in the
> words of influential Bishop Bull, virtually the whole of evan-
> gelical obedience—a moral life of good works lived in hope of
> acceptance at the last day.[48]

Whitefield believed that this sort of faith was not only "destructive nonsense," it was actually "blasphemous."[49] It was, he believed, "the religion of the natural man masquerading as Christianity" and was thus "the most common evil that was ever under the sun."[50] It produced "a religion of aspiration, perspiration, and in sensitive souls, periodic desperation."[51]

Nevertheless, such a religion was popular and accepted. It always is.

Thus despite the fact that Whitefield obviously struck a sensitive chord and won a wide following among the people when he proclaimed the old Puritan doctrines of grace, he just as obviously stirred up fierce opposition among both the ungodly and the religious—who always have been, and always will be, united in their animosity toward the Gospel.

Whitefield emphasized that a comprehension of grace would naturally prompt wholehearted righteousness—thus there was actually no contradiction between the requisites of Christian holiness and the prerogatives of Christian liberty. And that was equally an offense to the man who desired no accountability to a moral standard whatsoever and the man who desired to reduce the faith to a series of moral demands. To both the lawless and the legalist, Whitefield's message of life in Christ was intolerable.

It still is.

❖ TAKING THE OFFENSIVE

It seems that the balanced message of the prophet Micah was offensive to the people of his day. To some it smacked of overly spiritualized judgment (Micah 2:7). To others it seemed too worldly minded and secular (Micah 3:5–7). To all of them it was an unwelcome interruption of the status quo (Micah 2:6). It was an uncomfortable reminder that neither an obsession with the world that embraces the domination of evil nor a neglect of the world that concedes the domination of evil is acceptable in the sight of the Lord (Micah 3:8).

Thus, it seems that as it was in the beginning, is now, and ever shall be.

Eadburgh of Bicester, a princess of Mercia in seventh-century England known for her holy life and good deeds among the poor of Aylesbury, underscored the importance of fulfilling the Micah Mandate in the face of such tragic ironies:

> We do the lost and lonely, the desperate and deprived no
> favors by offering them anything less than the offense of the
> Gospel. There is no tenderness of heart, no sensitivity of soul,
> no generosity of spirit in accommodating men's sin in this life
> when the consequences be so dire in the next. Let us therefore
> hold firmly to this just cause, let us therefore raise up this just
> banner: His Word alone. In this fashion do we fulfill what the
> Lord requires: but to do justly."[52]

That may not appear to be either fish or fowl to the ideological minions of this poor fallen world—but it is right and good and true. And, it is just.

Truth, Justice, and the American Way

He has shown you, O man, what is good and what the Lord requires of you: to do justice, to love mercy, and to walk humbly with your God (Micah 6:8).

❖ Our conception of justice is so dominated by modern ideological categories that it is often difficult to see it in any other light. Why not make a conscious effort to redefine the concept from a Biblical perspective—entirely free of liberal or conservative proof texts or notions. Follow the word through the Scriptures to see how it is used—particularly notice how Micah's contemporaries Isaiah and Hosea used it in their prophecies.

❖ During the Reformation and then later during the American Revolution, the subject of justice was often addressed in sermons, tracts, and Christian books. Take some time to go to a library and read through some of these great works of the past to see how your vision of justice stacks up against that of those who have gone before us in faith.

❖ Justice is something that we do, not just something that we believe in. Are there injustices you are aware of that need to be rectified in your community? Is there something that you can do? Is there something that you *ought* to do? Well, what are you waiting for?

Good News vs. Nice News

It is to be steadily inculcated, that virtue is the highest proof of understanding, and the only solid basis of greatness. . . . Therein lies the hope of justice.

SAMUEL JOHNSON

That it does not matter what a man believes is a statement heard on every side today. The statement carries a fearful implication. The statement really means that it does not matter what a man believes so long as he does not take his beliefs seriously.

RICHARD WEAVER

It was late and I was tired. I had spoken five times that day at a large pro-life conference in Houston and I was really drained. My back ached, my throat was sore, the shower wasn't working properly in my hotel room, and I desperately missed my family. So, I decided to skip dinner and simply curl up with a good medieval mystery before turning in for the night. I was just getting comfortable when the phone rang.

I cringed. It was a local pastor, Ben Jackson, who had attended the conference and was now full of questions. He wanted to know if I had some time to talk. I was about to tell him that I just couldn't when he mentioned that he thought that we might want to step out for a barbecue brisket sandwich.

I have a particular weakness for barbecue. I've eaten at Arthur Bryant's in Kansas City, at Sonny's in Atlanta, at Red Bryan's in

Dallas, at Herbert's in Nashville, and at Bar-B-Q Baron's in Midland. I've had shredded pork in Knoxville, pit-roast in Richmond, honey-back in Charlotte, pollo loco in Miami, yankee links in New York, and charred cabritto in Santa Fe. I've even sampled Chen's Mongolian barbecue in London and Ferrot's Canadian ribs in Ottawa. But my favorite—by far—is Texas-style brisket.

Needless to say, I was sufficiently enticed to abandon my plans for a quiet evening.

Ben picked me up downstairs in the hotel lobby and we drove across the vast suburban landscape that surreally dominates the area just north of the city. What was little more than an uninhabited stretch of piney woods two decades ago is now a continuous sprawl of tacky strip shopping centers, gaudy oversized apartment complexes, and upper-middle-class bedroom communities. The drive seemed to go on forever and I was beginning to regret that I had consented to go along. Finally though, we stopped at Luther's—a Texas barbecue tradition that is now aggressively franchised all throughout the region.

As we found a quiet table in the corner of the barnlike restaurant, Ben told me that he had been pastoring for more than fifteen years. And everywhere he had served during those years, he had been met with great success. His current church had grown rather impressively from just under a hundred to more than seven hundred members during the last three years. He had undertaken two ambitious building programs, added three new staff members, and started a small mission project—all without incurring any long-term debt. He hosted a popular daily radio broadcast, he was recently elected chairman of the local minister's alliance, he had been asked to serve on the board of an independent community hospital, and was widely respected throughout the entire metropolitan area. He had an ideal home life—with a beautiful and talented wife and four "perfect" young children.

I kept waiting for the inevitable "but . . ." He was the picture of prosperity and achievement. Nevertheless, it was obvious that he was supremely dissatisfied.

Indeed, he went on to tell me that he felt trapped by the very success he had worked so hard for. He no longer felt that he could say what he needed to say, do what he needed to do. There was now too much at stake. He had too much to lose.

"Sometimes I feel as if I'm caught in a vise-grip of propriety. I know that I have an obligation to equip and inform the members of our church to deal with the grave problems of our culture, but to even raise those issues is offensive to many of them. They just immediately react. And that jeopardizes everything else that we're trying to do."

He explained to me his attempts over the last year or so to gently nudge the church toward involvement in any one of a number of projects—ranging from pro-life awareness to concern over pornography—all to no avail. Then last January he preached a sermon on the anniversary of Roe vs. Wade. He used a very familiar text: "The just shall live by faith" (Romans 1: 17).

"I said that though this verse was normally understood as an exhortation for believers to walk in faith, the apostle Paul makes it clear that the faithful believer was also to be *just*. I then dealt with the whole issue of Biblical justice and tried to apply it to the questions of abortion-on-demand and the runaway liberal activism of the courts," Ben told me.

Needless to say, the sermon did not go over too well with some of the folks who sat in the pews that morning. Ben was scolded by a handful of prominent members for getting "too political" from the pulpit. Several elders and deacons asked him to "tone it down" in the future. A few people even threatened to leave the church.

"They said my message was offensive. That I was bordering on intolerance. That I shouldn't deal with such complex issues as justice. That I should just stick with the Gospel and leave out all the controversial stuff."

What Ben wanted to know was how to deal with the tough

issues of our day without alienating people. He wanted a formula for continued success that would enable him to deal with offensive questions without being offensive.

"I think I'm pretty representative of a lot of people in the church today—whether they're in leadership or not. I don't want to run off the very people that I've tried so long to attract. I don't want to be judgmental, condemning, or close-minded. We live in a pluralistic society, after all. Times have changed."

I knew only too well the struggle that Ben was going through. We all want to be liked. We all want to be winsome. We want to present the world with a message that is attractive, uplifting, and cheery. We want to come across as friendly. We want to be nice. But the fact is that whenever we try to stand up for right against wrong, whenever we attempt to defend truth against deception, whenever we champion justice in the face of injustice, we're likely to ruffle some feathers. It can't be avoided.

The words *justice* and *judgment* are actually used interchangeably throughout the Bible. And for good reason. What is right and just and true inevitably contradicts and condemns what is evil and wicked and perverse. Whether we like to admit it or not, the Gospel draws lines of distinction and differentiation. And that is bound to be offensive to some people.

There was a long pause in our conversation. The jukebox was wailing a sad country song and the barbecue was getting cold. Finally, Ben said, "I'm not sure that it's possible to be both successful *and* faithful in America today."

"I guess it all just depends on how you define those terms," I replied.

❖ TAKING OFFENSE

A renowned English preacher of the last generation, D. Martyn Lloyd Jones, once remarked: "The great effect of our Lord's preaching was to make everybody feel condemned, and nobody likes that."[1]

On almost every page of the New Testament, we find Jesus offending someone. When He wasn't confronting the scribes and the Pharisees, He was rebuking the promiscuous and the perverse. When He wasn't alienating the Sadducees and the Herodians, He was reproving the tax collectors and the prostitutes. He even had a knack for estranging His own disciples with His "hard sayings" (John 6:60) and "mysteries of the kingdom" (Matthew 13:11).

Jesus "meek and mild" was rarely meek or mild when it came to sin. He pulled no punches. As philosopher and theologian Michael Bauman has commented:

> At various times, and when the situation demanded, Jesus publicly denounced sinners as snakes, dogs, foxes, hypocrites, fouled tombs, and dirty dishes. He actually referred to one of His chief disciples as Satan. So that His hearers would not miss the point, He sometimes referred to the objects of his most intense ridicule both by name and by position, and often face to face. . . . Christ did not affirm sinners; He affirmed the repentant. Others He often addressed with the most withering invective. God incarnate did not avoid using words and tactics that His listeners found deeply offensive. He well understood that sometimes it is wrong to be nice.[2]

He was an equal opportunity offender.

Christ came into this world to call all humanity unto repentance. Thus His message stands out as an unflinching condemnation of the fallen estate of all humanity: the great and the small, the good and the bad, the weak and the strong, the rich and the poor. It matters not who we may be or from whence we come, the Gospel is an affront to all that we have done and to all that we are: "There is none righteous, no, not one; there is none who understands; there is none who seeks after God. They have all turned aside; they have together become unprofitable; there is none who does good, no, not one" (Romans 3:10–12).

Such a message was never intended to be popular; it was intended to be true. There is no justice in a killing kindness; it may be attained only in the brutal apprehension of our dire need of Christ. We all desperately need Good News, not nice news.

And that is simply not a popular notion. Not now. Not ever. Thus, "He came to His own, and His own did not receive Him" (John 1:11).

Church growth experts tell us that controversial or confrontational preaching will do more to drive people away than to draw them in. They tell us that sermons ought to appeal to the lowest common denominator, that services ought to be simple and accessible, and that programs ought to be consumer-oriented and user-friendly—otherwise we may offend rather than attract. They tell us that substantive theology will at best confuse the average churchgoer, and at worst, alienate him.

And, they're probably right—as the ministry of Jesus so amply demonstrates. His insistence that the demands of justice ultimately had to be satisfied was an affront to virtually everyone who heard Him.

It still is.

The unvarnished truth is just as offensive to us as it was to Christ's contemporaries. We don't want to hear that our hearts are "deceitful above all things, and desperately wicked" (Jeremiah 17:9). We don't want to hear that we "all have sinned and fall short of the glory of God" (Romans 3:23) or that "the wages of sin is death" (Romans 6:23). We don't want to hear that our corrupt lives have resulted in a corrupt culture where the innocent are exploited, the helpless are despoiled, and the downtrodden are utterly forgotten. We don't want to hear that there are very real and tangible consequences to our sin that ultimately must be dealt with. We would much rather find a series of steps that would "enable" us, "empower" us, or help us to "recover," than hear the clear message of grace: "Repent therefore and be converted, that your sins may be blotted out, so that times of refreshing may come from the presence of the Lord" (Acts 3:19).

According to Lloyd-Jones:

> If Christ had come and told us that the way of salvation was to consider a great, noble, and wonderful teaching and then to set out and do it, why, we would have liked it. Thoughts of imitating Christ always please mankind, because they flatter us. They tell us that if we only use our wills we can do almost anything. . . . The world today in its state of trouble is very ready to listen to sermons that tell it somehow or another about the application of Christian principles. No one is annoyed at them. "What wonderful thoughts" people say. "What a wonderful conception." But the message of the Gospel is that, "The world is as it is because you are as you are. You are in trouble and confusion because you are not honoring God; because you are rebelling against Him; because of your self-will, your arrogance, and your pride. You are reaping," says the Gospel, "what you have sown." . . . We all dislike that, and yet it is always the message of Christ—He called upon men and women to repent, to acknowledge their sin with shame and to turn back to God in Him, but the message of repentance always has been and still is a cause of offense."[3]

As a result, "It is often our moral duty," says Oswald Chambers, "to give offense."[4]

And offense is easy enough to give. All we have to do is to say what the Bible says. All we have to teach is what the Bible teaches. We don't have to launch a crusade or provoke a revolution. We need not lower ourselves to rudeness, crudeness, or a lack of sophistication. The Bible is enough—*sola scriptura*—to send the purveyors of politically correct, multicultural fiddle-faddle into absolute conniptions. The Scriptural message of justice, mercy, and humble faith is "foolishness" to some (1 Corinthians 1:18). It is a "stumbling block" to others (1 Corinthians 1:23). But it is an "offense" to all who disbelieve (Galatians 5:11).

That is why people can't be ambivalent about Biblical justice.

That is why they have to react so violently to its demands. That is why they are able to be so tolerant of anything and everything else *except* the call to affirm Biblical standards of justice in our lives and in our communities. And that is why they are so intent on erecting new guidelines for an orthodoxy of their own making—a compromised hodgepodge of that "anything and everything" called "pluralism."

❖ PLURALISM

Like modern art, or an avant-garde poem, or the latest haute fashions, pluralism has always been hard to define. Though often stated with algebraic lucidity, its topsy-turvy logic is often as unintelligible as the dog-Latin of monkish hexameters. It is a kind of *upsidonia* as fully fantastic as Abbott's *Flatland* or Swift's *Liliput*. In practice, it is an odd attempt to forge a cultural consensus on the fact that there can be no cultural consensus. It is the unspoken assumption that a happy and harmonious society can be maintained only so long as the sole common belief is that there are no common beliefs. It is the reluctant affirmation that the only absolute is that there must not be any absolutes.

"Why can't we all just get along?" is the mantra of pluralism. Don't condemn anyone. Don't judge others. Respect diversity. Different strokes for different folks. *Que sera, sera.*

The advocates of pluralism claim that there is something more to the notion than this kind of blind toleration and naked diversity, of course. Walter Lippmann called this "something more" the "public philosophy,"[5] Jacques Maritain called it the "democratic faith,"[6] James Fallows called it "the radius of trust,"[7] and James Madison called it the "public good."[8]

According to Os Guinness, pluralism is the creation "out of the mosaic of religious and cultural differences, a common vision for the common good."[9] Many things are included in this "mostly unwritten" and "often half-conscious" sort of "common vision,"

THE FAITH THE JUST LIVE BY

He has shown you, O man, what is good and what the Lord requires of you: to do justice, to love mercy, and to walk humbly with your God (Micah 6:8).

One of the marks of the faithful church through the ages has been an unflinching commitment to Biblical standards of justice. Even when that commitment was slighted, scoffed, and scorned, the heroes of the faith stood their ground and asserted that ours was a moral universe created by a moral God and that His moral decrees were not to be trifled with but at great cost. Examples abound:

John Chrysostom (347–407) was one of the greatest preachers of the Patristic Age. His many extant sermons on family life, personal holiness, and Christian social responsibility remain models of wise erudition and faithful exposition while his liturgical reforms continue to define the parameters of orthodox worship to this day. A champion of charity to the poor, mercy to the lost, and tenderheartedness to the outcast, he was plainspoken about the ills and excesses of his day. As a result, although he was extremely popular among the people, his forthrightness earned him the enmity of many rich and powerful officials in the Byzantine court, including the empress. Eventually he was exiled and put through innumerable humiliations. Throughout his ordeals though, he remained steadfast, and even after his ignominious death, his impact upon the whole fabric of Byzantine culture was profoundly felt.

Bernard of Clairveaux (1090–1153) was one of the most brilliant Christian apologists, theologians, and Reformers of the high medieval period as well as the inspirational composer of innumerable hymns including the beloved "O Sacred Head Now Wounded." A determined holy life, a commitment to charitable compassion, and an unusual eloquence earned Bernard a reputation in his day as a wise and astute counselor to kings, emperors, and popes. Even so, his willingness to embrace unpopular truths often made his high profile a very precarious position. His ardor for Biblical justice combined with his passion for peace made him a key player in most of the great events of his day: monastic establishments, agrarian reforms, peasant revolts, ecclesiastical reconciliations, Teutonic crusades, and attempts to liberate Jerusalem and the old Christian realms of the East.

Girolamo Savonarolla (1452–1498) was an early Italian Reformer and the composer of the beautiful hymn "Glorious, All Glorious He." During the moral and social tumult of the Medici reign in Florence he captured the attentions of the populace, attacking every sort of laxity with special eloquence. For several years he stood practically alone as a stalwart defender of all that was good and just. When the Medicis were finally deposed in 1494, the city turned to the fiery preacher for leadership and guidance. He instituted dizzying reforms and quickly distanced the city from the corruptions of both the empire of Charles VII and of the papal see of Alexander VI. Eventually, the political intrigues of his opponents succeeded in turning the tide of public opinion against him and he was convicted of heresy, treason, and schism. Nevertheless, his commitment to justice became one of the chief inspirations of the Reformation just a few years later and formed the basis for the Western conception of liberty under law.

Dozens of others could be cited throughout the wide span of history: Fabiola Fabii (d. 399), Dympna Caelrhynn (d. 682), Elizabeth of Portugal (d. 1336), Charles Borromeo (d. 1584), Henry Martin (d. 1812), Elizabeth Fry (d. 1845), and Robert Caldwell (d. 1891). Each took a bold stand for that which was good and just and true. Each risked the ire of all those around them who took offense at unvarnished Biblical truth. And as a result, each remains a paragon of courage and virtue even today.

he says.[10] Those things range from "shared ideals, such as honesty and loyalty" to "shared understandings, such as the relationship of religion and public life."[11]

But that is just so much wishful thinking. We no longer share the ideals of honesty and loyalty—if we ever did. And we certainly don't have shared understandings about the place of religion in public life—just ask the ACLU. To pretend otherwise is worse than naiveté. It is willful denial.

Ours is a society that has lost whatever ethical cohesion we once had—what James Q. Wilson has called the "moral sense"[12] and what William Bennett says was the "locus of virtue."[13] And as a result we are embroiled in an intractable conflict—what James Dobson has dubbed the "civil war of values"[14] and what James Davison Hunter has called the "culture war."[15]

Who decides what is and what is not a part of pluralism's "common vision"? Who defines just what "honesty" entails? Or "loyalty"? Or any other "ideal," for that matter? At what point does "diversity" become "fragmentation"? Are the momentary whims of the majority sufficient to steer a society clear of the dangerous shoals of distention and dissolution?

And what is justice? What can we legitimately criminalize or stigmatize if our ultimate values have to be continuously updated by sifting them through the filter of popular opinion and the will of the 51 percent? Have we really reduced the notion of truth to *Vox Populi, Vox Dei?* Is the public opinion poll our only source of the voice of virtue?

The advocates of naked pluralism have yet to supply ready answers to such plaguing dilemmas. Nevertheless, pluralism— along with its sundry vagaries—is now the assumed basis for American culture and life.

Just before landing at Salem, John Winthrop stood aboard the *Arbella* and addressed the brave Pilgrim pioneers, saying: "It is of the nature and essence of every society to be knit together by some covenant, either expressed or implied."[16]

Two centuries later, Alexis de Tocqueville agreed:

> "Without such common belief no society can prosper; nay,
> rather, no society can exist; for without ideas held in common
> there is no common action, and without common action there
> may still be men, but there is no social body.[17]

We need not appeal to such distant authorities as Winthrop and de Tocqueville, though. It ought to be obvious enough that any society that has ceased to hold in common certain essential assumptions about life and morals cannot long survive. A hazy and nebulous pluralism—with its lowered standards, diluted ethics, and compromised integrity—is not only insufficient to hold a society together, it actually militates against the very possibility of cohesion. Justice is necessarily tossed to and fro on waves of doubt. Truth changes from one day to the next. And anarchy or tyranny actually becomes the best of a host of other undesirable options.

It is just as absurd to say that *any* idea is as valid as *every* idea as it is to say that bad ideas are as helpful as good ideas. It is equally ridiculous to say that there is no difference between right and wrong as it is to say that there is no difference between right and left. We all know that too many chiefs and not enough Indians will inevitably result in chaos, and yet we have somehow failed to grasp the fact that too many moralities and not enough morals will likewise result in chaos.

By drenching the notion of pluralism in what C. S. Lewis called "a perpetual lukewarm shower bath of sentimentality"[18] we have obscured its disastrous illogic. But no amount of rhetorical pleasantries about unity in diversity can obscure its results.

❖ HELL ON EARTH

An avalanche of perversity has crashed over our land in recent years, laying waste to nearly everything in its path. A veritable Pandora's box of evils has been unleashed by the champions and purveyors of pluralism. Thus, rampant immorality has begun to significantly erode the stability of our cultural foundations.

Pornography has become a frighteningly powerful multi-billion-dollar-a-year industry in the United States and Canada—with higher sales figures than even McDonald's.[19] It has, in fact, become the fastest growing segment of the American "entertainment" industry.[20] With its very clear connections to violent crime, organized crime, and societal dysfunction, all of the various manifestations of pornography—soft porn, hard porn, child porn, violent porn, live porn, video porn, phone porn, cable porn, peep porn, and snuff porn—are dangerous incursions on the security and liberty of us all.[21]

Prostitution, like pornography, is becoming an ever more dominant factor in the economic ecology of our nation.[22] With the proliferation of bathhouses, massage parlors, escort services, nude bars, and swank bordellos in virtually every region and locale, the once seedy and shadowy profession has been transformed into a far-flung modern industry bringing in millions of dollars a year—in many places legal, in most others, entirely unregulated.[23]

Unchecked promiscuity now runs rampant. The "sexual revolution" has come and gone, leaving in its wake innumerable casualties—as all revolutions are wont to do.[24] Recent studies indicate that the residual damage is even worse than what we might expect.[25] Only 31 percent of American women wait until marriage before engaging in sexual relations.[26] Only 20 percent of men do.[27] Forty-three percent of all teens under the age of seventeen have already initiated sexual activity.[28] Perhaps we should not be surprised then that more than half of all marriages in America today fail within the first seven years—they are on shaky ground before they even begin.[29]

It is now difficult to keep track of the vast array of publicly endorsed and institutionally supported sexual aberrations—from homosexuality and lesbianism to pedophilia and necrophilia.[30] And the rate of infection from a panoply of sexually transmitted diseases—from syphilis and herpes to gonorrhea and AIDS—has reached epidemic proportions.[31]

Add to this litany of woes the abortion holocaust, the rapid encroachment of euthanasia, and the dramatic increase in drug abuse, and you have all the ingredients for complete cultural disaster.

In a pluralistic society though, each of these woes falls into the gray and hazy domain of "victimless crimes"—in other words, no one is involved and no one is harmed except "consenting adults." And so, they fall beyond the pale of justice. Advocates of pluralism maintain—in both their literature and in the innumerable court cases they have undertaken—that such issues should fall entirely outside the concern of the community or the citizenry.[32] They argue that to impose any "community standards" of ethics and decency is "a violation of the spirit of American democracy" and a "contradiction of our most basic constitutional tenets."[33]

Any attempt to do so is instantly dubbed "intolerance," "bigotry," "zealotry and insensitivity," or "the excesses of religious fundamentalism."[34]

Amazingly, the vast proportion of the modern church has accepted this notion—if not in principle, then in practice. We shy away from the Biblical imperative to "do justice, to love mercy, and to walk humbly" with our God (Micah 6:8). We don't want to get sidetracked by a lot of peripheral issues that might deflect interest in the Gospel. We don't want to offend anyone.

"And besides," we carefully reason "you can't legislate morality in a pluralistic society."[35]

❖ LEGISLATING MORALITY

On the contrary, as D. James Kennedy has so often asserted, "Morality is the only thing you can legislate."[36] That's what legislation is. It is the codification in law of some particular moral concern—generally so that the immorality of a few is not forcibly inflicted on the rest of us. Legislating morality is the very cornerstone of justice.

Murder is against the law because we recognize that the premeditated killing of another human being is a violation of a very basic and fundamental moral principle—a moral principle that most of us still cherish: the sanctity of human life. Theft is against the law because we recognize that taking someone else's belongings without permission is a breach of another one of our most basic and fundamental ethical standards: the inviolability of private property. The fact is, all law is some moral or ethical tenet raised up to social enforceability by the civil sphere.

Thus, the question is not Should we legislate morality? Rather, it is, Whose morality should we legislate? What moral standard should we use when we legislate? Will it be the unchanging, unerring Scriptural prescription for justice, or will it be the ever-shifting, ever-changing notion of pluralistic accommodation?

The fact is, genuine pluralism is a practical impossibility.

Robert Goguet, in his authoritative history of the develop-ment of judicial philosophy in this country, argued that the Founding Fathers, though often not personally Christian them-selves, recognized the importance of choosing some identifiable objective standard upon which to build cultural consensus. The precedence they gave to Biblical morality was a matter of sober-headed practicality:

> The more they meditated on the Biblical standards for civil morality, the more they perceived their wisdom and inspira-tion. Those standards alone have the inestimable advantage never to have undergone any of the revolutions common to all human laws, which have always demanded frequent amend-ments; sometimes changes; sometimes additions; sometimes the retrenching of superfluities. There has been nothing changed, nothing added, nothing retrenched from Biblical morality for above three thousand years.[37]

The framers of the Constitution were heavily influenced by the writings of Thomas Hooker, founder of the city of Hartford in the Connecticut Colony and learned Puritan divine. Thus they agreed wholeheartedly with his oft-quoted maxim on the well-spring of law and order in society:

> Of law there can be no less acknowledged, than that her seat is in the bosom of God, her voice in the harmony of the world. All things in heaven and on earth do her homage; the very least as doing her care, and the greatest as not exempt from her power. Both angels and men, and creatures of what condition soever, though each in a different sort of name, yet all with one uniform consent, admire her as the mother of their peace and joy.[38]

John Jay, the first chief justice of the Supreme Court, similarly affirmed the necessity of a standard of virtue for the proper main-tenance of civil stability and order:

> No human society has ever been able to maintain both order

and freedom, both cohesiveness and liberty apart from the
moral precepts of the Christian Religion applied and accepted
by all the classes. Should our Republic ere forget this fundamental precept of governance, men are certain to shed their
responsibilities for licentiousness and this great experiment
will then surely be doomed.[39]

Thus, a brash and cavalier attitude toward any exclusive
standard of goodness and morality is perhaps the single most distressing trait of modern pluralism. In the name of civil liberties,
cultural diversity, and political correctness it has pressed forward
a radical agenda of willy-nilly moral corruption and ethical
degeneration.

Ironically, its brazen disregard for any objective standard of
decency and its passionately undeterred defense of perverse impro-
priety have actually threatened our liberties and diversity because
they have threatened the foundations that made those things possible in the first place.

Pluralism wants the privileges of America bestowed upon the
citizenry as an unearned, undeserved, and unwarranted entitlement. Apart from the grace of God though, there simply cannot
be any such entitlement in human societies. Great privileges bring
with them great responsibilities. Our remarkable freedom has
been bought at a price. And that price was moral diligence, virtuous sacrifice, and ethical uprightness. The legal commitment of
pluralism to any and all of the fanatically twisted fringes of
American culture—pornographers, gay activists, abortionists, and
other professional liberationists—is a pathetically self-defeating
crusade that has confused liberty with license.

Gardiner Spring, the eloquent pastor-patriot during the early
nineteenth century in New York, persuasively argued that the
kind of free society America aspired to be was utterly and completely impossible apart from moral integrity:

> Every considerate friend of civil liberty, in order to be consis-
> tent with himself must be the friend of the Bible. No tyrant

has ever effectually conquered and subjugated a people whose liberties and public virtue were founded upon the Word of God. After all, civil liberty is not freedom from restraint. Men may be wisely and benevolently checked, and yet be free. No man has a right to act as he thinks fit, irrespective of the wishes and interests of others. This would be exemption from all law, and from the wholesome influence of social institutions. Heaven itself would not be free, if this were freedom. No created being holds any such liberty as this, by a divine warrant. The spirit of subordination, so far from being inconsistent with liberty, is inseparable from it.[40]

Similarly, Aleksandr Solzhenitsyn, the brilliant Russian novelist, historian, and Nobel laureate, has said:

Fifty years ago it would have seemed quite impossible in America that an individual be granted boundless freedom with no purpose but simply for the satisfaction of his whims. The defense of individual rights has reached such extremes as to make society as a whole defenseless. It is time to defend, not so much human rights, as human obligations.[41]

According to James Q. Wilson, the shabby ambiguities of pluralism are a kind of riot of second-bests:

Many people have persuaded themselves that no law has any foundation in a widely shared sense of justice; each is the arbitrary enactment of the politically powerful. This is called *legal realism*, but it strikes me as utterly unrealistic. Many people have persuaded themselves that children will be harmed if they are told right from wrong; instead they should be encouraged to discuss the merits of moral alternatives. This is called *values clarification*, but I think it a recipe for confusion rather than clarity. Many people have persuaded themselves that it is wrong to judge the customs of another society since there are no standards apart from custom on which such judgments can rest; presumably they would oppose infanticide only if it involved their own child. This is sometimes called tolerance; I think a better name would be barbarism.[42]

The dumb certainties of experience weigh heavily against the practical viability of pluralism. But perhaps the strongest argument against pluralism is the simplest: it is the existence of hell.

It is not sound logic, practical politics, reasoned jurisprudence, cultural preference, economic feasibility, or even forensic necessity that makes the eclectic pipe dreams of pluralism so hirsute and fabulous. It is the fact that God will one day judge all men. It is the fact that His judgment is unqualified and final. It is the fact that the demands of justice ultimately must be satisfied.

It only makes no difference what people do or believe if it actually does not *matter* what they do or believe. But hell offers vivid testimony that it does indeed matter. Moral absolutes matter. Ethical standards matter. Virtue and vice matter. Right and wrong matter. Good and bad matter. Justice and injustice matter. They matter because the eternal destiny of men hangs upon their determination.

The entire witness of Western civilization bears this out. Thus, through the ages faithful men have boldly cut across the grain of comfort and convention, warning sinners of their dire danger.

❖ HELLFIRE AND BRIMSTONE

Unlike his friend George Whitefield, Jonathan Edwards was not a particularly enthralling master of pulpit theatrics or hermaneutical technique.[43] Instead, he won his reputation as a thinker. He was highly regarded as a "precise dogmatician."[44] He was widely admired as a "careful systemizer."[45] And he was deeply appreciated as a "cogent preceptor."[46]

As a philosopher, his greatness was unmatched.

Thomas Chalmers said that he was "undoubtedly the greatest of all the theologians."[47] Benjamin Franklin said that he "had a rational mind unmatched for generations untold."[48] Daniel Webster offered that his books were among the "greatest achievements of the human intellect."[49] James Hollister said he was "the most gifted man of the eighteenth century, perhaps the most profound thinker in the world."[50] Robert Hall mused that "he was the greatest of the sons of men."[51] Moses Tyler said he was "the most original and acute thinker yet produced in America."[52] And Georges Lyon said he was "superior to Locke, Newton, Descartes, and a couple of Pascals combined."[53]

But as a preacher, he apparently left a little something to be desired.

In fact, he read his densely theological and tautly philosophical sermons from painstakingly researched longhand manuscripts—often in a flat, monotonous voice. Only rarely did he deign to make eye contact with his congregation. Though not unpleasant in demeanor, he hardly cut a dashing or charismatic figure.

A member of his church described these deficiencies sympathetically:

> His appearance in the pulpit was with a good grace, and his delivery easy, natural, but very solemn. He had not a strong voice but appeared with such gravity, and spake with such distinctness and precision—his words so full of ideas and set in such a plain and striking light—that few speakers have been so able to demand the attention of an audience as he. His words often discovered a great degree of inward fervor, without much noise or external emotion, and fell with great weight on the minds of his hearers. He made but little motion of his head or hands in the pulpit, but spake as to discover the motion of his own heart, which tended in the most natural and effectual manner to move and affect others.[54]

But another said:

> I can little explain how the assembly remains awake during his discourses—which are over-long, boorish, and often incomprehensible to the simple man. Though there is evidence of some great passion in thought, yet to the eye and ear, little or none.[55]

Nevertheless, on July 8, 1741, Edwards traveled a few miles from his home into western Connecticut and read to a small congregation assembled there "the most famous sermon ever delivered in the history of America."[56]

Entitled *Sinners in the Hands of an Angry God*, the sermon was an exposition of the text "Their foot shall slip in due time" (Deuteronomy 32:35). Its subject was the imminence of judgment and the horrors of perdition. It was about what we today derisively call "hell-fire and damnation."

Later described by literary and historical critics as a "rhetorical masterpiece,"[57] the sermon was astonishingly gripping and terrifyingly vivid:

> Yea, God is a great deal more angry with great numbers that are now on the earth; yea doubtless, with many that are now in this congregation, who it may be are at ease, than He is with many of those who are now in the flames of Hell. The wrath of God burns against them, their damnation does not slumber; the pit is prepared, the fire is made ready; the furnace is now hot ready to receive them; the flames do now rage and glow; the glittering sword is now whet and held over them. Unconverted men walk over the pit of Hell on a rotten covering, and there are innumerable places in this covering so weak that they will not bear their own weight, and these places are not seen.[58]

The sermon caused an immediate sensation in the town of Enfield where it was preached. According to historian John Currid, even before the sermon was finished, "people were moaning, groaning and crying out" such things as "What shall I do to be saved?"[59] In fact, there was such a "breathing of distress and weeping" that Edwards had to quiet and calm the people several times so he could conclude.[60] The fervor of the Great Awakening, which had thus far bypassed Enfield, now swept through the little town with a white-hot intensity. Suddenly the people were "bowed down with an awful conviction of their sin and danger."[61]

And a "great outpouring of the Holy Spirit" came with "amazing and astonishing power" evidenced by the fact that "several souls were wrought upon" in that place of "former antipathy."[62]

In short order, the sermon was printed and widely distributed throughout the Americas. It not only won for Edwards even greater renown than he already enjoyed, but it provoked a further awakening among its distant readers. Since then it has been reprinted hundreds of times—perhaps thousands. To this day it is not only a standard text for the study of great preaching, but it also has passed into the realm of classic literature—and thus is the most anthologized sermon in the English language.

Though obviously anointed with divine favor, *Sinners in the Hands of an Angry God*—like so much of the rest of his vast body of work—was not without controversy. Many said that Edwards illegitimately played upon people's emotions.[63] Others said that he shamelessly exploited the popular fears and phobias of the day.[64] Still others said that he appealed to the innate intolerance, bigotry, and mob instincts of unsuspecting simple-minded people.[65]

For the record, Edwards claimed that all of his sermons—and there were many on the subject of hell, some even more vivid than the one he preached in Enfield—were modeled on the admonition of the apostle Paul, "Knowing, therefore, the terror of the Lord, we persuade men" (2 Corinthians 5:11). He told his own parish: "I don't desire to go about to terrify you needlessly or represent your case worse than it is, but I do verily think that there are a number of people belonging to this congregation in imminent danger of being damned to all eternity."[66]

It was that kind of pastoral concern and evangelistic passion that enabled Edwards to wisely lend leadership and direction to the Great Awakening—perhaps the most sweeping revival in modern history.[67] It enabled him to become the "acknowledged dean" of American Evangelicalism.[68] And it thrust him into the international limelight alongside Whitefield and Wesley as a spokesman for Christian unity and cooperation.[69]

Even so, the controversy stirred by his unbending commitment to an unadulterated proclamation of the Gospel never entirely went away. After nearly a quarter century of service to his Northampton congregation, a small disgruntled faction—advocates of what historian Perry Miller called a kind of "early pluralism"[70] who desired less stringent moral standards for church membership than Edwards would allow—secured his ouster.[71] They were apparently offended by his insistence that the message of justice—temporal and eternal—was inseparable from the message of faith. He was exiled to the frontier where he lived out his days as a missionary to the Indians.

But he had no regrets. He knew that the Biblical imperative of justice is not a matter to be trifled with. He knew that both the imminence and the finality of eternal judgment mitigated against lowering the standards, diluting the ethics, or compromising the integrity of temporal judgment. He knew that hell was the best argument against muddled and mitigated morals.

And yet, the controversy still rages. The argument continues apace.

❖ TRUTH, JUSTICE, AND THE AMERICAN WAY

The Good News is that the bad news is bad—and yet hope remains. Knowing this, Jonathan Edwards threw caution to the wind and pled for his congregation to hear and heed the Gospel:

> You hang by a slender thread, with the flames of divine wrath flashing about it, and ready every moment to singe it and burn it asunder. God hath had it on His heart to show angels and men, both how excellent His love is, and also how terrible His wrath is.[72]

And so ought we to plead with all men.

But we don't. If we issue any warning at all, it is an inauspicious, self-conscious, uncertain one—more often than not couched in the congested compromise of pluralism. We almost act as if we are indifferent to the fate of the myriads of men and nations.

J. I. Packer has lamented:

> At no time, perhaps, since the Reformation have Christians as a body been so unsure, tentative, and confused as to what they should believe and do. Certainty about the great issues of Christian faith and conduct is lacking all along the line. The outside observer sees us as staggering on from gimmick to gimmick and stunt to stunt like so many drunks in a fog, not knowing at all where we are or which way we should be going. Preaching is hazy; heads are muddled; hearts fret; doubts drain our strength; uncertainty paralyzes action. . . . We know in our bones that we were made for certainty, and we cannot be happy without it. Yet unlike the first Christians who in three centuries won the Roman world, and those later Christians who pioneered the Reformation, and the Puritan awakening, and the Evangelical revival, and the great missionary movement of the last century, we lack certainty.[73]

We lack certainty. As Ben Jackson confided to me, most of us are not too sure that we can be both successful and faithful in America today. And so like the people in the days of Micah the prophet we cry, "Do not prattle. . . . So they shall not prophesy to you" (Micah 2:6). We shy away from the harsh truth—thinking that surely the Word of the Lord only brings good things (Micah 2:7).

We want to present the world with an upbeat message. We want to create a positive image. We want to emphasize the many and substantial benefits of the Christian life. We want to put on a happy face. We want to proclaim a Gospel of "peace."

The problem is, "There is no peace . . . for the wicked" (Isaiah 48:22).

A. W. Tozer decried this accommodated version of the Gospel as a "spiteful cruelty to the lost and languishing—a cruelty misguidedly offered in the name of comfort."[74] This updated "message of indifference" does not "slay the sinner; it redirects him."[75] Furthermore:

> It gears him into a cleaner and jollier way of living and saves his self-respect. To the self-assertive it says, "Come and assert yourself for Christ." To the egotist it says, "Come and do your boasting in the Lord." To the thrill-seeker it says, "Come and enjoy the thrill of the Christian life." The idea behind this kind of thing may be sincere, but its sincerity does not save it from being false.[76]

Is there any wonder then that our influence is so slight and our impact so minuscule in this day of great need? Instead of nurturing God's people with the rich truths of practical Biblical instruction, we have indulged in theological junk food. Instead of building every discipline on the unwavering foundation of God's Word, we have humored ourselves with intellectual white elephants. Instead of standing for justice in this day of grave injustice, we have squirreled away the offense of the Gospel deep in the bowels of an evangelical ghetto.

If we refuse the prophetic mantle of John the Baptist (Matthew 14:3–12), of Elijah (1 Kings 21:1–25), and of Nathan (2 Samuel 12:1–13), in exposing the evil deeds of darkness in our day, announcing God's just wrath, and proclaiming the only sure and certain hope, not only are the innocent and the helpless sure to perish, but God's vast army will slumber through one debilitating Meggido after another.

"For if the trumpet makes an uncertain sound, who will prepare for battle?" (1 Corinthians 14:8) and "Where there is no revelation, the people cast off restraint" (Proverbs 29:18).

It is a terrible indictment that the civil message of pluralism sounds to us "more loving and Christlike" than the once common warnings of perdition, judgment, and divine justice. It is a frightful thing that we are more at home with the pleasant, nonconfrontational, least common denominator messages and methodologies of our culture than we are with the holy alarms of

Scripture. It is a senseless tragedy that we have carelessly foisted the fierce injustice of our own recalcitrance upon a hellbound world.

Thus, G. K. Chesterton remarked: "If the world grows too worldly, it can be rebuked by the church; but if the church grows too worldly, it cannot be adequately rebuked for worldliness by the world."[77]

The Micah Mandate provokes us to an unflinching demonstration of justice—in both word and deed—that not only guards our culture from the awful errors of naked pluralism but guards all those within the culture from any grand illusions about the awful horrors of perdition as well.

Doing Justice

He has shown you, O man, what is good and what the Lord requires of you: to do justice, to love mercy, and to walk humbly with your God (Micah 6:8).

❖ Survey the messages of the Minor Prophets—from Hosea to Malachi—and notice how often the issue of justice recurs. Then read the Sermon on the Mount or the Epistle of James to see how these themes are woven into the message of the New Testament.

❖ It is easy to talk about justice in the abstract. To make the issue more practical and tangible consider starting a list of all the kinds of questions the Bible addresses in terms of justice— from care of the poor to the protection of the innocent. Then assess how your life and faith stack up when it comes to "doing justice."

❖ Is there someone you know—perhaps someone in your church—who is known for their commitment to justice? Maybe they're involved in the pro-life movement, or they volunteer at the local shelter for the homeless, or they work on behalf of Christian political candidates. Have you ever asked them how or why they got started? Perhaps they would consider walking you through the process of deciding how to best get involved in doing justice yourself. Strike up a friendship. Discover what it is that makes them tick—it may be one of the best decisions you've ever made.

❖ Do you see a need that has not been addressed? If you do, it's probably a call. Get busy. Go to work.

Part Three
Mercy: To Do Good

❖

*Nothing could more testify the opposition between the
nature of God and moral evil, or more amply display His
justice, to men and angels, to all orders and successions of
beings, than that it was necessary for the highest and
purest nature, even for Divinity itself, to pacify the
demands of vengeance, by a painful death, of which the
natural effect will be, that when justice is appeased, there
is a proper place for the exercise of mercy.*

Samuel Johnson

*One of the strangest disparities of history lies between the
sense of abundance felt by older and simpler societies and
the sense of scarcity felt by the ostensibly richer societies of
today.*

Richard Weaver

5

Living as If People Mattered

It is natural to mean well, when only abstracted ideas of virtue are proposed to the mind, and no particular passion turns us aside from rectitude; and so willing is every man to flatter himself, that the difference between approving laws, and obeying them is frequently forgotten.

SAMUEL JOHNSON

That curious modern hypostatization "service" is often called in to substitute for the now incomprehensible doctrine of vocation.

RICHARD WEAVER

I remember only too well the first time I met Francis Schaeffer.

I was puttering around in one of my favorite used book-stores—on Locust Street, just a couple of blocks from the beautiful Christ Church Cathedral in downtown St. Louis. The cathedral's magnificent altarpiece and Caen-carved reredos—soaring nearly forty feet above the choir and stretching across the entire breadth of the nave—draw me like a magnet whenever I am in the city. The matching narthex and bell tower have always inspired me—a vivid reminder to me of the remarkable flowering of creativity and beauty that the Gospel has always provoked through the ages.

Just out of sight of the great Easter pinnacle is a little row of quirky stores and businesses. There are a couple of musty antique dealers, a disreputable-looking chili restaurant, a jaunty coffee shop, a bizarre boutique specializing in platform shoes from the seventies, and of course, the bookstore—stocking a rather eccentric jumble of old magazines, cheap paperbacks, and fine first editions arranged in no apparent order.

I had just discovered a good hardback copy of Scott's *Ivanhoe* and a wonderful turn-of-the-century pocket edition of Ruskin's *Seven Lamps of Architecture*—both for less than the cost of a new paperback copy—when I rounded a corner and bumped into Dr. Schaeffer. Literally.

I had been reading his books since the late sixties and looked to him as my spiritual and intellectual mentor. Not only did he express his orthodox Reformed faith in a clear and thoughtful fashion, his appreciation for the great heritage of Christendom's art, music, and ideas and his commitment to practical justice and true spirituality made him a beacon light of hope to me. In 1948, he had gone to live in the Swiss Alps just below Villars. There, in a little mountain chalet, he established a unique missionary outreach to whoever might find their way to his door.

Over the years, literally thousands of students, skeptics, and searchers found their way to that door. He named the ministry *L'Abri*—a French word meaning "shelter"—an apt description for the function it served to the rootless generation of the Cold War era. It had always seemed to me that L'Abri was precisely the kind of witness that the church at the end of the twentieth century desperately needed.

I'd like to say that at that moment, as I stood face to face with my hero, I was able to articulate my appreciation for all that he had done for my faith and my walk with Christ. I'd like to say that I was able to express my gratitude and then perhaps struck up a stimulating conversation about, say, epistemological self-consciousness. I'd like to say that as the opportunity that providence had afforded dawned on me I was able to think of all the questions that I'd always wanted answered. Unfortunately, that was not the case.

Instead, the first thought that sprang into my mind was: *Oh my, he's short!*

My second thought was: *What a haircut!*

My third thought was: *And what's the deal with the knickers?*

In shock, I realized that I couldn't think of a single intelligent thing to say. I had fallen epistemologically unconscious.

Evidently, Dr. Schaeffer could read the awkward consternation in my eyes. He just chuckled, introduced himself to me, and struck up a conversation. Amid my embarrassed befuddlement he was cheerfully gracious and kind. He commended me on my selections and then showed me a couple of other books he thought I might like—a fine paperback copy of Van Til's *The Calvinistic Concept of Culture* and a rare edition of Schaff's *The Principle of Protestantism*.

Here was one of the brightest minds of our generation giving of his time and attentions to a gawky young Christian who couldn't even string together a coherent sentence. I later discovered that this was typical of him. Though he was often passionate, stubborn, and irascible, his life was suffused with a clear sense of calling—a calling to serve others. He demonstrated that calling on a daily basis—not just through heroic feats of sacrifice but through the quiet virtue of ordinary kindness. He believed that the Reformation doctrine of the priesthood of all believers was best portrayed in the beauty of caring human relationships. And so he listened. He cared. He gave. He put into motion Christ's tender mercies through the simplest acts of humble service.

I came away from that first brief encounter with Dr. Schaeffer with an entirely new understanding of Biblical mercy. With a servant's heart, he treated me as if I mattered. He treated me the way we are all to treat one another.

❖❖ SERVICE

Service is a much ballyhooed concept these days. The burgeoning literature of business success and personal management tosses it about rather profligately.

We are told for instance, that our dominant industrial economy has been almost completely transformed into a service economy by the advent of the information age. The service factor is the new byword for success in the crowded global marketplace. Good service guarantees customer loyalty, management efficiency, and employee morale. It provides a competitive edge for companies in an increasingly cutthroat business environment. It is the means toward empowerment, flexibility, and innovation at a time when those qualities are essential for business survival. It prepares ordinary men and women to outsell, outmanage, outmotivate, and outnegotiate their competition. It enables them to "swim with the sharks without being eaten alive."[1]

According to Jack Eckerd and Chuck Colson, service on the job and in the workplace can mean many things: "Valuing workers. Managing from the trenches. Communicating. Inspiring excellence. Training. Using profits to motivate."[2]

Virtually all the corporate prognosticators, strategic forecasters, motivational pundits, and management consultants agree—from Tom Peters, John Naisbitt, and Stephen Covey to Richard Foster, Michael Gerber, and Zig Ziglar. They all say that service is an indispensable key to success in business or success in life.

According to these analysts service is essentially a complex combination of common courtesy, customer satisfaction, and the "spirit of enterprise." It is simply realizing that the customer is always right and then going the extra mile. It is a principle-centered approach to human relationships and community responsibilities. It is putting first things first.[3]

This new emphasis on service is not just confined to the corporate world. It has also suddenly reappeared as a stock-in-trade public virtue in the discourse of politics. Candidates now offer themselves for public service rather than to merely run for office. They invoke cheery images of community service, military service, and civic service as evidence of their suitability to govern the affairs of state. Once in office they initiate vast federal programs for national service. They charge the lumbering government bureaucracy with the task of domestic service. And they offer special recognition for citizens who have performed exemplary volunteer service.

Again, service is defined rather broadly in a series of happy platitudes—as an expansive sense of public-spiritedness, good neighborliness, community-mindedness, or big-hearted cooperativeness.[4]

All of these things are certainly admirable. They are fine and good as far as they go. But they are not at all what the Bible has in mind when it speaks of service—as Francis Schaeffer would no doubt have readily attested.

Biblical service isn't a tactic designed to boost profit margins, to protect market shares, to keep customers happy, or to improve employee relations. It isn't a strategy designed to inculcate patriotism, strengthen community relations, or attract more investments. It is not a technique to pad résumés, garner votes, or patronize constituents. It isn't a style of leadership, a personality bent, or a habit of highly effective people.

Instead, Biblical service is a priestly function of mercy. The Hebrew word often used for service in the Old Testament is *sharath*. It literally means "to minister" or "to treat with affection." Similarly, in the New Testament the Greek word *diakoneo* is often used. It literally means "to care for" or to "offer relief." In both cases, the priestly connotations and the merciful intentions of service are quite evident. In both cases, the emphasis is on the interpersonal dimension rather than the institutional dimension, on mercy rather than management, on true righteousness rather than mere rightness. Biblical service is far more concerned about taking care of souls than about taking care of business.

This fastidious distinction between the ministry of service and the business of service is like the difference between faith in God and faith in faith.[5]

❖ DOING UNTO OTHERS

God is merciful and just.

He works righteousness and justice for all (Psalm 33:5). Morning by morning, He dispenses His justice without fail (Zephaniah 3:5) and without partiality (Job 32:21). All His ways are just (Deuteronomy 32:4) so that injustice is an abomination to Him (Proverbs 11:1).

Thus, He is adamant about ensuring the cause of the meek and the weak (Psalm 103:6). Time after time, Scripture stresses this important attribute of God:

> But the Lord shall endure forever;
> He has prepared His throne for judgment.
> He shall judge the world in righteousness,
> And He shall administer judgment for the peoples in uprightness.
> The Lord also will be a refuge for the oppressed,
> A refuge in times of trouble. (Psalm 9:7–9)

> "For the oppression of the poor, for the sighing of the needy,
> Now I will arise," says the Lord;
> "I will set him in the safety for which he yearns." (Psalm 12:5)

> A father of the fatherless, a defender of widows,
> Is God in His holy habitation.
> God sets the solitary in families;
> He brings out those who are bound into prosperity;
> But the rebellious dwell in a dry land. (Psalm 68:5–6)

> The poor and needy seek water, but there is none, their tongues fail for thirst. I, the Lord, will hear them; I, the God of Israel, will not forsake them. I will open rivers in desolate heights, and fountains in the midst of the valleys; I will make

the wilderness a pool of water, and the dry land springs of water. I will plant in the wilderness the cedar and the acacia tree, the myrtle and the oil tree; I will set in the desert the cypress tree and the pine and the box tree together, that they may see and know, and consider and understand together, that the hand of the Lord has done this, and the Holy One of Israel has created it. (Isaiah 41:17–20)

God cares for the needy. And His people are to do likewise.

God desires that we follow Him (Matthew 4:19). We are to emulate Him (1 Peter 1:16). We are to do as He does. In effect, we are to do unto others as He has done unto us. That is the ethical principle that underlies the Golden Rule (Matthew 7:12; Luke 6:31).

If God has comforted us, then we are to comfort others (2 Corinthians 1:4). If God has forgiven us, then we are to forgive others (Ephesians 4:32). If God has loved us, then we are to love others (1 John 4:11). If He has taught us, then we are to teach others (Matthew 28:20). If He has borne witness to us, then we are to bear witness to others (John 15:26–27). If He has laid down His life for us, then we are to lay down our lives for one another (1 John 3:16).

Whenever God commanded the priestly nation of Israel to imitate Him in ensuring justice for the wandering homeless, the alien, and the sojourner, He reminded them that they were once despised, rejected, and homeless themselves (Exodus 22:21–27; 23:9; Leviticus 19:33–34). It was only by the grace and mercy of God that they had been redeemed from that low estate (Deuteronomy 24:17–22). Thus they were to exercise compassion to the brokenhearted and the dispossessed. They were to serve.

Priestly privilege brings priestly responsibility. If Israel refused to take up that responsibility then God would revoke their privilege (Isaiah 1:11–17). If they refused to exercise reciprocal mercy then God would rise up in His anger to visit the land with His wrath and displeasure, expelling them into the howling wilderness once again (Exodus 22:24). On the other hand, if they fulfilled their calling to live lives of merciful service then they would ever be blessed (Psalm 41:1–2).

The principle still holds true. Those of us who have received the compassion of the Lord on high are to demonstrate tenderness in kind to all those around us. This is precisely the lesson Jesus was driving at in the parable of the unmerciful slave:

> Therefore the kingdom of heaven is like a certain king who wanted to settle accounts with his servants. And when he had begun to settle accounts, one was brought to him who owed him ten thousand talents. But as he was not able to pay, his master commanded that he be sold, with his wife and children and all that he had, and that payment be made. The servant therefore fell down before him, saying, "Master, have patience with me, and I will pay you all." Then the master of that servant was moved with compassion, released him, and forgave him the debt. But that servant went out and found one of his fellow servants who owed him a hundred denarii; and he laid hands on him and took him by the throat, saying, "Pay me what you owe!" So his fellow servant fell down at his feet and begged him, saying, "Have patience with me, and I will pay you all." And he would not, but went and threw him into prison till he should pay the debt. So when his fellow servants saw what had been done, they were very grieved, and came and told their master all that had been done. Then his master, after he had called him, said to him, "You wicked servant! I forgave you all that debt because you begged me. Should you not also have had compassion on your fellow servant, just as I had pity on you?" And his master was angry, and delivered him to the torturers until he should pay all that was due to him. So My heavenly Father also will do to you if each of you, from his heart, does not forgive his brother his trespasses. (Matthew 18:23–35)

The moral of the parable is crystal clear. The needy around us are living symbols of our own former helplessness and privation.

We are therefore to be living symbols of God's justice, mercy, and compassion. We are to do as He has done (John 15:1–8).

God has set the pattern by His gracious working in our lives. Now we are to follow that pattern by serving others in the power of the indwelling Spirit (John 14:15–26).

In other words, the Gospel calls us to live daily as if people really matter. It calls us to live lives of selfless concern. We are to pay attention to the needs of others—in both word and deed, in both thought and action we are to weave ordinary kindness into the very fabric of our lives (Deuteronomy 22:4).

But this kind of ingrained mercy goes far beyond mere politeness. We are to demonstrate concern for the poor (Psalm 41:1). We are to show pity toward the weak (Psalm 72:13). We are to rescue the afflicted from violence (Psalm 72:14). We are to familiarize ourselves with the case of the helpless (Proverbs 29:7), give of our wealth (Deuteronomy 26:12–13), and share of our sustenance (Proverbs 22:9). We are to "put on tender mercies, kindness, humility, meekness, longsuffering" (Colossians 3:12). We are to become "a father to the poor," and to search out the case of the stranger (Job 29:16). We are to love our neighbors as ourselves (Mark 12:31) and "deliver those who are drawn toward death" (Proverbs 24:10–12), thus fulfilling the law (Romans 13:10).

According to the Scriptures, this kind of comprehensive servanthood emphasis is, in fact, a primary indication of the authenticity of our faith: "Pure and undefiled religion before God and the Father is this: to visit orphans and widows in their trouble, and to keep oneself unspotted from the world" (James 1:27).

We are called to do justice and to love kindness (Genesis 18:19). We are to be ministers of God's peace (Matthew 5:9), instruments of His love (John 13:35), and ambassadors of His kingdom (2 Corinthians 5:20). We are to care for the helpless, feed the hungry (Ezekiel 18:7), clothe the naked (Luke 3:11), shelter the homeless (Isaiah 16:3–4), visit the prisoner (Matthew 25:36), and protect the innocent (Psalm 82:4).

We are to live lives of merciful service:

> Is this not the fast that I have chosen: to loose the bonds of
> wickedness, to undo the heavy burdens, to let the oppressed go
> free, and that you break every yoke? Is it not to share your
> bread with the hungry, and that you bring to your house the
> poor who are cast out; when you see the naked, that you cover
> him, and not hide yourself from your own flesh? Then your
> light shall break forth like the morning, your healing shall
> spring forth speedily, and your righteousness shall go before
> you; the glory of the Lord shall be your rear guard. Then you
> shall call, and the Lord will answer; you shall cry, and He will
> say, "Here I am." If you take away the yoke from your midst,
> the pointing of the finger, and speaking wickedness, if you
> extend your soul to the hungry and satisfy the afflicted soul,
> then your light shall dawn in the darkness, and your darkness
> shall be as the noonday. The Lord will guide you continually,
> and satisfy your soul in drought, and strengthen your bones;
> you shall be like a watered garden, and like a spring of water,
> whose waters do not fail. Those from among you shall build
> the old waste places; you shall raise up the foundations of
> many generations; and you shall be called the Repairer of the
> Breach, the Restorer of Streets to Dwell In. (Isaiah 58:6–12)

The balanced Christian life necessarily includes merciful service.

❖ GOOD DEEDS

In writing to Titus, the young pastor of Crete's pioneer church, the
apostle Paul pressed home this fundamental truth with a clear
sense of persistence and urgency. The task before Titus was not an
easy one. Cretan culture was terribly worldly. It was marked by
deceit, ungodliness, sloth, and gluttony (Titus 1:12). Thus, Paul's
instructions were strategically precise and right to the point. Titus
was to preach the glories of grace, but he was also to make good
deeds evident. Priestly mercy and selfless servanthood were to be
central priorities in his new work:

For the grace of God that brings salvation has appeared to all
men, teaching us that, denying ungodliness and worldly lusts,
we should live soberly, righteously, and godly in the present
age, looking for the blessed hope and glorious appearing of our
great God and Savior Jesus Christ, who gave Himself for us,
that He might redeem us from every lawless deed and purify
for Himself His own special people, zealous for good works.
(Titus 2:11–14)

Paul tells Titus he should actually build his entire fledgling
ministry around works of mercy: He was "to be a pattern of good
works" (Titus 2:7). He was to teach the people "to be ready for
every good work" (Titus 3:1). The older women and the younger
women were to be thus instructed, so "that the word of God may
not be blasphemed" (Titus 2:5); and the bond slaves, "that they
may adorn the doctrine of God our Savior" in every respect
(Titus 2:10). They were all to "learn to maintain good works to
meet urgent needs, that they may not be unfruitful" (Titus 3:14).
There were those within the church who professed "to know God,
but in works they deny Him, being abominable and disobedient,
and disqualified for every good work" (Titus 1:16). Titus was to
"rebuke them sharply, that they may be sound in the faith"
(Titus 1:13). He was to speak confidently, "that those who have
believed in God should be careful to maintain good works"
(Titus 3:8).

As a pastor, Titus had innumerable tasks that he was responsible to fulfill. He had administrative duties (Titus 1:5), doctrinal
duties (Titus 2:1), discipling duties (Titus 2:2–10), preaching
duties (Titus 2:15), counseling duties (Titus 3:1–2), and arbitrat-
ing duties (Titus 3:12–13). But intertwined with them all, fundamental to them all, were his servanthood duties.

And what was true for Titus then, is true for us all today, for
"these things are good and profitable to [all] men" (Titus 3:8).

ZEALOUS FOR GOOD DEEDS

He has shown you, O man, what is good and what the Lord requires of you: to do justice, to love mercy, and to walk humbly with your God (Micah 6:8).

Through the ages, the great heroes of the faith were regarded as much for their charity and kindness as they were for their doctrinal fidelity. They were invariably men and women of mercy who lived lives of selfless service. Examples abound:

Not only did *John Wyclif* (1329–1384) revive interest in the Scriptures during a particularly dismal and degenerate era with his translation of the New Testament into English, he also unleashed a grassroots movement of lay preachers and relief workers that brought hope to the poor for the first time since the unlanding of the peasants more than two generations before. Those common Lollards—as they were most often called—carried Wyclif's determined message of grace and mercy to the entire kingdom, laying the foundations for the Reformation in England more than a century and a half later.

John Calvin (1509–1564) established Geneva as the epicenter of the Reformation with his profound theological insight and his rich devotional piety. His careful and systematic codification of the Biblical foundations for Reform was like a magnet for the best and brightest throughout Christendom. The city quickly became an island of intellectual integrity and economic prosperity. In addition though, it became renowned for its charitable compassion. It was a kind of safe haven for all of Europe's poor and persecuted, dispossessed and distressed. There they found that Calvin had not only instructed the people in such things as the providence of God, but he had also taught them the importance of mercy in balancing the Christian life.

Dwight L. Moody (1837–1899) was America's foremost evangelist throughout the difficult days that immediately followed the cataclysm of the War Between the States and disruption of Reconstruction. Literally thousands came to know Christ because the former shoe salesman faithfully proclaimed the Gospel wherever and whenever he had opportunity—pioneering the methods of both modern crusade evangelism and Sunday school outreach. But in addition to preaching to the masses, he cared for the masses. He was responsible for the establishment of some 150 schools, street missions, soup kitchens, clinics, colportage societies, and other charitable organizations. He believed it was essential that Christians proclaim the Gospel in both word and deed. As a result, his impact on the nation is still felt—

through many of those institutions that continue their vital work—
nearly a century after his death.

Dozens of others could be cited throughout the wide span of history: Polycarp (d. 155), Ambrose (d. 397), Angelica of Brescia (d.
1540), Edmund Arrowsmith (d. 1628) David Brainerd (d. 1747),
George Muller (d. 1898), and Florence Nightingale (d. 1910). Each
made the priestly message of their lips manifest by the servanthood
message of their hands. Thus, each became an emblem of mercy in
this often merciless world.

❖ TO THE UTTERMOST

Paul called himself a servant (Galatians 1:10). That's all he ever
aspired to be (Romans 1:1). Similarly, James, Peter, Epaphroditus,
Timothy, Abraham, Moses, David, and Daniel were all called servants.[6] In fact, even before they were called "Christians," all of the
first-century believers were called "slaves" (1 Corinthians 7:22).

Whenever and wherever the Gospel has gone out, the faithful have emphasized the priority of good works, especially works of
compassion toward the needy. Every great revival in the history of
the church, from Paul's missionary journeys to the Reformation,
from the Alexandrian outreach of Athanasius to the Great
Awakening in America, has been accompanied by an explosion of
priestly service. Hospitals were established. Orphanages were
founded. Rescue missions were started. Almshouses were built.
Soup kitchens were begun. Charitable societies were incorpo-
rated. The hungry were fed, the naked clothed, and the unwanted
rescued. Word was wed to deeds.[7]

This fact has always proved to be the bane of the church's enemies. Unbelievers can argue theology. They can dispute philosophy. They can subvert history. And they can undermine character.
But they are helpless in the face of extraordinary feats of selfless
compassion.[8]

Thus, Martin Luther said: "Where there are no good works, there is no faith. If works and love do not blossom forth, it is not genuine faith, the Gospel has not yet gained a foothold, and Christ is not yet rightly known."[9]

Likewise, the *Westminster Confession* asserted:

> Good works, done in obedience to God's commandments, are the fruits and evidences of a true and lively faith: and by them believers manifest their thankfulness, strengthen their assurance, edify their brethren, adorn the profession of the Gospel, stop the mouths of the adversaries, and glorify God whose workmanship they are, created in Christ Jesus thereunto; that, having their fruit unto holiness, they may have the end, eternal life."[10]

All too often in our own day though, we have tended to abrogate those priestly responsibilities—yielding the work of service to government bureaucrats or professional philanthropists. Grave societal dilemmas that before have always busied the church—like defending the sanctity of life, caring for the aged, and protecting the helpless—have been mentally and practically separated from our other "spiritual" responsibilities. They have been relegated to the status of "issues."

From a Biblical perspective though, these things are not "issues"; they cannot be separated from our tasks as believer-priests. They are our tasks as believer-priests. They are central to our purpose and calling in the world.

Many Christians have observed—only partly in jest—that if God doesn't judge America soon, He's probably going to have to apologize to Sodom and Gomorrah. That may well be true—but not for the reason that we think. God did not judge Sodom and Gomorrah because of their rampant greed, perversity, and corruption. He judged them because those who were charged with serving, didn't (Ezekiel 16:49–50). If God's wrath ever does utterly consume America, it will be for precisely the same reason. When Biblical service is replaced by its sundry worldly counterfeits, the deleterious effects go far beyond rising taxes, bloated bureaucracies, welfare graft, urban blight, and sundered families. When we fail to do the priestly work of mercy and compassion, judgment becomes inevitable.

Sava of Trnova, writing at the end of the seventh century, said:

> The chief spiritual works in the world are sevenfold: to admonish sinners, to instruct the ignorant, to counsel the doubtful, to comfort the sorrowful, to suffer wrongs patiently, to forgive injuries, and to pray for all men at all times. Thus, we are to feed the hungry, give drink to the thirsty, to clothe the naked, to ransom the captives, to shelter the homeless, to visit the sick, and to rescue the perishing, for only in these corporal acts of service may this world of carnality be guarded from the full consequences of judgment.[11]

The Bible tells us that if we will obey the command to be generous to the poor, we ourselves will taste joy (Proverbs 14:21). If we will serve the needy, God will preserve us (Psalm 41:1–2). If we will offer priestly mercy to the afflicted, we ourselves will be spared (Proverbs 28:27). We will prosper (Proverbs 11:24), our desires will be satisfied (Proverbs 11:25), and we will even be raised up from beds of sorrow and suffering (Psalm 41:3). God will ordain peace for us (Isaiah 26:12), authenticate our faith (James 2:14–26), and bless our witness to the world (Isaiah 58:6–12).

But only if we will serve.

Charles Haddon Spurgeon, the great Victorian pastor, not only was a masterful pulpiteer, a brilliant administrator, a gifted writer, and a selfless evangelist, he was a determined champion of the deprived and the rejected. He spent more than half of his time in an incredibly busy schedule on one or another of the sixty organizations or institutions he founded for their care and comfort. Explaining his furious activity on behalf of the poor and needy, Spurgeon said:

> God's intent in endowing any person with more substance than he needs is that he may have the pleasurable office, or rather the

delightful privilege, of relieving want and woe. Alas, how many there are who consider that store which God has put into their hands on purpose for the poor and needy, to be only so much provision for their excessive luxury, a luxury which pampers them but yields them neither benefit nor pleasure. Others dream that wealth is given them that they may keep it under lock and key, cankering and corroding, breeding covetousness and care. Who dares roll a stone over the well's mouth when thirst is raging all around? Who dares keep the bread from the women and children who are ready to gnaw their own arms for hunger? Above all, who dares allow the sufferer to writhe in agony uncared for, and the sick to pine into their graves unnursed? This is no small sin: it is a crime to be answered for, to the Judge, when He shall come to judge the quick and the dead.[12]

Nathaniel Samuelson, a Puritan divine of some renown, was another great spokesman for Christ who devoted his life and ministry to the poor. He established a network of clinics, hospitals, and rescue missions that in later years served as the primary inspiration for William Booth in founding the Salvation Army. In a sermon that he reportedly preached more than three hundred times throughout England, he said:

Sodom was crushed in divine judgment. And why, asks me? Was it due to abomination heaped upon abomination such as those perpetuated against the guests of Lot? Nay, saith Scripture. Was it due to wickedness in commerce, graft in governance, and sloth in manufacture? Nay, saith Scripture. In Ezekiel 16:49, thus saith Scripture: "Behold this, the sin-guilt of thine sister Sodom: she and her daughters wrought arrogance, fatness, and ill-concern, but neglected the help of the poor and need-stricken. Thus, they were haughty, committing blasphemy before me. Therefore, I removed them in judgment as all see." Be ye warned by Sodom's ensample. She was crushed in divine judgment simply and solely due to her selfish neglect of the deprived and depressed.[13]

Wherever committed Christians have gone, throughout Europe, into the darkest depths of Africa, to the outer reaches of

China, along the edges of the American frontier, and beyond to the Australian outback, this kind of selfless care for the needy has been in evidence. In fact, most of the church's greatest heroes are those who willingly gave the best of their lives to the less fortunate. Service was their hallmark. Mercy was their emblem.

"Then the word of God spread" (Acts 6:7).

❖ A LIFE OF SERVICE

According to the majority of eighteenth- and nineteenth-century historians, the most remarkable event during America's Founding Era did not take place on a battlefield. It did not occur during the course of the constitutional debates. It was not recorded during the great diplomatic negotiations with France, Spain, or Holland. It did not take place at sea, or in the assemblies of the states, or in the counsels of war. It was instead when the field commander of the continental armies surrendered his commission to the congressional authorities at Annapolis.

It was instead a humble demonstration of servanthood. It was when General George Washington resigned his officer's commission.

At the time, he was the idol of the country and his soldiers. The army was unpaid, and the veteran troops, well armed and fresh from their victory at Yorktown, were eager to have him take control of the disordered country. Some wanted to crown him king. Others thought to make him a dictator—rather like Cromwell had been a century earlier in England.

With the loyal support of the army and the enthusiasm of the populous, it would have been easy enough for Washington to make himself the ruler of the new nation. But instead, he resigned. He appeared before President Thomas Mifflin and his cabinet and submitted himself to their governance.

According to Henry Cabot Lodge, what he said on that occasion was "one of the two most memorable speeches ever made in the United States."[14] Thus it was on December 23, 1783, that the general said:

> Mr. President, the great events on which my resignation depended having at length taken place, I have now the honor of offering my sincere congratulations to Congress, and of presenting myself before them, to surrender into their hands the trust committed to me and to claim the indulgence of retiring from the service of my country. Happy in the confirmation of our independence and sovereignty, and pleased with the opportunity afforded the United States of becoming a respectable nation, I resign with satisfaction the appointment I accepted with diffidence. The successful termination of the war has verified the most sanguine expectations, and my gratitude for the interposition of Providence and the assistance I have received from my countrymen increases with every review of the momentous contest. I consider it an indispensable duty to close this last solemn act of my official life by commending the interests of our dearest country to the protection of Almighty God, and those who have the superintendence of them to His holy keeping. Having now finished the work assigned me, I retire from the great theater of action, and, bidding an affectionate farewell to this august body, under whose orders I have so long acted, I here offer my commission and take my leave of all the employments of public life.[15]

Writing of this remarkable scene, Henry Wadsworth Longfellow, exclaimed:

> Which was the most splendid spectacle ever witnessed—the opening feast of Prince George in London, or the resignation of Washington? Which is the noble character for after-ages to admire—yon fribble dancing in lace and spangles, or yon hero who sheathes his sword after a life of spotless honor, a purity unreproached, a courage indomitable, and a consummate victory?[16]

The answer to most Americans was obvious: Washington was "first in war, first in peace, and first in the hearts of his countrymen."[17]

Though he had often wrangled in disagreement with his superiors over matters of military strategy, pay schedules, supply shipments, troop deployment, and the overlap of civil and martial responsibilities, there was never any question of his ultimate loyalty or allegiance. In the end, he always submitted himself to the authority God had placed over him.

And that was no mean feat.

Washington had faithfully served under eleven different American presidents at a time of severest crisis. The first two held office prior to the signing of the Declaration of Independence— Peyton Randolph of Virginia and Henry Middleton of South Carolina. The next six held office between the time of the Declaration and the ratification of the first constitution—John Hancock of Massachusetts, Henry Laurens of South Carolina, John Jay of New York, Samuel Huntington of Connecticut, Samuel Johnson of North Carolina, and Thomas McKean of Delaware. The last three held office under the Articles of Confederation—John Hanson of Maryland, Elias Budinot of New Jersey, and finally, Thomas Mifflin of Pennsylvania. Another four presidents would hold office during Washington's short interlude away from public life prior to the ratification of the current constitution—Richard Henry Lee of Virginia, Nathaniel Gorham of Massachusetts, Arthur St. Clair of Pennsylvania, and Cyrus Griffin of Virginia. During all those trying days, under each of those varied men, General Washington gave himself wholeheartedly to the loyal task of selfless service.

He obeyed orders. He rendered due respect. He yielded to the authority of lawful office and jurisdiction. He met the sundry needs of the hour. He set aside personal ambition, personal preference, personal security, and at times, personal opinion in order to serve.

Of this remarkable posture before God and men, Lodge wrote: "Few men in all time have such a record of achievement. Still fewer can show at the end of a career so crowded with high deeds and memorable victories a life so free from spot, a character so unselfish and pure."[18]

"His true greatness was evidenced," said the pundit Henry Adams, "in the fact that he never sought greatness, but rather service."[19] The dean of American historians, Francis Parkman, concurred that it was this "remarkable spirit of the servant" that ultimately "elevated him even higher in his countrymen's estimations than he already was."[20] And biographer Paul Butterfield wrote, "He never countenanced the sin of omission when it came to duty to God or country. His was a life of constant service in the face of mankind's gravest need."[21] Thus, historian John Richard Green commented, "no nobler figure ever stood in the forefront of a country's life. Never did he shrink from meeting the need of the hour. He was our national guardian."[22]

George Washington lived a life of service. He practiced what we today call servant-leadership. He would settle for nothing less. He would strive for nothing more. And he left the disposition of the matter of his life and fortune in the hands of God.

Though we generally think of mercy more in terms of charity or philanthropy, Washington's balanced and selfless perspective actually comes closer to the Biblical ideal. Kindness, helpfulness, compassion, and care are the natural outgrowths of a servant's heart. Where personal ambition and a lust for self-fulfillment are subdued, true mercy is sure to follow.

❖ GOOD SERVICE

The prophet Micah condemned the people of his day for their heartless neglect of the needy (Micah 2:1–2). He asserted that the imminent judgment of their land was a result of their refusal to undertake their servanthood responsibilities (Micah 3:2–4). Instead, they were concerned only with their own comforts and pleasures (Micah 2:8–11). They were intent on their own personal peace and affluence, often at the cost of oppression and exploitation (Micah 3:5–11). They had thus violated the covenant (Micah 5:10–15).

Where there is no mercy there is no hope.

Thus, the Micah Mandate was not only a call to the people to repent and to return to the path of righteousness, but it was also a proclamation of reconciliation and healing. It was a promise of better things to come. The prophet asserted that the remnant would be regathered (Micah 4:6). The shame of affliction would be lifted (Micah 4:7). And the lost fortunes of the land would be restored (Micah 4:8).

Where there is mercy there is hope.

The great American pastor and theologian Jonathan Edwards understood this all too well. Thus he regularly exhorted his congregation to adhere to the tenets of the Micah Mandate and exercise priestly service to the needy:

> That religion which God requires, and will accept, does not consist in weak, dull, lifeless wishes, raising us but a little above a state of indifference. God in His Word, greatly insists upon it, that we be in good earnest, fervent in spirit, and our hearts vigorously engaged in mercies.[23]

Therefore let us, too, be "zealous for good works" (Titus 2:14).

Do a Good Turn Daily

He has shown you, O man, what is good and what the Lord requires of you: to do justice, to love mercy, and to walk humbly with your God (Micah 6:8).

❖ There is an entire catalog of Scriptural exhortations to act mercifully to those around us.[24] Do a brief concordance study—looking up the verses that deal with mercy, kindness, and compassion—to get a good overview of the subject.

❖ Try to make a list—from memory, if possible—of all the saints and heroes of the past whose stories of mercy, service, and compassion you have heard before in sermons, Sunday School, missions conferences, Bible studies, or devotions. What does your list tell you about the import and impact of mercy ministry on the overall history of the church?

❖ There are needs all around us. It doesn't matter what section of the country we live in. It doesn't matter what kind of neighborhood we call home. There are single mothers silently struggling to make ends meet. There are elderly couples trying to get by on fixed incomes. There are young families stymied by debt, underemployment, illiteracy, physical handicaps, or prejudice. There are undernourished and poorly clothed children. There are third and fourth generation welfare dependents. There are hurting, lonely, desperate people. They may be right next door, down the street, around the block, across the tracks, or on the other side of town. But they are there. Stop. Look. Listen. See if you can't develop new eyes to see those needs where they are.

❖ Now, get busy. You may not have abundant resources or even much time to spare, but none of us are too strapped to care about—and then do something about—the needs of others.

6

Oddities and Rarities

It is an act of the highest charity to represent the calamities which not only virtue has suffered, but virtue has incurred; to inform men that one evidence of a future state is the uncertainty of any present reward for goodness.

SAMUEL JOHNSON

We cannot expect a more cordial welcome than disturbers of complacency have received in any other age.

RICHARD WEAVER

The hot kelvin lights bore down on us. Cameras whirred. Production personnel bustled. The host prodded and cajoled. Nervous tension filled the air like the saccharined stench of freshly machined steel.

What had already been an unpleasant enough exchange was charged with even more tension as we raced toward the end. A staffer from the multi-billion-dollar abortion behemoth, Planned Parenthood, looked fiercely across the impeccable set and sallied a few final clichés. I rhetorically riposted.

In desperation as the seconds slipped away, she made one last lunging stab: "What I don't understand about you anti-choicers is where you've been all these years." The camera moved in to capture the high drama. Passion shone from her anguished features. Beads of sweat trickled down her perfectly sculpted brow. "Women have been suffering for centuries. The antiabortion movement didn't even exist until 1973. You're just a bunch of extremists, opportunists, and Johnny-come-latelies."

My turn. The camera zoomed in to catch my reaction.

I just smiled. "Ah, but once again, there is where you are so very wrong: The pro-life movement is not a recent phenomenon or innovation," I said. "It is two thousand years old. You see, the pro-life movement was inaugurated on an old rugged cross, on a hill far away. It is best known as Christianity. Standing against the oppression, tyranny, and exploitation of things like abortion, cannibalism, euthanasia, ethnic cleansing, and immolation has always been a part of our witness to this poor fallen world. The earliest extant Christian documents, outside of the canonical books of the New Testament, are pastoral warnings against the sin of child-killing and other heinous abuses of the innocent. Caring for the helpless, the deprived, and the unwanted is not simply what we do. It is what we are. It always has been. It always will be."

"That's just ridiculous," she scoffed. "Wishful thinking. Nostalgia doesn't wash these days, at least not in the real world of public policy and legitimate political discourse. But then, you just can't bear to face the facts, can you? Admit it."

She was really agitated now and was practically yelling across the soundstage. "But no, you people just don't get it. The jig is up. You've lost. Give it up. It's over. The fat lady has sung."

I took a long, deep breath. Then I quietly replied, "No. I'm afraid it's you that just doesn't get it. Though at times it may appear that our cause is lost, though the barometer of public opinion may bode ill for us, we will never concede. We will never yield. You see, it's not over when the fat lady sings. It's over when the trump sounds. And until that trump sounds we will proclaim Christ's truth in both word and deed, just as all those who have preceded us did. Until that trump sounds we will quietly do the work the Lord has placed before us—and we'll leave the results to Him. Until that trump sounds."

Cut. Break for commercial and the prerecorded wrapup.

Stung by her little sound-bite setback, the Planned Parenthood staffer gathered up her gaggle of local supporters and proponents and stormed out of the television studio. The host of the local program sauntered off to some comfortable corner to sulk and primp. And my little pro-life contingent in the audience became unusually ecstatic.

I have to say that that reaction took me by surprise.

Certainly, I wasn't surprised that my sparring partner was a bit incensed. I wasn't even surprised by the cool dismissal of my host. What caught me off guard was the serendipitous reaction of my friends in the pro-life movement:

"Wow. I'd never heard *anything* like that before."

"Was there *really* a pro-life movement *before* 1973?"

"I didn't even know that abortion was an *issue* before *Roe v. Wade*."

"Do you really think that we will be able to stand firm through thick and thin?"

"Will we *really* be able to hold on until the trump sounds?"

Over the next several months, as I traveled around the country working with pro-life leaders from virtually every major organization, across all ecclesiastical boundaries, and in every stratum of life, I was rather astonished to discover a similar unfamiliarity with our rich heritage of mercy ministry—and a corresponding uncertainty about the future. People who had been valiant in defense of the innocent were generally unaware of the fact that the battle had already been fought and won—several times—by Christian pro-life stalwarts generations, and even centuries ago.

And I was entirely unprepared for that.

After all, here we were, decades into a ferocious new life-and-death struggle over abortion, infanticide, and euthanasia. So, how could we be so negligently uninformed of our own legacy? How could we be incognizant of the wealth of wisdom and experience from the past? Why does it seem that we are perpetually stuck at square one—always having to start from scratch? Why are we incessantly trying to reinvent the wheel? Why aren't we building on the successes of those who have gone before us?

That so many of us have forgotten that vaunted heritage is bad enough, but what is worse is that because we have forgotten it, we have begun to lose the ability to see beyond our present difficulties and circumstances. And consequently, we have begun to lose heart.

Distracted by the blinding oblivion of the moment, we have almost abandoned the crucial work at hand. We have begun to doubtfully waver in the face of temporary setbacks and defeats. We have practically lost sight of the fact that the church is a perpetually defeated thing that always survives its conquerors. We have even started to despair of being able to hold on until the trump sounds.

And that is a dangerous situation. It makes our merciful work in the world all but impossible.

❖ WINNERS AND LOSERS

Everyone loves a winner. The sweet smell of success draws nearly all of us like moths to a candle flame. Popularity, celebrity, prominence, and fame are not only the hallmarks of our age, they are just about the only credentials we require for adulation or leadership.

As a result, we are generally not too terribly fond of the peculiar, the obscure, or the unpopular. At best we reserve pity for losers. In fact, we view with suspicion anyone who somehow fails to garner kudos from the world at large. If they have fallen prey to vilification, defamation, or humiliation we simply assume that they must somehow be at fault.

There was a time when martyrdom was among the church's highest callings and greatest honors. Early on, Christians embraced the truth that "all who desire to live godly in Christ

Jesus will suffer persecution" (2 Timothy 3:12). The heroes of the faith have always been those who actually sacrificed their lives, fortunes, and reputations for the sake of the Gospel.

But no longer. There is almost a kind of shame that we attach to those who suffer persecution or isolation in our culture. If their cause does not meet with quick success, we are only too hasty to abandon them. Maybe they didn't try hard enough. Maybe they just made a couple of dumb mistakes. Maybe they had faulty theology. Maybe they just failed to marshal effective public relations techniques. But however they got into the mess they're in, we are all but certain that they are not the kind of models we ought to follow.

E. M. Bounds, the great nineteenth-century pastor and evangelist who penned several classic books on prayer, asserted it was "all too often the case" that "when the church prospers it loses sight of the very virtues from whence its prosperity has sprung." According to Bounds those virtues "invariably have sprung out of either the suffering of believers or their response to the suffering of others."[1]

That insight was honed from his own personal experience. Throughout his long earthly service to Christ, Bounds suffered both fierce persecution and enforced obscurity. During the calamitous War Between the States, he was imprisoned by Northern troops—despite the fact that he was a loyal Unionist in a border state—simply because he refused to surrender his congregation's property to federal regulators. Later he suffered scorn at the hands of liberal denominational administrators who objected to his unswerving evangelical orthodoxy. Even at the end of his life, he was unable to enjoy success—he was sorely neglected by publishing executives who believed that his brilliant doctrinal and devotional writings were too rigid, too legalistic, or too harsh. He was beaten, ridiculed, defrocked, and defamed. He suffered poverty, isolation, betrayal, and disgrace.

Through it all though, Bounds said that he found solace in the fact that the Christian vocation does not depend on the confirmation of worldly notions of success and thus does not need to adjust to the ever-shifting tides of situation or circumstance. He knew that the blood, toil, tears, and sweat of the faithful are the seeds of real success and that our diligent, unflagging efforts on behalf of the despised and rejected are our most potent caveats to the worldly-wise.

Though that may be an alien notion to us today, it has been the common experience of virtually all those who have gone before us in faith: apostles, prophets, martyrs, confessors, pastors, evangelists, missionaries, reformers, and witnesses. They tasted the bittersweet truth that the kingdom of heaven belongs to "those who are persecuted for righteousness' sake" (Matthew 5:10) and that great blessings and rewards eventually await those who have been insulted, slandered, and sore vexed who nevertheless persevere in their high callings (Matthew 5:12-13).

And so, though they often suffered the slanging ridicule and irate torments of the world, they remained steadfast, continued their course, and walked in grace. They did their jobs.

According to the Scriptures it is incumbent upon us to "comfort those who are in any trouble, with the comfort with which we ourselves are comforted by God" (2 Corinthians 1:4). We are to "bear one another's burdens, and thus fulfill the law of Christ" (Galatians 6:2). We are to "encourage one another and build up one another" (1 Thessalonians 5:11). The mandate to care for one another and all those who suffer—even in the midst of our own travail—rings as clear as a clarion down through the ages:

> Be kindly affectionate to one another with brotherly love, in honor giving preference to one another; not lagging in diligence, fervent in spirit, serving the Lord; rejoicing in hope, patient in tribulation, continuing steadfastly in prayer; distributing to the needs of the saints, given to hospitality. Bless those who persecute you; bless and do not curse. Rejoice with those who rejoice, and weep with those who weep. Be of the

same mind toward one another. Do not set your mind on high things, but associate with the humble. (Romans 12:10–16)

The tenderest stories, the greatest adventures, and the most inspiring examples of faith across the wide span of history are invariably those instances when the Family of God has actually acted like a family and when the Household of Faith has actually functioned as a household. Those instances have occurred when the church served as Christ's own instrument of mercy, when it became a kind of medicine of immortality to the dying minions of the world.

Like so many before him—and so many who would follow—E. M. Bounds discovered the beauty of fellowship, the strength of communion, and the brilliance of grace at a time when ugliness, weakness, and dullness seemed most certain to prevail in his life. "It was in those darkest hours" he would later write, "that the radiant glory of Christ's redemptive work was made plain to me through the commonest of courtesies conveyed by the brethren. It was then that the powerful solace of works of mercy became evident to me."[2] Indeed, it was only as he witnessed the constant and fervent service of the true church during his bitterest days of adversity that he began to comprehend the place and power of prayer—a comprehension that would in later years bring blessing and strength to generations of Christian readers through his many incisive books.

Merciful service in the face of suffering is "often the glue that holds together the varied fragments of the confessing church" says the remarkable Romanian pastor Josef Tson.[3] It affords the church "strong bonds of unity, compassion, and tenderheartedness" says Russian evangelist Georgi Vins.[4] It "provokes the very best in us, demonstrating grace to a watching world, working out that which God has worked in," according to Indian apologist Vishal Mangalwadi.[5] It "lays sure foundations for evangelism and discipleship simply because in the face of tyranny, oppression, and humiliation, the church has no option but to be the church," asserts Croatian pastor Josep Kulacik.[6] "Disguised as evil, persecution comes to us as an ultimate manifestation of God's good providence" says Bosnian pro-life leader Frizof Gemielic. "It provokes us toward a new-found dependence upon His grace, upon His Word, and upon His people. It is in that sense a paradoxical blessing perhaps even more profound than prosperity."[7]

Our response to the "fragrance of oppression," as historian Herbert Schlossberg has dubbed the persecutions and sufferings of our world,[8] is perhaps the single most significant indicator of the health and vitality of the church. It is in "tribulations, in needs, in distresses, in stripes, in imprisonments, in tumults, in labors, in sleeplessness, in fastings" (2 Corinthians 6:4–5) that our mettle is proven.

E. M. Bounds has said it well:

> The easy smile, the temperate deportment, and the contented visage of a successful and prosperous Christians can but impress few, but the determined faithfulness, the long-suffering fellowship, and the stalwart compassion of yokefellows in hardship is certain to convey the hope of grace to many.[9]

Everyone loves a winner. That's not all bad—as long as our understanding of who the real winners are conforms to Biblical standards.

But then that's the rub, isn't it?

❖ PEER PRESSURE

It appears that Pogo was right: "We have met the enemy and he is us."[10]

We have so completely capitulated to worldly standards of success that the modern church is awash in compromise. Our flippant commitment to the slick contemporaneity, razzle-dazzle modernity, and gee-whiz fashionability of the world has made us very nearly indistinguishable from any other social institution or philanthropic enterprise in America. Our mimicry of the world and the ways of the world has transformed virtually aspect of ministry from pastoral care and foreign missions to church growth and Sunday worship. It is almost as if we've caught the spirit of the age like a virus. As a result, we are afflicted by what Kenneth Meyers calls a "plague of terminal trendiness."[11] It is no longer a joke: We have actually become the "church of what's happenin' now."[12]

The result is that we have utterly lost what Steve Brown has called "old fashioned stick-to-it-iveness."[13] The difficult vocation of what Eugene Peterson has vividly dubbed "a long obedience in the same direction" is almost entirely missing from our lives and ministries.[14] Even in evangelical congregations, the Gospel has been squeezed into the mold of this world with amazing alacrity. We tone down our denunciations of sin lest we be accused of being "judgmental"; we minimize doctrinal distinctives lest we be accused of being "divisive"; we blur the boundaries between virtue and vice lest we be accused of being "legalistic"; we brush off heresy and heterodoxy lest we be accused of being "intolerant"; and we veil our concerns about societal disarray lest we be accused of being "political."

According to David Wells in his astonishing and revealing book *No Place for Truth*: "Even the mildest assertion of Christian truth today sounds like a thunderclap because the well-polished civility of our religious talk has kept us from hearing much of this kind of thing."[15]

Indeed, the well-polished civility of our religious talk has all but eliminated true religion from our talk—to say nothing of our lives. Thus, recovery seems to have replaced repentance; dysfunction seems to have replaced sin; drama seems to have replaced dogma; positive thinking seems to have replaced passionate preaching; subjective experience seems to have replaced propositional truth; a practical regimen seems to have replaced a providential redemption; psychotherapy seems to have replaced discipleship; encounter groups seem to have replaced evangelistic teams; the don't-worry-be-happy jingle seems to have replaced the prepare-to-meet-thy-God refrain; the Twelve Steps seem to have replaced the One Way.

Today it is far better to be witty than to be weighty. We want soft-sell. We want relevance. We want acceptance. We want an upbeat, low-key, clever, motivational, friendly, informal, yuppiefied, and abbreviated faith. No ranting; no raving; no Bible-thumping; no heavy commitments; no strings attached. No muss; no fuss. We want the same salvation as in the Old Time Religion—but with half the hassle and a third less guilt.

Thus, our public services have become little more than entertainment extravaganzas. Pragmatic methodology has all but displaced dogmatic theology. Christian publishing now emphasizes self-improvement or private diversion and only rarely concentrates on theological or Biblical studies. Ministry has become a consumer-driven commodity—determined by a demographic study, a niche group analysis, or a market focus survey—all in an attempt to attract the baby-boomer, the channel-surfer, and the media-savvy unbeliever.

Chuck Colson tells the story of a typical megachurch built upon this conception:

> A Baptist congregation was worried about declining membership and decided to do something about it. First, the pastor commissioned a market survey of the neighborhood. The survey found that people were put off by the word *Baptist*. So the church changed its name. Then the survey showed that people liked accessibility. So the congregation built a new building right by the freeway. They took down the crosses and other religious symbols and constructed a huge building with beamed ceilings and a stone fireplace. It looked more like a dude ranch than a church. Next the church threw out theological terminology. As the pastor explained, "If we use the words redemption and conversion, people think we are talking about bonds." So he banished all difficult or unpleasant terms

from his sermons—like *sin* and *guilt*. The pastor even produced an abridged, easy-to-read Bible. In the end, the church became wildly successful. People loved it. It was McChurch for religious consumers.[16]

In our haste to present the Gospel in this kind of fresh, innovative, and user-friendly fashion, we have come dangerously close to denying its essentials altogether. We have made it so accessible that it is no longer Biblical. When Karl Barth published his liberal manifesto *Romerbrief* in 1918, it was said that he had "exploded a bomb on the playground of theologians."[17] But the havoc wreaked by the current spate of evangelical compromise may well prove to be far more devastating. As pastor Ben Patterson has observed: "Of late, evangelicals have out-liberaled the liberals, with self-help books, positive-thinking preaching, and success gospels."[18]

Predictably, the erosion of the distinctiveness of the Gospel has wrought an avalanche of decadence. The moral practices of the average Christian today are not discernibly different from the average non-Christian.[19] It doesn't take a rocket scientist or a social ethicist to figure out that does not bode well for us. What we do or don't do, how we act or don't act, what we want or don't want, are all likely to be practically identical to what our unbelieving neighbors do, act, or want.

According to John White this woeful state of affairs is due to the fact that we are "flirting with the world."[20] John Gerstner attributes it to the fact that we have for too long indulged in "wrongly dividing the Word of truth."[21] Michael Scott Horton asserts it is due to our attempt to "domesticate God."[22] Dave Hunt and T. A. McMahon claim it is because we have yielded to the "seduction of Christianity,"[23] while Gary DeMar and Peter Leithart assert it is attributable to the fact that we have succumbed to the "reduction of Christianity."[24] John MacArthur simply says it is because we are "ashamed of the Gospel."[25]

Whatever the cause, it is clear that unfettered compromise is now the modern church's most damning dilemma. Theologian

Howard Snyder has said:

> Worldliness is the greatest threat to the church today. In other
> ages the church suffered from dead orthodoxy, live heresy,
> flight from the world, and other maladies. But the painful
> truth today is that the church is guilty of massive accommoda-
> tion to the world.[26]

The Bible calls us to stand out as a "special treasure" unto the
Lord (Exodus 19:5), a "special people, zealous for good works"
(Titus 2:14). Instead though, it seems we have done our utmost to
blend in. The Bible says that we are to "come out" from the world
(2 Corinthians 6:17), to be "set apart" from it (Exodus 13:12), and
to be "undefiled [and] separate" from it (Hebrews 7:26). Instead,
by all appearances we have endeavored to be completely accepted.
The Bible says that such carnality is at odds with true spirituality
(1 Corinthians 3:1), but we seem to have placed our confident
new carnality on a par with spirituality.

And worst of all, most of us never even noticed.

The worldliness of the modern church is thus not really a matter of hypocrisy. Instead it is something far more insidious. Ethicist
Peter Kreeft writes:

> A prominent Christian businessman is exposed as a crook and
> a bigamist. A historic Christian denomination goes on record
> as favoring a woman's right to abortion. The second fact is
> even more shocking than the first. Why? A brilliant Christian
> writer and pastor leaves his wife and children and runs off
> with another woman. Then he writes a book justifying it. The
> second fact is more shocking than the first. Why? Nearly as
> many of the marriages of Christians end in divorce as those of
> non-Christians. Most Christian denominations permit divorce,
> though Christ did not. The second fact is more shocking than
> the first. Why? In each of these cases, the first statement
> shows only the perennial fact of hypocrisy, of not practicing
> what one preaches. But the second statements are something
> altogether new. They represent a changing of the rules that
> makes hypocrisy impossible. The first set of facts shows a lack

of virtue; the second shows a lack of knowledge of virtue. Christians, like other sinners, have always been susceptible to vice, but today we no longer seem to know what vice and virtue are.[27]

All the towering materialism of modern evangelicalism rests on one assumption—a false assumption. It is that substantive spirituality can be had apart from disciplined maturity and diligent labor. The fact is, the compromise of the church is not so much rooted in a revolt against sexual mores, or against financial scruples, or against gender roles, or against spiritual integrity. It is instead rooted in the infantilization of the faith. It is rooted in the dumbing-down and the easing-up of the demands of the Gospel. It is rooted in the oversimplification and the underestimation of discipleship. It is rooted in an aversion to work, perseverance, and holy patience. It is rooted in a revolt against maturity.

Mercy ministry is a function of diligence, faithfulness, and maturity. It does not survive in an environment of childish compromise. Thus, the modern church's revolt against maturity has all but eliminated works of compassion from our lives.

❖ COMPROMISE

Though a member of the despised Jewish exile community, the prophet Daniel had risen to a place of great power and influence in Babylonian politics and cultures as a fairly young man. Not surprisingly, he attracted the jealous attentions of many within the empire's cutthroat governing elite:

> So the governors and satraps sought to find some charge
> against Daniel concerning the kingdom; but they could find
> no charge or fault, because he was faithful; nor was there any
> error or fault found in him. Then these men said, "We shall
> not find any charge against this Daniel unless we find it
> against him concerning the law of his God." So these gover-

nors and satraps thronged before the king, and said thus to
him: "King Darius, live forever! All the governors of the kingdom, the administrators and satraps, the counselors and advi-
sors, have consulted together to establish a royal statute and to
make a firm decree, that whoever petitions any god or man for
thirty days, except you, O king, shall be cast into the den of
lions. Now, O king, establish the decree and sign the writing,
so that it cannot be changed, according to the law of the
Medes and Persians, which does not alter." Therefore King
Darius signed the written decree. (Daniel 6:4–9)

Daniel was a man of principle. He was a man of conviction.
He refused to be drawn into the petty world of party pandering
and peccant patronizing. He was a wise man who simply would
not sacrifice integrity for mere pragmatism.

He had been providentially raised up to a position of tremendous cultural influence by the Lord God (Daniel 1:4, 17–20), and
so he owed his first allegiance to Him (Daniel 6:10–11). He would
not, and he could not, compromise that commitment. God's will,
God's purpose, and God's agenda for his life were completely non-
negotiable as far as he was concerned:

> Now when Daniel knew that the writing was signed, he went
> home. And in his upper room, with his windows open toward
> Jerusalem, he knelt down on his knees three times that day,
> and prayed and gave thanks before his God, as was his custom
> since early days. (Daniel 6:10)

Daniel refused to yield to the pressure of the world. That did
not mean that he was inflexible, archaic, and moss-backed. On
the contrary, he was remarkably creative (Daniel 1:12–13). He
was capable and discerning (Daniel 1:4). He was learned and
facile (Daniel 1:20). He was dedicated and teachable
(Daniel 1:17–18). He was selfless and discreet (Daniel 2:14–18).
His extraordinary wisdom and insight won for him the audience of
earthly kings (Daniel 5:13–14), and his extraordinary piety and
devotion won for him the audience of heavenly hosts

(Daniel 9:3–22). He was highly esteemed by men (Daniel 4:18), by angels (Daniel 10:11), and by God (Daniel 9:23).

Still, his unswerving commitment and his righteous determination were inimitable. He was forthright in his condemnation of sin (Daniel 4:27). He was unguarded in his pronouncement of truth (Daniel 5:13–28). He was single-minded in his adherence to the Word of God (Daniel 6:5) and the worship of God (Daniel 6:10).

Daniel dutifully obeyed the clear command of Scripture to be steadfast and unwavering:

- "Therefore be very courageous to keep and to do all that is written in the Book of the Law of Moses, lest you turn aside from it to the right hand or to the left . . . but you shall hold fast to the Lord your God, as you have done to this day" (Joshua 23:6, 8).

- "Therefore, my beloved brethren, be steadfast, immovable, always abounding in the work of the Lord, knowing that your labor is not in vain in the Lord" (1 Corinthians 15:58).

- "Blessed is the man who walks not in the counsel of the ungodly, nor stands in the path of sinners, nor sits in the seat of the scornful. But his delight is in the law of the Lord, and in His law he meditates day and night" (Psalm 1:1–2).

A stand like that can be costly though, and it nearly cost Daniel everything.

Think of it. He had power (Daniel 6:3). He had influence (Daniel 5:12). He had prominence (Daniel 5:14). But he risked it all for the sake of conscience. A simple compromise anywhere along the way would have preserved his power, influence, and prominence. But he refused to compromise.

He could have tried to work within the system. He could have tried to wait out the edict. He wouldn't have had to *deny* his faith, just keep it *quiet* for a little while. He could have tried conciliation, accommodation, or negotiation. Why waste everything that he had gained over such a small matter? Why not just play along, attempting to do good as the opportunity presented itself?

But no. Not for Daniel. He refused to compromise—risking prison and even death. He refused for three reasons.

First, Daniel understood who really governs men and nations. He did not need to tremble before mere human edicts. God and God alone directs the ebb and flow of history:

- "The king's heart is in the hand of the Lord, like the rivers of water; He turns it wherever He wishes" (Proverbs 21:1).

- "For I know that the Lord is great, and our Lord is above all gods. Whatever the Lord pleases He does, in heaven and in earth, in the seas and in all deep places" (Psalm 135:5–6).

Daniel knew that the resolution of any power, influence, or prominence that he might have depended upon God's sovereign purpose. His only responsibility was his own personal covenantal loyalty and obedience:

> See, I have set before you today life and good, death and evil, in that I command you today to love the Lord your God, to walk in His ways, and to keep His commandments, His statutes, and His judgments, that you may live and multiply; and the Lord your God will bless you in the land which you go to possess. (Deuteronomy 30:15–16)

Daniel knew that the outcome of all events lay in providence—which was thankfully beyond his purview or control. Compromise was out of the question. Thus, he could rest in the Lord's wisdom and concentrate on simply doing his job.

Second, Daniel understood the nature of his opposition. He knew that his enemies would not be satisfied with anything less than the assassination of his faith and the obliteration of his privilege. Compromise would have been fruitless. It wouldn't have accomplished anything more than a watering down of his message.

He knew that the truth always invites opposition. There is no way around it. No amount of compromise can divert it. Persecution is inevitable.

Jesus explained this fact to His disciples:

> If the world hates you, you know that it hated Me before it hated you. If you were of the world, the world would love its own. Yet because you are not of the world, but I chose you out of the world, therefore the world hates you. Remember the word that I said to you, "A servant is not greater than his master." If they persecuted Me, they will also persecute you. If they kept My word, they will keep yours also. (John 15:18–20)

Thus, no matter what concessions or accommodations Daniel would have made, his enemies would have continued their assaults against him. Compromise would have done little more than buy some time.

Third, Daniel understood the fundamental truth that God "causes all things [to] work together for good to those who love God, to those who are the called according to His purpose" (Romans 8:28). By refusing to compromise, he knew that he was risking prison or death. But he also knew that the threat of both prison and death could easily become marvelous opportunities under the sovereign direction of God Almighty.

The testimony of Scripture in this matter is clear:

- Like Daniel, Joseph risked everything by refusing to compromise his obedience to God (Genesis 39:7–16). As a result, he was thrown into prison (Genesis 39:19–20). But God used that prison experience as the first stage of his ultimate victory. Before long, Joseph was raised up out of the depths to exercise authority over the whole land (Genesis 41:37–45).

- Similarly, David risked everything by refusing to compromise his obedience to God (1 Samuel 18:1–16). As a result, he was cast into exile (1 Samuel 19:11–18). But God used the experience of exile as the first stage of his ultimate victory. Before long, David was raised up out of the depths to exercise authority over the whole land (2 Samuel 2:4).

- The early Christians also risked everything by refusing to compromise their obedience to God (Acts 4:19–20). As a result, they were thrown into prison (Acts 5:19). But God used that prison experience as the first stage of their ultimate victory. Before long they were raised up out of the depths to exercise authority over the whole land (Acts 19:26).

This pattern of reaction-repression-resurrection runs all throughout the Bible. It underlies the stories of Esther (Esther 3:6–15; 8:1–17), Job (Job 1:13–22; 42:10–15), Jeremiah (Jeremiah 37:11–16; 39:11–12), Elijah (1 Kings 17:1–16; 18:20–46), Hosea (Hosea 1:2–9; 3:1–5), Micaiah (1 Kings 22:7–12, 24–40), and the apostle Paul (Philippians 1:7; 3:8–16). Like Daniel, each of these heroes of the faith witnessed the resurrection power of almighty God. Each of them saw the most difficult and oppressive circumstances providentially transformed into glorious victory. Each of them went from death to life, from bondage to liberty, from prison to promise. Each of them mirrored and illuminated in their lives and experiences the outline of the Gospel of grace: "For I delivered to you first of all that which I also received: that Christ died for our sins according to the Scriptures, and that He was buried, and that He rose again the third day according to the Scriptures" (1 Corinthians 15:3–4).

Jesus refused to compromise His message and mission, of course (Luke 22:42; Philippians 2:5–8). As a result, He was thrown into the prison of the grave (Matthew 16:21). But God used that prison experience as the first stage of His ultimate victory. On the third day Jesus arose out of the depths to exercise authority—to rule and reign—over the whole world (Philippians 2:9–11). This is the essence of the salvific work.

So, Daniel's uncompromising stand was rooted in his understanding of God's absolute sovereignty and man's resolute opposition. But it was also rooted in his comprehension of the privilege of prison and the promise of resurrection. He could remain steadfast because he was wise enough to recognize that the reaction-repression-resurrection pattern in his own experience was designed to forge a new level of maturity in his life and to lay the foundations of some future victory. He could therefore "walk by faith, not by sight" (2 Corinthians 5:7).

❖ STEADFASTNESS

An uncompromising stance before the watching world is all too often mistaken for prideful self-assurance. Because he understood who really governs men and nations, because he understood the nature of his opposition, and because he understood that God would transform prison into promise, Daniel refused to hedge God's statutes (Daniel 1:8; 6:5). He remained resolutely "peculiar" (Exodus 19:5). His enemies took this to be mere hardheaded stubbornness (Daniel 6:13). They presumed that Daniel was just another in a long line of self-confident, egotistical, and dogmatic poseurs.

Virtually all of God's heroes throughout history have been accused of having a self-indulgent, self-inflating, and self-assuming attitude at one time or another:

- Joseph's older brothers assumed that he was little more than a swaggering, self-promoting braggart after he revealed his dreams to them (Genesis 37:8).
- Moses was accused of being self-centered and pompous by the very people he was trying to save (Exodus 2:14).
- Job's friends denounced what they perceived as his prideful attitude toward both God and man (Job 8:2).
- David came under the fierce condemnation of Saul when the king began to suspect the young shepherd of royal aspirations (1 Samuel 18:8).
- Even Jesus was accused by the scribes in His day of the sins of blasphemy and pride (Matthew 9:3).

Uncompromising steadfastness is almost always confused with unreasoning pontification. Righteousness is thus inevitably

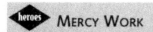

MERCY WORK

He has shown you, O man, what is good and what the Lord requires of you: to do justice, to love mercy, and to walk humbly with your God (Micah 6:8).

Mercy ministry has always been the primary work of Christians in the world—serving as the conduit for evangelism, pastoral care, and cultural influence. From the beginning, the heroes of the faith have been those who have at great risk refused to compromise with the world and instead worked hard to show forth mercy and compassion. Examples abound:

Alban of Verlamium (154–191) is widely venerated as the first Christian martyr on the Island of Britain. During the last few decades of the second century he offered refuge to those fleeing the persecution against the church. He succored the sick, cared for the poor, and saved abandoned children from certain death. Bede the historian records his brutal martyrdom on Holmhurst Hill after he tried to intercede on behalf of a pitiful family of refugees. Though his work in the world was brief, his uncompromising commitment to mercy continues to inspire the faithful to fulfill their callings regardless of the opposition they may face.

When *Hugh Goldie* (1706–1881) joined a mission station in Old Calabar on the West Coast of Africa early in the nineteenth century, he was horrified by many of the things he found there. The living conditions of the people were utterly deplorable. Their nutrition was abominable. Their hygiene was disgraceful. Their social and commercial arrangements were in utter disarray. But it was their cavalier attitude to the sanctity of human life that most disturbed him. Although they had recently abandoned the centuries-old practice of human sacrifice, they still freely practiced abortion, abandonment, and infanticide. Goldie was met with stiff opposition by the tribal chiefs—and even by many of his fellow missionaries who felt that his pro-life convictions would compromise their evangelistic efforts—he stood firmly on the integrity of the whole counsel of God. Finally, as a result of his lifelong crusade for life, tribal decrees in 1851 and 1878 banned the terrible customs. He went on to his eternal reward having "fought the good fight, . . . finished the race, [and] kept the faith" (2 Timothy 4:7).

Joseph Damien de Veuster (1840–1889) grew up in the lowlands of Belgium. After posting a promising academic record, he disappointed his family's expectations of a brilliant professional career in business, law, or politics by submitting to a call to the mission field. Assigned to the newly reopened islands of Hawaii, he served as a pastor in the burgeoning village of Honolulu for nearly a decade. His concern for the sanctity of all human life led him not only to fight against the few remaining abortionists among the natives, but to eventually request a transfer to the wretched leprosarium on Molakai. There, Damien helped the people to build homes, schools, roads, civic halls, and treatment clinics. He protected the integrity of each resident from persecution and rejection—both from within and without the colony. Encouraging the essential Christian values of faith, family, and work, he helped restore dignity, hope, and purpose to the despised and rejected. His sacrificial character was soon lauded around the globe. Even the renowned literary skeptic Robert Louis Stevenson was struck by Damien's saintly service to the unwanted—actually risking his fortune and his reputation by publishing a defense of the great man. Eventually contracting leprosy himself, Damien died at the age of forty-nine. On his tombstone were engraved the words, "Died a Martyr of Charity."

Dozens of others could be cited throughout the wide span of history: Barlaam of Antioch (d. 327), Dunstan of Canterbury (d. 988), Cajetan Gaetano (d. 1547), Zephaniah Swift (d. 1834), Anna Bowden (d. 1844), Lemuel Whitman (d. 1846), and Booker T. Washington (d. 1915). Each buckled down to the tasks at hand in this poor fallen world: demonstrating obedience to Christ, mercy to the afflicted, and diligence despite opposition.

labeled "intolerant," "judgmental," and "biased." Righteous men and women are always popularly diagnosed as "suffering from delusions of grandeur."

But nothing could be farther from the truth.

Uncompromising believers throughout the ages who have "subdued kingdoms, worked righteousness, obtained promises, stopped the mouths of lions, quenched the violence of fire, escaped the edge of the sword, out of weakness were made strong," did so "through faith" (Hebrews 11:33–34). In other words, they trusted God rather than themselves. Far from having confidence or certainty in their own flesh, their own ideas, their own understanding, their own abilities, their own strength, and their own ingenuity, they put their full reliance on God (Philippians 3:3). They obtained victory even amid great difficulty, not because they were domineering and proud, but because they were submissive to continue in the tasks placed before them, because they yielded humbly to their particular calling (Matthew 5:3–12).

The Bible is crystal clear in this matter:

> Rest in the Lord, and wait patiently for Him;
> Do not fret because of him who prospers in his way,
> Because of the man who brings wicked schemes to pass.
> Cease from anger, and forsake wrath;
> Do not fret—it only causes harm.
> For evildoers shall be cut off;
> But those who wait on the Lord,
> They shall inherit the earth.
> For yet a little while and the wicked shall be no more;
> Indeed, you will look carefully for his place,
> But it shall be no more.
> But the meek shall inherit the earth,
> And shall delight themselves in the abundance of peace.
> (Psalm 37:7–11)

Jesus reiterated this same truth:

You know that the rulers of the Gentiles lord it over them, and those who are great exercise authority over them. Yet it shall not be so among you; but whoever desires to become great among you, let him be your servant. And whoever desires to be first among you, let him be your slave—just as the Son of Man did not come to be served, but to serve, and to give His life a ransom for many. (Matthew 20:25–28)

Notice that in times of travail or persecution, believers are to bear up under the strain simply by continuing in their regular work of merciful service. They are to carry on by meeting the needs of others. There is no special trick to avoiding the pitfalls of compromise. There is no gimmick of spiritual whoop-de-doo warfare. It does not require a steely resolve or an iron will. It is instead found in a mature and contented attention to the details of our daily labor and our common calling.

The enemies of the Gospel often mistake this single-minded dedication to the work at hand as a kind of prideful know-it-all aloofness. That many Christians today make the same mistake is a telling commentary on the modern evangelical mindset.[28]

❖ WORK

We may not like to admit it, but work is the heart and soul, the cornerstone, of man's created purpose. It is the basis of all ministry and it is the foundation upon which true compassion is built. God's first word to man was definitive: "Be fruitful and multiply; fill the earth and subdue it; have dominion over the fish of the sea, over the birds of the air, and over every living thing that moves on the earth" (Genesis 1:28). In other words: *Work*.

The Bible is replete with teaching on work. But its basic thrust may be reduced to four basic points.

First, the Bible teaches that all honorable work is holy: "Nothing is better for a man than that . . . his soul should enjoy good in his labor" (Ecclesiastes 2:24; 3:22).

Far from being a bitter consequence of the Fall, work is a vital aspect of God's overall purpose for man in space and time. For that reason, He has typically used workmen, ordinary laborers, in the enactment of that purpose. He has used shepherds like Jacob and David. He has used farmers like Amos and Gideon. He has used merchants like Abraham and Lydia. He has used craftsmen like Aquilla and Paul. He has used artists like Solomon and Bezalel. And the men He chose to revolutionize the Roman Empire in the first century were a motley band of fishermen and tax collectors.

The great Puritan Hugh Latimer best captured the Biblical emphasis on the holiness of man's work when he wrote: "Our

Savior, Christ Jesus, was a carpenter and got his living with great labor. Therefore, let no man disdain to follow Him in a common calling and occupation."[29]

The fourth commandment, though commonly and correctly understood as prohibition against working on the Sabbath, has another all too often neglected injunction: "Six days you shall labor and do all your work" (Exodus 20:9). And so Richard Steele, another of the great Puritans, could confidently write that it is in the shop "where you may most confidently expect the presence and blessing of God. Work is holy unto the Lord, ordained by His immutable Way."[30]

Second, the Bible teaches that God calls each person to his or her work: "There are diversities of gifts, but the same Spirit. There are differences of ministry, but the same Lord. And there are diversities of activities, but it is the same God who works all in all" (1 Corinthians 12:4–6).

The doctrine of calling was once the distinctive pennon of the Reformation. And rightly so. As Martin Luther wrote long ago: "The world does not consider labor a blessing, therefore, it flees and hates it . . . but the pious who fear the Lord, labor with a ready and cheerful heart; for they know God's command and will, they acknowledge His calling."[31]

Similarly, Cotton Mather, the great American Colonial preacher, wrote:

> A Christian should follow his occupation with contentment. Is your business here clogged with any difficulties and inconveniences? Contentment under those difficulties is no little part of your homage to that King who hath Placed you where you are by His call.[32]

And William Tyndale inveyed: "If we look externally there is a difference betwixt the washing of dishes and preaching of the Word of God; but as touching to please God, in relation to His call, none at all."[23]

Third, the Bible teaches that work is intended for the benefit of the community. It is not just to benefit ourselves. By work, we are to uphold our responsibility to provide for our family (1 Timothy 5:8), build the work of Christ's kingdom (Deuteronomy 8:18), and share with those in need (Ephesians 4:28). Work *is* mercy. It *is* service.

As John Calvin so aptly asserted: "We know that all men were created to busy themselves with labor . . . for the common good."[34]

And Martin Luther wrote: "All stations are so oriented that they serve others."[35]

Fourth, the Bible teaches that, because of sin's devastation, the high ideals of the work ethic can be attained only through Christ's restoration, imparted to us in the Gospel.

The Fall has disrupted and obstructed the blessings of work. Man cannot, and will not, work as he should (Genesis 3:17-19). Sin blinds, and binds us, so that our divine commission is left unfulfilled.

"Adam refused to work as priest of God's creation," says theologian James B . Jordan: "He rejected the true meaning and direction of his life. As a result, he became dead and impotent. His work was cursed to futility, and he was cast out of the pleasant land of Eden into a howling wilderness."[36]

In a very real sense, everything that the Bible teaches about the benefits of work can stand only as a condemnation to fallen man (Romans 7:10–11). Such things as poverty and privation in our midst are but standing reminders of this fact.

Thanks be to God, in Jesus Christ we are restored (Romans 7:24–25). In Him our lives and our work are redeemed from futility and made meaningful once again (Ephesians 2:10). As Langdon Lowe, a nineteenth-century Southern Presbyterian, wrote: "Man was made for work. The Fall unmade him. Now, in Christ made anew, man can once again work. But he must be ever mindful of the salvific connection: the call to work must not, cannot, go out unaccompanied by the call to salvation."[37]

Whenever the peculiar people of God have tended to their

work and left the outcome of external events to the care of providence they have successfully resisted the temptation to compromise. Like Daniel, when they have simply fulfilled their calling and done their jobs they have been able to avoid accommodation with the world. And they have been able to fulfill their calling as agents of mercy in this fallen world.

❖ BEYOND THE WICKET GATE

Next to the Bible, the best-loved and most-read book during the first three hundred years of American Colonial and national life was John Bunyan's *Pilgrim's Progress*. Its plot was familiar to every schoolchild. Its characters became cultural icons. Its imagery was seamlessly woven into the art, music, literature, and ideas of the people.

The opening lines of the saga were etched into the memories of untold thousands and became a kind of yardstick against which to measure literary and devotional excellence:

> As I walked through the wilderness of this world, I lighted on a certain place where was a den, and I laid me down in that place to sleep, and as I slept I dreamed a dream. I dreamed, and behold I saw a man clothed in rags, standing in a certain place, with his face from his own house, a book in his hand, and a great burden on his back. I looked and saw him open the book, and read therein; and as he read he wept and trembled, and not being able to longer contain, he brake out with a lamentable cry, saying: What shall I do?[38]

First published in 1678, the vivid allegory detailed the trials and tribulations of a young man named Christian as he made his way through the treacherous world. He was a pilgrim—journeying toward his ultimate home, the Celestial City. Along the way he passed through such tempestuous places as Vanity Fair, the Slough of Despond, Strait Gate, the Hill of Difficulty, Delectable Mountains, By-Path Meadow, Lucre Hill, Doubting Castle, and

Mount Caution. Those inhospitable locales were populated by a variety of carefully drawn villains such as Obstinate, Pliable, Mr. Worldly-Wiseman, Mistrust, Timorous, Wanton, Talkative, Envy, Mr. Money-Love, Faint-Heart, and Little-Faith. Despite the fact that he was helped from time to time by a whole host of heroic characters such as Evangelist, Faithful, Good Will, Hopeful, Knowledge, Experience, Watchful, and Sincere, the hapless pilgrim had to struggle through one difficulty or distraction after another. Again and again he was forced to decide between compromise or faithfulness, between accommodation with the world or holy perseverance, between the wide way to destruction or the narrow road to glory.

After overcoming a number of chilling risks and hazards, the story was ultimately resolved—like virtually all great classic works of literature—with a happy ending.

Though written in a coarse, speech-patterned prose—a far cry from the polite literary convention of the seventeenth century—the book was almost immediately acclaimed as a masterpiece of imagination and inspiration. Even those Christians who chafed a bit at Bunyan's gallant Puritan theology, his stalwart Calvinistic doctrine, and his intrepid nonconformist practice readily identified with his beautifully realized vision of life in this poor fallen world. What appeared on the surface to be little more than an episodic series of adventures or a blithe narrative of folk-tale ups and downs, was in fact a penetrating portrayal of the universal human experience.

Pilgrim's Progress struck a nerve.

The reason was simple enough: The question of compromise is one that nags at all of us. The pressure to accommodate ourselves to the pattern of this world is an almost omnipresent and ubiquitous dilemma. It is no less real to the banker in New York, the grocer in Kansas City, the salesclerk in Houston, the professor in San Diego, the housewife in Seattle, or the restaurateur in Toronto than it was to Christian in the Wicket-Gate.

Bunyan knew this only too well—from painful personal experience. As the pastor of a small separatist congregation during a time of fierce persecution, he was repeatedly flogged and imprisoned for his faith. Once he spent nearly twelve years in Bedford's little jail perched over the River Ouse. At any time he could have ensured his release—if he would only promise not to preach without approval or license.

All he had to do was to compromise his principles and he could have been reunited with his impoverished wife and children. All he had to do was to accommodate himself to the realities of life under the restored Stuart monarchy and he could have continued with a full—albeit quiet—ministry among his neighbors. All he had to do was to renounce his peculiar bias, his odd methods, his curious lifestyle. All he had to do was to fit in.

Though his resolve undoubtedly wavered from time to time, in the end he remained steadfast. Like Christian, he persevered.

It was during those tortured years of confinement that Bunyan wrote his allegorical story. Drawing from obvious autobiographical details, he threw the searchlight of understanding on the soul of Everyman.

As literary critic Roger Sharrock said: "A seventeenth-century Calvinist sat down to write a tract and produced a folk-epic of the universal religious imagination instead."[39]

In our own day, when compromise is more prevalent than ever before, Bunyan's classic is perhaps more relevant than ever before.

❖ DONE WITH

In his final message to the church in the twentieth century, Francis Schaeffer bemoaned evangelicalism's tragic flight from work and its consequent immature accommodation to the world:

> Have we as evangelicals been on the front lines contending
> for the faith and confronting the moral breakdown over the
> last forty to sixty years? Have we even been aware that there is

a battle going on—not just a heavenly battle, but a life and death struggle over what will happen to men and women and children in both this life and the next? If the truth of the Christian faith is in fact *truth*, then it stands in antithesis to the ideas and immorality of our age, and it must be practiced in both teaching and practical action. Truth demands confrontation. It must be loving confrontation, but it must be confrontation nonetheless. Sadly we must say that this has seldom happened. Most of the evangelical world has not been active in the battle, or even been able to see that we are in a battle. And when it comes to the issues of the day the evangelical world most often has said nothing; or worse has said nothing different from what the world would say. Here is the great evangelical disaster—the failure of the evangelical world to stand for truth as truth. There is only one word for this— namely accommodation: the evangelical church has accommodated to the world spirit of the age.[40]

Similarly, Martin Luther asserted:

If I profess with the loudest voice and clearest exposition every portion of the truth of God except precisely that little point which the world and the devil are at the moment attacking, I am not confessing Christ, however boldly I may be professing Christ. Where the battle rages, there the loyalty of the soldier is proved and to be steady on all the battle front besides, is mere flight and disgrace if he flinches at that point.[41]

The prophet Micah reminded the people of his day that this kind of simple and balanced attentiveness to the work at hand was the most merciful caveat to the smothering conformity of the world and the best antidote to the withering accommodation of the world (Micah 4:4–5). Though such a lifestyle is a rebuke to the world (Micah 4:3), it is nevertheless ultimately quite alluring and enticing to it (Micah 4:1–2). Thus the Micah Mandate affords us the resources to maintain our peculiarity before a watching world.

John Bunyan knew that only too well.

In the center of Bedford, England, there stands a statue of Bunyan carrying a tinker's burden upon his back and a Bible in his hand. It marks the place where that great Puritan spent the long years of his imprisonment for the offense of teaching and preaching without proper state certification. Near the foot of the statue is a little bronze plaque. On it are engraved the words of the prosecutor—the Lord Judge Magistrate of Bedford—spoken at Bunyan's sentencing in 1673. The judge said: "At last we are done with this tinker and his cause. Never more will he plague us: for his name, locked away as surely as he, shall be forgotten, as surely as he. Done we are, and all eternity with him."[42]

Of course, it is not Bunyan that is forgotten. Instead, it is the Lord Judge Magistrate of Bedford that remains unnamed and unremembered. Bunyan foiled the plans of the powers and the principalities by holding fast to that which was once and for all delivered unto the saints: a world and life view rooted in the grace of a sovereign God and the uncompromised maturity of diligence in daily work.

Tough and Tender Mercies

He has shown you, O man, what is good and what the Lord requires of you: to do justice, to love mercy, and to walk humbly with your God (Micah 6:8).

❖ Have you ever noticed how work and mercy are connected throughout the Bible? Do a quick topical study of the way that diligence in our calling actually leads to effective service and compassion. A good Bible dictionary is a good place to start—but you might also want to simply follow the marginal references in a study Bible.

❖ Think about the unexpected opportunities God has afforded you to do acts of mercy while on the job, while exercising your

calling, or while developing your gifts. Make a list of the ways
you think you might be able to be used sometime in the future.

❖ What do you want to be doing and where do you want to be
in two years? In five years? In ten years? How do your dreams
coincide with your calling? And how do they together relate
to your past opportunities to live mercifully and compassion-
ately?

❖ Different seasons of life provide different opportunities to use
our gifts, our callings, and our vocations to serve others. What
should you be doing at this particular time in your life? Now,
just do it.

Part Four:
Humility: To Do Well

❖

The men who can be charged with the fewest failings, either with respect to abilities or virtue, are generally most ready to allow them.

Samuel Johnson

Exertion, self-denial, endurance, these make the hero, but to the spoiled child they connote the evil of nature and the malice of man.

Richard Weaver

7

Our Codependent Love

Everyone should consider himself as entrusted not only with his own conduct, but with that of others; and as accountable, not only for the duties he neglects or the crimes which he commits, but for the negligence and irregularity which he may encourage or inculcate.

SAMUEL JOHNSON

Like peace, regeneration caries a price which those who think of it idly will balk at.

RICHARD WEAVER

For several years now I have been a fascinated student of the early years of American life and liberty. Admittedly, separating fact from fiction, exactitude from nostalgia, and actuality from myth is often more than a little difficult, but I have found it to be well worth the effort. Though I do not have anything like an idealized perception of that great epoch, I am nevertheless constantly amazed by the breadth and depth of the fledgling American culture and by the substantive character of the people who populated it. Living in a day when genuine heroes are few and far between—at best—those pioneers and the times they vivified provide a startling contrast.

The fact is Colonial America produced an extraordinary number of prodigiously gifted men. From William Byrd and George Wythe to Thomas Hutchinson and William Stith, from Robert

Beverley and Edward Taylor to Benjamin Franklin and John Bartram the legacy of the seventeenth-century's native-born geniuses remains unmatched. Their accomplishments—literary, scientific, economic, political, and cultural—are staggering to consider. According to historian Paul Johnson, "Never before has one place and one time given rise to so many great men."[1]

As a child, my attentions were naturally drawn to such men as Washington, Hamilton, Adams, Lee, Laurens, Hancock, and the other leaders of the Revolution. But as I have grown older, it has been the men who preceded the so-called "Founding Fathers" that most evidently captivate my interests. Men like Cotton Mather.

I have often reflected that it is a cruel irony of history that Mather is generally pictured unsympathetically as the archetype of a narrow, intolerant, severe Puritanism, who proved his mettle by prosecuting the Salem witch debacle of 1692. In fact, he never attended the trials—he lived in the distant town of Boston—and actually denounced them. And as for his Puritanism, it was of the most enlightened sort. Mather was a man of vast learning, prodigious talent, and expansive interests. He owned the largest personal library in the New World—consisting of nearly four thousand volumes ranging across the whole spectrum of classical learning. He was also the most prolific writer of his day, producing some 450 books on religion, science, history, philosophy, biography, and poetry. His style ranged from *Magnalia Christi Americana*, dripping with allusions to classical and modern sources, to the practical and straightforward *Essays to Do Good*, said to be the most influential book ever written in this hemisphere.

He was the pastor of the most prominent church in New England—Boston's North Church. He was active in politics and civic affairs, serving as an advisor to governors, princes, and kings. He taught at Harvard and was instrumental in the establishment of Yale. He was the first native-born American to become a member of the scientific elite in the Royal Society. And he was a pioneer in the universal distribution and inoculation of the smallpox vaccine.

His father, Increase Mather, was the president of Harvard, a gifted writer, a noted pastor, and an influential force in the establishment and maintenance of the second Massachusetts Charter. In his day he was thought to be the most powerful man in New England—in fact, he was elected to represent the colonies before the throne of Charles II in London. But according to many historians, his obvious talents and influence actually pale in comparison to his son's.

Likewise, both of Cotton Mather's grandfathers were powerful and respected men. His paternal grandfather, Richard Mather, helped draw up the *Cambridge Platform*, which provided a constitutional base for the Congregational churches of New England. And with John Eliot and Thomas Weld, he prepared the *Bay Psalm Book*, which was the first text published in America, achieved worldwide renown, and remains a classic of ecclesiastical literature to this day. His maternal grandfather was John Cotton, who wrote the important Puritan catechism for children, *Milk for Babes,* as well as drawing up the *Charter Template* with John Winthrop as a practical guide for the governance of the new Massachusetts Colony. The city of Boston was so named in order to honor him—his former parish work in England was at St. Botolph's Boston.

According to historian George Harper, together these men laid the foundations for a lasting "spiritual dynasty" in America.[2] Even so, according to his lifelong admirer, Benjamin Franklin, "Cotton Mather clearly out-shone them all. Though he was spun from a bright constellation, his light was brighter still."[3]

Mather was assuredly a man of splendid talents and varied interests whose impact covered the whole field of human endeavor, but his greatest contribution may well have been pioneering a theology of Biblical balance—one that ultimately gave shape to early American culture and life. Again, according to George Harper:

His supreme achievement lay in drawing on the perspectives of English Puritans like Richard Baxter and German Pietists like August Hermann Francke to forge a distinctive American theology. This new piety would finally come into its own with the flowering of evangelicalism in the nineteenth and twentieth centuries. Mather's ministry bridged the gap between what was and what was to be.[4]

Though some might doubt the influence of the otherworldly German Pietism in Mather's thought, there is no doubt that he was able to combine deep devotion and strident action into a single and cohesive vision for life and ministry that gave a unique tenor to the nascent American mindset.[5] He proclaimed a careful balancing of "word and deed, of hand and heart, of the life in the heavenlies and the life of this earth, of personal piety and corporate responsibility."[6]

For Mather this balance was supremely Scriptural—drawn from the very nature and character of God. "Cognizant of His sovereignty, alert to His providence, and respectful of His majesty," Mather believed there was no alternative but to "yield to every dimension of true discipleship," regardless of the "adjustments of life and comfort" such yielding "might effectuate."[7] It was simply a matter "demanded by the very attributes of the Lord."[8]

Mather's influence on my own life has been profound. The fact that he could be so active and at the same time so devout impresses me as the very kind of balance that we all ought to strive for. But the fact that this balance was invigorated in his life by an apprehension of God's own character and nature is more impressive still.

Mather wasn't just an overachiever, a pioneer workaholic. He was a man who knew God, disciplined the protocol of his life accordingly, and thereby was used in the good providence of God to alter the destiny of this nation forever.

That is the kind of example I have always desired to follow.

❖ KNOWING GOD

The *Westminster Confession of Faith* was written between 1643 and 1648 by a remarkable group of English Reformers. The cornerstone of its magnificent formulation of Biblical orthodoxy is its conception of God's nature and character:

> There is but one only living and true God, who is infinite in being and perfection, a most pure spirit, invisible, without body, parts, or passions, immutable, immense, eternal, incomprehensible, almighty; most wise, most holy, most free, most absolute, working all things according to the counsel of His own immutable and most righteous will, for His own glory; most loving, gracious, merciful, long-suffering, abundant in goodness and truth, forgiving iniquity, transgression and sin; the rewarder of them that diligently seek Him; and withal most just and terrible in His judgments; hating all sin, and who will by no means clear the guilty.[9]

This precise perception of God's regal character is matched in the Confession by a sober realization of His sovereign attributes:

> God hath all life, glory, goodness, blessedness, in and of Himself; and is alone in and unto Himself all-sufficient, not standing in need of any creatures which He hath made, nor deriving any glory from them, but only manifesting His glory in, by, unto, and upon them: He is alone the foundation of all being, of whom, through whom, and to whom are all things; and hath most sovereign dominion over them, to do by them, for them, or upon them whatsoever Himself pleaseth. In His sight all things are open and manifest; His knowledge is infinite, infallible, and independent upon the creature; so as nothing is to Him contingent or uncertain. He is most holy in all His counsels, in all His works, and in all His commands.[10]

Thus, the *Confession* concludes with a practical admonition: "To Him is due from angels and men, and every other creature, whatsoever worship, service, or obedience He is pleased to require of them."[11]

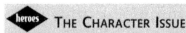 **THE CHARACTER ISSUE**

He has shown you, O man, what is good and what the Lord requires of you: to do justice, to love mercy, and to walk humbly with your God (Micah 6:8).

Through the ages, Christian heroes have demonstrated their fullest comprehension of God's character and attributes as they have humbly centered their lives and ministries in the work of the church in the world. They exercised careful stewardship over the little time they were alotted on this earth to walk in a circumspect fear of the Almighty. Examples abound:

The legendary generosity and charity of *Wenceslas of Bohemia* (907–929), is no mere Christmas fable. The young prince lived a life fraught with conflict and tragedy. Both his mother and grandmother—victims of court intrigue and anti-Christian conspiracy—were murdered when he was young. He himself was the object of several assassination attempts and revolts. Yet, despite such adversity, he was a model Christian regent. He outlawed child abandonment. He criminalized abortion. He reformed the penal system. And he exercised great compassion on the poor. All this because he took seriously the high call of discipleship and a life of service in the church. When he was finally killed by rival heathen elements in the court, his short life was grievously mourned by his subjects and he became for all time the symbol of a holy dependence on a sovereign God.

John Eudes (1570–1649) was born in Normandy at a time when anticlerical and anti-Christian sentiment there were at a fever pitch. Because his parents remained pious, he tasted the bitter draught of discrimination early in life. Not surprisingly, as an adult he dedicated himself to the care of the persecuted—refugees, the feeble-minded, Jews, the sick, Huguenots, and mendicants. He even organized teams of Christian women to care for women reclaimed from prostitution. His fearless and selfless care of the dying distinguished him during two virulent epidemics that swept through France in 1634 and 1639. But it was for his piety before the Lord and his devotion to the church that he was best known. He was unswerving in his commitment to utilize every moment he had breath to serve his sovereign Lord.

Louise De Marillac (1626–1691) married a high official of the French court and enjoyed a life of privilege and pleasure. Her husband's shocking death left her a widow at the age of thirty-three. That tragedy effected in her a deep desire to serve Christ and she committed herself to His kingdom. Shortly thereafter, she became a companion and coworker of Vincent De Paul in Paris, caring for the sick and helpless. With him, she launched a sheltering ministry for women in crisis. At the time of her death, the ministry had more than forty houses throughout France and twenty-six more in Paris where abused and exploited women could learn to rebuild their lives. But as with the others, this service was simply the outward expression of an inward committment to yield every aspect of her life to the ministry of the church and its sovereign King and Savior.

Dozens of others could be cited throughout the wide span of history: Clement of Rome (d. 100), Severinus Boethius (d. 524), Susanna Wesley (d. 1742), Count von Zinzendorf (d. 1760), Howell Harris (d. 1773), Samuel Crowther (d. 1891), and John Mott (d. 1955). Each was committed to serve others through the aegis of the church—not out of a sense of guilt or obligation but out of a solemn recognition of just who God is. And each laid the groundwork for us to live similar lives of submission and obedience.

Though such an understanding of God formed the backdrop of the thinking of men like Cotton Mather—and thus, in turn, much of the fabric of early American culture—it is a far cry from our own comprehension of God today. In fact, the doctrinal precision of the Westminster divines necessarily sounds rather foreign to our ears, not just because they made liberal use of an exacting tone and a majestic language at odds with our relaxed syntax and egalitarian prose, but because their very perception of God is foreign to us.

We are prone to think of God—when we think of Him at all—as wonderful. We are less likely to see Him as willful. Certainly He is both, but the overwhelming emphasis of Scripture is upon the will rather than the wonder. It is upon the exercise of God's prerogative rather than the expiation of our pleasure. The difference is probably a matter of slights rather than slanders. Nevertheless, it is a difference that makes for rather dramatic consequences.

Thus, to some of us God is little more than a cosmic vending machine in the sky, designed to dispense our every want and whim. To others of us He is a grandfatherly sage who lives to patiently offer us certain therapeutic benefits and baubles from His largess. To still others He is a kind of Santa figure—jolly, unflappable, and determined to bestow goodies upon incognizant masses. Invariably though, we moderns tend to see God in terms of ourselves—in terms of our wants, our needs, our preferences, and our desires. We have apparently, as Voltaire accused, "made God in our own image."[12]

To the Westminster divines, such a conception of God would have been altogether unrecognizable as the God of the Bible. Such a conception would have been incapable of laying foundations for Cotton Mather's theology of balance—thus rendering the flowering of American civilization utterly impossible.

In fact, according to psychologist Paul Vitz, such a conception is not knowledge of God at all, but a form of "self-worship."[13] According to the revered Anglican pastor J. C. Ryle it is "the cruelest of all delusions" because "by it men think they have come to a knowledge of God when in fact they have done nothing of the sort."[14] Thus, Lutheran theologian Joseph Aulen has argued that "the vast proportion of modern Christians have a vastly mistaken knowledge of the person and work of the Almighty."[15]

According to D. Martyn Lloyd-Jones, "because men do not know God or the nature of God—particularly those who claim to be Christians—all of the problems of life and culture are amplified even more."[16] Andrew Murray asserts that it is due to the fact that Christians do not "properly entertain a knowledge of God" that "societies fall into such disarray as we have in the modern world."[17] And A. W. Tozer has said that "a lack of a true knowledge of God's attributes and character" is the "root of the indecisiveness, imbalance, and ineffectiveness" of the contemporary church.[18]

That is a tragedy in more ways than one. J. I. Packer, in his devotional masterpiece, *Knowing God*, has said:

> What were we made for? To know God. What aim should we set ourselves in life? To know God. What is the "eternal life"

that Jesus gives? Knowledge of God. What is the best thing in life, bringing more joy, delight, and contentment, than anything else? Knowledge of God. What, of all the states God ever sees man in, gives Him most pleasure? Knowledge of Himself.[19]

Therefore, if we fail to come to a full and accurate knowledge of God—if it is shallow, or superficial, or self-centered, or supercilious, as our modern evangelical conception of God is apt to be—then we are not only likely to miss God's purpose and will for our lives, we are likely to make a mess of the world around us as well.

And so we have.

❖ THE EARTH IS THE LORD'S

Nebuchadnezzar, the great king of the Babylonian empire during the sixth century before Christ, might sympathize:

All this came upon King Nebuchadnezzar. At the end of the twelve months, he was walking about the royal palace of Babylon. The king spoke, saying, "Is not this great Babylon, that I have built for a royal dwelling by my mighty power and for the honor of my majesty?" While the word was still in the king's mouth, a voice fell from heaven: 'King Nebuchadnezzar, to you it is spoken: the kingdom has departed from you! And they shall drive you from men, and your dwelling shall be with the beasts of the field. They shall make you eat grass like oxen; and seven times shall pass over you, until you know that the Most High rules in the kingdom of men, and gives it to whomever He chooses." (Daniel 4:28–32)

He was the greatest king of the ancient world. His reign was resplendent with glory, honor, and power. The city that he built was utterly magnificent, unrivaled in its scope and vision. The empire that he assembled was mythically proportioned, unrivaled in its strength and valor. The reputation that he forged was terrifyingly universal, unrivaled in its supremacy and vastness. And yet, Nebuchadnezzar was still but a man.

He thought he was something more. He imagined for himself a majesty that transcended that of all other men. He reveled in the storehouse of his great pride. He boasted of his invincibility.

And so, God humbled him. He decreed that Nebuchadnezzar would be reminded of the frailty of human flesh. He decreed that the great king would be forced to acknowledge a King greater still:

> That very hour the word was fulfilled concerning Nebuchadnezzar; he was driven from men and ate grass like oxen; his body was wet with the dew of heaven til his hair had grown like eagles' feathers and his nails like birds' claws. (Daniel 4:33)

The complete demise of Nebuchadnezzar was a vivid demonstration to all the citizens of Babylon that God alone is sovereign and all-mighty (Revelation 17:14), that God alone is to be exalted and praised (Psalm 148:13), that God alone is the possessor of all greatness, power, glory, and majesty in heaven and on earth (1 Chronicles 29:11).

The lesson was not lost on the king or his subjects:

> And at the end of the time I, Nebuchadnezzar, lifted my eyes to heaven, and my understanding returned to me; and I blessed the Most High and praised and honored Him who lives forever: For His dominion is an everlasting dominion, and His kingdom is from generation to generation. All the inhabitants of the earth are reputed as nothing; He does according to His will in the army of heaven and among the inhabitants of the earth. No one can restrain His hand or say to Him, "What have You done?" At the same time my reason returned to me, and for the glory of my kingdom, my honor and splendor returned to me. My counselors and nobles resorted to me, I was restored to my kingdom, and excellent majesty was added to me. Now I, Nebuchadnezzar, praise and extol and honor the King of heaven, all of whose works are

truth, and His ways justice. And those who walk in pride He is able to put down. (Daniel 4:34–37)

Nebuchadnezzar learned the most central truth in all the cosmos: God sovereignly rules over all things (Psalm 103:19). He learned that God and God alone is supreme (Isaiah 40:17–18), that God is the "King of kings and Lord of lords" (1 Timothy 6:15).

God sovereignly rules because He is the creator and owner and sustainer of all things above and below:

- "The Lord, God Most High, the Possessor of heaven and earth" (Genesis 14:22).
- "Indeed, heaven and the highest heavens belong to the Lord your God, also the earth with all that is in it" (Deuteronomy 10:14).
- "The earth is the Lord's, and all its fullness, the world and those who dwell therein. For He has founded it upon the seas, and established it upon the waters" (Psalm 24:1–2).

Nebuchadnezzar had to learn the hard way that the whole universe is in a very real sense a *theocracy* (*theos* = God, *kratos* = rules). It is a theocracy now. God's rule is not something we must wait for. It is not something that we must attempt to usher in through the manipulations of the political process or the revolutionary subversion of human governments. It is a reality right this very moment. "Alleluia! For the Lord God Omnipotent reigns!" (Revelation 19:6)

The Bible is absolutely clear on this point. There is nothing in heaven above or on earth below that escapes His jurisdiction. God rules.

God sovereignly rules the forces of creation:

- "I know that the Lord is great, and our Lord is above all gods. Whatever the Lord pleases He does, in heaven and in earth, in the seas and in all deep places. He causes the vapors to ascend from the ends of the earth; He makes lightning for the rain; He brings the wind out of His treasuries" (Psalm 135:5–7).

- "He sends out His command to the earth; His word runs very swiftly. He gives snow like wool; He scatters the frost like ashes; He casts out His hail like morsels; who can stand before His cold? He sends out His word and melts them; He causes His wind to blow, and the waters flow" (Psalm 147:15–18).

- "For of Him and through Him and to Him are all things" (Romans 11:36).

God also sovereignly rules the course of history. The ultimate destiny of both men and nations lie in His hands:

- "[He] works all things according to the counsel of His will" (Ephesians 1:11).

- "Remember the former things of old, for I am God, and there is no other; I am God, and there is none like Me, declaring the end from the beginning, and from ancient times things that are not yet done, saying, "My counsel shall stand, and I will do all My pleasure" (Isaiah 46:9–10).

- "Let all the earth fear the Lord; let all the inhabitants of the world stand in awe of Him. For He spoke, and it was done; He commanded, and it stood fast. . . . The counsel of the Lord stands forever, the plans of His heart to all generations" (Psalm 33:8–9, 11).

God sovereignly rules the hearts and minds and ways of men as well. Though He yields us extraordinary freedoms, we remain under the discretion of His divine purpose and plan:

- "A man's heart plans his way, but the Lord directs his steps" (Proverbs 16:9).

- "For in Him we live and move and have our being" (Acts 17:28).

- "It is God who works in you both to will and to do for His good pleasure" (Philippians 2:13).

God even sovereignly rules the nations of the earth. He is King over all kings and Lord over all lords:

- "For the kingdom is the Lord's, and He rules over the nations" (Psalm 22:28).

- "Why are the nations in an uproar, and the peoples devising a vain thing? The kings of the earth take their stand, and the rulers take counsel together against the Lord and against His Anointed: 'Let us tear their fetters apart, and cast away their cords from us!' He who sits in the heavens laughs, the Lord scoffs at them. Then He will speak to them in His anger and terrify them in His fury" (Psalm 2:1–5).

- "The Lord brings the counsel of the nations to nothing; He makes the plans of the peoples of no effect" (Psalm 33:10).

The fact is God rules everything and everyone, everywhere and at all times. He is the one true Master of the universe. Again, this is not something that we have to somehow confirm through political or cultural processes. It is a temporal objective that we must strive toward. God is even now on the throne. For, "The Lord has established His throne in heaven, and His kingdom rules over all (Psalm 103:19).

❖ THE CHRISTIAN LIFE

Clearly then, the goal of Christian living in the world is not to usher in some new theocratic order or enforce some new theocratic code. It is instead to simply acknowledge the theocracy that already exists by virtue of the nature and character of God (Proverbs 3:6). It is to know God for who He actually is and to live accordingly. It is to "glorify God and to enjoy Him forever."[20]

Christian activity in the world therefore is not supposed to attempt an imposition of a messianic kingdom from the top down. Only God can lawfully control the hearts of men by imposing His rule. The balanced Christian life before the watching world is thus merely a public expression of our fealty to Him and our submission to the Word, which reveals Him in His fullness—it is an outward expression of our humility before almighty God. The daily Christian walk is therefore a bottom-up and inside-out process in the light of our knowledge of God.

The Bible asserts that the administration of the theocracy, the government of God, rests on the shoulders of Jesus Christ (Isaiah 9:6–7). It is His robe of glory (Revelation 19:11–16). So the Christian life is simply a recognition of and a submission to that fact. It is an active affirmation in word and deed that Christ is the creator and sustainer of the universe (Colossians 1:16–17), that even now He upholds "all things by the word of His power" (Hebrews 1:2), and that there will be no end to the increase of His government or of peace (Isaiah 9:7). It freely confesses what Nebuchadnezzar was forced to admit: "His dominion is an everlasting dominion, and His kingdom is from generation to generation" (Daniel 4:34). The balanced Christian life is nothing more and nothing less than the daily and ubiquitous declaration: "Jesus is Lord"—the most basic of all Christian declarations (Romans 10:9).

Sadly, most of us have repeatedly made Nebuchadnezzar's foolish mistake—we are so self-centered and self-consumed that we actually fail to take the nature and character of God into account. We have thus been entirely unaware of the fact that Christ bears the ensigns of the theocracy of heaven and earth: a crown of glory and honor (Hebrews 2:9), a sword of truth and justice (Revelation 1:16; 2:16), a scepter of righteousness and authority (Hebrews 1:8), a crest of promise and consolation (Revelation 5:5), a name of prerogative and transcendence (Philippians 2:9–10), and a title deed of absoluteness and finality (Matthew 11:29). We have acted as if the lordship of Christ was not the least bit real in terms of the management of our daily schedules and agendas.

We have acted like Nebuchadnezzar.

As a result, we have often, like Nebuchadnezzar, suffered utter humiliation. The enemies of the Gospel scoff and ridicule. They persecute and antagonize. They run roughshod over the weak and helpless. They pollute the land with abomination and desecration. And all the while, we are scuttled off to pasture like so many bovine indigents (Daniel 4:33). All for the lack of the knowledge of God. All for the lack of a simple comprehension of the fact that Christ is the Lord over the totality of life—that God rules.

Of course, Nebuchadnezzar learned his lesson. His humiliation convinced him beyond any shadow of a doubt that it is God who "removes kings and raises up kings" (Daniel 2:21); it is God who appoints over the land whomsoever He will (Daniel 5:21); it is God who rules on earth as He does in heaven (Psalm 110:1–3). Nebuchadnezzar learned his lesson and changed his heart and his life.

What about us?

❖ FEAR OF GOD

According to South African theologian and pastor Brendan de Prinster, the clearest evidence that we "have not a true knowledge of God" is that we have ceased to adequately fear Him:

> It is a matter of pride. We have made God into our buddy. We have made Him into our supernatural mascot. We have made Him our co-pilot. Gone is the righteous and royal dread of the Holy One of Israel. Gone is the sense of awe at His Majesty. Gone is the knowledge of His vast power, His unswerving justice, and His uncompromising standards. Gone altogether.[21]

And yet the Bible makes it clear that a correct comprehension of God and His attributes will inevitably result in a holy fear of God. Again and again the refrain sounds:

- "The fear of the Lord is the beginning of wisdom; a good understanding have all those who do His commandments. His praise endures forever" (Psalm 111:10).

- "The fear of the Lord is the beginning of knowledge, but fools despise wisdom and instruction" (Proverbs 1:7).

- "The fear of the Lord prolongs days, but the years of the wicked will be shortened" (Proverbs 10:27).
- "In the fear of the Lord there is strong confidence, and His children will have a place of refuge. The fear of the Lord is a fountain of life, to turn one away from the snares of death" (Proverbs 14:26–27).
- "Better is a little with the fear of the Lord, than great treasure with trouble" (Proverbs 15:16).

A nation whose leaders fear God will suffer no want (Psalm 34:9). It will ever be blessed (Psalm 115:13). It will be set high above all the nations of the earth (Deuteronomy 28:1). Ancient Israel's greatness can be directly attributed to her leaders' fear of God: Abraham was a God-fearer (Genesis 20:11); Joseph was a God-fearer (Deuteronomy 10:12); as were Job (41:23), Joshua (Joshua 24:14), David (2 Samuel 23:3), Jehoshaphat (2 Chronicles 19:4), Hezekiah (Jeremiah 26:19), Nehemiah (Nehemiah 5:15), and Jonah (Jonah 1:9).

According to the great Puritan Richard Baxter: "The proper knowledge and fear of God leads us to but two postures of the spiritual service of worship: corporately in yielding of our praise in the church and individually in the yielding of our time in the world."[22]

The balanced Christian life always maintains this twofold expression of holy knowledge and fear: putting a high priority on the centrality of the church and sanctifying whatever time God grants us.

❖ THE CHURCH

Though all men are naturally like Nebuchadnezzar: deaf, dumb, and blind to a genuine knowledge of God (Jeremiah 9: 23–26), though we are bound instead into a selfish covenant with ignorance, defilement, and death (Isaiah 28:15), and though we pursue it (Proverbs 21:6), choose it (Jeremiah 8:3), and embrace it

(Proverbs 2:8), deep down we desire to escape its wretched shackles (Ecclesiastes 11:1–10).

Though we may vociferously deny it, the truth of God is written on the fleshly tablets of our hearts (Romans 2:14–15). In fact, we must actively restrain or suppress that truth in order to carry on with our destructive ways (Romans 1:18). Though we deliberately debase ourselves with futile thinking, foolish passions, and filthy behavior, we actually know what is right (Romans 1:19–24, 26–27). Though we consciously choose the precepts of alienation from God, we cannot escape the awful conviction of the ordinances of intimacy with God (Romans 1:28–31).

That is why all men so desperately need the church.

Only the church—as it holds steadfastly to the Word revealed, the Word made manifest, and the Word vivified—is able to effect the kind of comprehensive and reinforced transformation necessary to snap the spell with which sin and ignorance grip each and every one of us—and our society.

This is due to several great truths. First, the church renews the minds of fallen men through the teaching and preaching of the Bible—the Word revealed. Right doctrine shatters old habits, explodes perverse ideas, and establishes real hope. The Gospel changes people by the power of the Holy Spirit (Romans 1:16). Men trapped in the snares of death and darkness need good news. They need the Good News. And thus God has entrusted the crucial task of publishing that Good News among the nations to the church—and only to the church.

Second, the church readjusts men to genuine life through sacramental worship—the Word made manifest. Worship is not simply an indulgence in abstract theological rituals. Instead, it is a tangible offering to God, a consecration before God, a communion with God, and a transformation before God. In the simple yet profound act of worship, the meaning and value of life are revealed and fulfilled. It reorients men to God's plan, God's purpose, and God's program (Psalm 73:1–28). Once again, God has entrusted this vital function to the church—and only to the church.

Third, the church reforms the lifestyles of men through discipleship—the Word vivified. The disciplined accountability of life in a local church community repatterns a man's ways according to the ways of the Lord. By instilling in them godly habits they learn "the way [they] should go" (Proverbs 22:6). Through ritual and repetition they are trained to walk "the paths of justice" (Proverbs 2:8) and to avoid "the ways of darkness" (Proverbs 2:13). Through routines of righteousness they are established in "every good path" (Proverbs 2:9) so that ever afterward they may "trust in the Lord with all [their] heart, and lean not on [their] own understanding; in all [their] ways [acknowledging] Him" (Proverbs 3: 5–6). Thus, men are reformed through the church—and only through the church.

The church has the keys to the kingdom (Matthew 16:19). It has the power to bind and loose (Matthew 18:18). It has the authority to prevail over the very gates of hell (Matthew 16:18). It offers men the water of life (Revelation 22:17), the Bread of Life (John 6:31), and the Word of Life (John 1:1), because its Head is the Author of Life (Acts 17:25).

Presbyterian pastor and theologian Peter Leithart in his brilliant book, *The Kingdom and the Power,* makes it clear that in the good providence of God, the church is *Plan A* and there is no *Plan B.* Nevertheless, he says:

> Many treat the church as a more or less helpful addendum to the Christian life—if, that is, one can get free on Sunday mornings. The church is an aid to devotion, like rosary beads or a crucifix. If that makes you feel closer to God, fine. If not, well, one can surely be a Christian without being a member of the church. For all the professed religiosity of Americans, comparatively few believe that regular association with a specific group of people is a necessary and central part of a genuinely Christian life. Fewer still think of the church as an institution with real authority over her members; ask any pas-

tor who has tried to enforce discipline, and he will show you his scars.[23]

In contrast, however, he argues that a genuine knowledge and fear of God will ultimately provoke the process of "rediscovering the centrality of the church."[24]

Through the ages, the best and the brightest, the kindest and the holiest, have inevitably been those who have walked in awe of almighty God by making the fellowship, accountability, and ministry of the local church central to their lives and callings. They have invariably been churchmen.

❖ TIME

A genuine knowledge and fear of God will also provoke the process of sanctifying our time as well.

Virtually every Biblical injunction about the Biblical use of time underlines the importance of each moment that passes. It is an ethical imperative to act and act quickly when lives are at stake, when justice is perverted, when truth is in jeopardy, when mercy is at risk, when souls are endangered, and when the Gospel is assaulted.

We are admonished to make the most of our time (Ephesians 5:15–16). We are to redeem the time (Colossians 4:5). We are to utilize every day to the utmost (Hebrews 3:13). In short, we are to sanctify the time (Ecclesiastes 3:1–8).

According to the Bible, our time is not our own. It is not ours to dispose of as we choose. We have been "bought at a price" (1 Corinthians 6:20). Therefore we are to set our days, weeks, and years apart to the Lord for His glory (Romans 14:6–12).

In the Old Testament, the days were therefore carefully divided into eight distinct periods: dawn, morning, midday, dark, evening, and three night watches. These were distinguished in the lives of believers by times and seasons of prayer (Psalm 55:17;

Daniel 6:10). In the New Testament, the value of this kind of liturgical clock was affirmed by the followers of Christ who punctuated and accentuated their urgent task of evangelization with the discipline of regular spiritual refreshment (Acts 3:1).

Similarly, the weeks of God's people were ordered with purposeful sanctity. In the Old Testament, the week centered around the Sabbath and the attendant sacrifices. In the New Testament, the week revolved around the Lord's Day and the sacraments. Thus, each week had its own pace, its own schedule, its own priorities, and its own order. Believers were able to give form to function and function to form (Deuteronomy 5:12; Hebrews 10:24–25). The liturgical calendar enabled them to wait on the Lord and thus to "run and not be weary" and to "walk and not faint" (Isaiah 40:31).

Even the years were given special structure and significance to reinforce the Biblical conception of decisive urgency. In ancient Israel, feasts, fasts, and festivals paced the community of faith in its progression through the months (Exodus 13:6–10; Psalm 31:15). The early church continued this stewardship of time, punctuating the years with liturgical seasons—with Advent, Christmas, Epiphany, Lent, Easter, Ascension, and Pentecost. Thus, God's people were enabled and equipped to run the race (Philippians 2:16), to fight the fight (Ephesians 6:10–18), to finish the course (2 Timothy 4:7), and to keep the faith (2 Timothy 3:10).

In order to maintain a sense of balance it is essential that we maintain the knowledge and fear of God by pacing our efforts through the sanctification of our time. We will thus be able to risk all, remain decisive, and persevere with single-mindedness. We will thus be able to affirm with the psalmist:

> I hear the slander of many;
> Fear is on every side;
> While they take counsel together against me,
> They scheme to take away my life.

But as for me, I trust in You, O Lord;
I say, "You are my God."
My times are in Your hands;
Deliver me from the hand of my enemies,
And from those who persecute me. (Psalm 31:13–15)

Clearly, there is no room for procrastination or contemplation in light of the nature and character of God. We are called to seize the day. Decisiveness, determination, single-mindedness, constancy, diligence, and passion must inform our agenda. The pace we set should be fervent—because the task before us is urgent.

But just as we are to live our lives in holy fear of God with a clear sense of urgency, we are also to measure out that urgency with patience. Victory will not be won in a day, however fervently we act. It will take time—perhaps generations. It has always been that way. It always will be.

In the interim, we are to rest and rely on God's "exceedingly great and precious promises" (2 Peter 1:4). We are to trust that His sovereign working will indeed make all things right (Romans 8:28) and that His good providence will by no means be thwarted (Ephesians 1:11).

Though the times are hard and all the earth cries out under the burden of wickedness, injustice, and perversion, we can relax in the assurance that God is playing the keys of providence according to the score of His own devising. We need not be anxious (Philippians 4:6). We need not worry (Matthew 6:25). We need not fret (Luke 12: 22).

Such is the characteristic of holy patience.

Patience is actually an attribute of God Himself (2 Peter 3:9–15). In addition though, it is a command from on high—a nonoptional mandate for every believer (Ephesians 4:2). It is a fruit of the spirit (Galatians 5:22). It is an evidence of love (1 Corinthians 13:4). It is an ensign comfort (2 Corinthians 1:6). And, it is a qualification for church leadership (2 Timothy 2:24).

In times of persecution (1 Peter 2:20), suffering (James 5:10), and confrontation (1 Thessalonians 5:14), patience is to be the Christian's overriding concern. We are to be patient in hope (Romans 8:5). We are to be patient in affliction (Romans 12:12). We are to be patient in our preaching (2 Timothy 4:2). We are to clothe ourselves in patience (Colossians 3:12). And we are to endure in patience (Revelation 3:12). The pace we set must be steady. Because the task we face will not soon be dispatched.

All through the Scriptures this lesson is emphasized:

- "Rest in the Lord, and wait patiently for Him; do not fret because of him who prospers in his way, because of the man who brings wicked schemes to pass. Cease from anger, and forsake wrath; do not fret—it only causes harm. For evildoers shall be cut off; but those who wait on the Lord, they shall inherit the earth. For yet a little while and the wicked shall be no more; indeed, you will look carefully for his place, but it shall be no more. But the meek shall inherit the earth, and shall delight themselves in the abundance of peace" (Psalm 37:7–11).

- "He who is slow to anger is better than the mighty, and he who rules his spirit than he who takes a city" (Proverbs 16:32).

- "The discretion of a man makes him slow to anger" (Proverbs 19:11).

- "The end of a thing is better than its beginning; the patient in spirit is better than the proud in spirit. Do not hasten in your spirit to be angry, for anger rests in the bosom of fools. Do not say, 'Why were the former days better than these?' For you do not inquire wisely concerning this. Wisdom is good with an inheritance, and profitable to those who see the sun" (Ecclesiastes 7:8–11).

- "By long forbearance a ruler is persuaded, and a gentle tongue breaks a bone" (Proverbs 25:15).

According to the Bible, we are to imitate others who have

manifested a spirit of patience (Hebrews 6:12). Thus, Abraham (Hebrews 6:15), Noah (1 Peter 3:20), and the apostle Paul (2 Corinthians 6:6) are to be our models—as are the legions of other faithful heroes that have gone before us. They faced seemingly insurmountable odds with the calm assurance and the quiet confidence that could have come only from holy patience.

❖ INFORMED BALANCE

The grave sin of the people in Micah's day was that they had grown weary of the Lord (Micah 6:3). Obviously, they did not have a proper knowledge of God (Micah 1:2–5). Like Nebuchadnezzar they had become prideful (Micah 2:6), selfish (Micah 2:2), and decadent (Micah 2:1). They had become altogether alienated from the truth of God (Micah 6:10–11). They could not even understand the concept of repentence (Micah 6:6–7). And the result was a nation and a culture under judgment (Micah 2:10).

According to Cotton Mather, the only possible remedy for such a situation is a restoration of a humble recognition of the person and work of the Lord God:

> The pride of man bars him from the utterly base dependence upon gracious providence and from the sheer amenability of life within covenantal bounds. It debilitates both men and nations. Only the swift embrace of a holy and fearful apprehension of Christ Almighty may stay the dire consequences of such a reprobation. Such pride is a destroyer.[25]

Similarly, C. S. Lewis has said:

> The essential vice, the utmost evil, is pride. Unchastity, anger, greed, drunkenness, and all that are mere flea-bites in comparison: it was through pride that the devil became the devil: pride leads to every other vice: it is the complete anti-God state of mind.[26]

While all the world runs from dependency and co-dependency, the knowledge of God beckons us to humbly welcome them both—the former as we fearfully acknowledge God's sovereign rule and reign in the world and the latter as we yield to the gracious provisions of the church in space and time. Living the balanced Christian life demands both.

Indeed, as Otto Blumhardt once asserted:

> When our hearts, and souls, and minds are filled with the knowledge of the Most High and Living God then we are most prone to bow before the throne in trembling awe. And then we are most prone to depend upon one another as well. For as we humbly acknowledge the Lord's sovereign dominion over all things, we are best able to see our proper place in accord with His perfect will—and that is a fearsome thing indeed.[27]

With Fear and Trembling

> He has shown you, O man, what is good and what the Lord requires of you: to do justice, to love mercy, and to walk humbly with your God (Micah 6:8).

❖ Though we know that the Bible describes the church as the "holy preisthood" and the "spiritual house" of God's kingdom (1 Peter 2:5–9) we only rarely think of it in monarchical terms. Why not do a study of the way God has established the church and its ministries as a royal court on this earth? How would a more regal perspective of God's monarchical reign affect our vision of the church? Does our American democratic orientation sometimes cause us to miss key insights about the character of God and the way He desires to walk in this world?

❖ How central is the life and work of your local church to you and your family? Do you regularly pray for its leadership? Do you seek out ways to integrate your spiritual concerns into its overall outreach? Do you strive to make your gifts available to its various ministries? What can you do to make the tie that binds more secure?

❖ Time-management techniques and systems abound—but they rarely reflect the Biblical emphasis of stewardship. Evaluate how you manage your time—maybe you're fanatical about keeping a daily planner or maybe you're a little less than organized. Either way, assess how well your approach facilitates your walk with the sovereign Lord. And then make the changes necessary to bring your days and seasons under His rule and reign.

8

Just Do It

*As pride sometimes is hid under humility, idleness is often cov-
ered by turbulence and hurry.*

SAMUEL JOHNSON

*The whole tendency of modern thought, one might say its whole
moral impulse, is to keep the individual busy with endless
induction.*

RICHARD WEAVER

As is often the case for young aspiring authors, my first attempts
at writing took the form of poetry. It was not a promising start.
Most of those teenage compositions were rather soppy, maudlin,
and sentimental reflections on the shallower things in life. Like
the early *ex nihilo* realms of creation, they were "formless and
void."

It wasn't long before I realized that I wasn't getting anywhere
writing free verse. So, I decided to try my hand at a few of the
more traditional forms of poetry: iambic pentameter, trachaic
trimeter, anapestic heptameter, and dactylic dimeter. I wrote qua-
trains, elegies, odes, idylls, ballads, and sonnets. But it was not
until I hit upon the limerick that I found a rhyming scheme that
actually suited my utter lack of lyrical discipline—and if the truth
be told, my utter lack of lyrical talent. Limericks are not, after all,
too terribly demanding.

Perhaps that is why, unlike me, Edward Lear always hated to

admit that his own career was launched by this peculiar five-line lyrical form—even though his name is practically inseparable from it today. Though he was unquestionably the father of the limerick, Lear actually didn't invent it. Its origins lie shrouded somewhere back in the hoary mists of Irish folklore, fairy tales, and nursery rhymes. In fact, some of the most ancient and familiar lines in English poetry are counted among its number:

> There was an old lady of Leeds
> Who spent all her time in good deeds.
> She worked for the poor
> Till her fingers were sore
> This pious old lady of Leeds.[1]

> Hickory, dickory, dock.
> The mouse ran up the clock.
> The clock struck one
> And down he'd run.
> Hickory, dickory, dock.[2]

But, even though the form was already a time-honored convention, it was Lear who first brought the odd pun-filled limerick into popular favor and international fame. He did it quite by accident—and much to his chagrin.

You see, Lear was a mature professional, not a teenage neophyte—his paintings of birds were often compared with Audubon's, his watercolors were hung in the Louvre, his criticism was widely respected and heeded during his day, and he was often retained to give composition lessons to the sons and daughters of royalty. He apparently was desperate to make his mark in history as a serious artist.

Yet it is for his nonsense verses that he is best remembered:

> There was an old man in a tree,
> Who was horribly bored by a bee.
> When they said, "Does it buzz?"
> He replied, "Yes it does!
> It's a regular brute of a bee."[3]

There was an old man who supposed
That the street door was partially closed;
But some very large rats
Ate his coats and his hats,
While that futile old gentleman dozed.[4]

Though this kind of nonsense rhyme made him both rich and famous, Lear rather despised them—as a kind of literary junk food. In fact, late in life he said they were "awful and noxious distractions."[5] Despite his protestations, limericks became one of the most popular forms of versifying during the Victorian age on both sides of the Atlantic. Their infectious rhythm and lilt appealed to wits and wags of every stripe.

The form flourished:

There was a young lady of Niger
Who smiled as she rode on a tiger.
They returned from the ride
With the lady inside
And the smile on the face of the tiger.[6]

There was an old man of Blackheath
Who sat on his set of false teeth.
Said he with a start,
Well, bless my heart!
I've bitten myself underneath.[7]

A tutor who tooted the flute
Tried to tutor two tooters to toot
Said the two to the tutor
Is it harder to toot?
Or to tutor two tooters to toot?[8]

A fly and a flea in a flue
Were imprisoned, so what could they do?
Said the fly, "Let us flee."
"Let us fly," said the flea.
So they flew through a flaw in the flue.[9]

The more we hear them, the more likely we'll agree with Lear's stern assessment: Limericks are rather silly. Often only mildly humorous. Fluff really. Not at all the stuff of serious literature.

Actually, according to Lear limericks do the very opposite of what "good poetry" is supposed to do. He said:

> Good poetry focuses the attentions of the reader while limericks merely scatter those attentions. Good poetry attaches itself to a clear idea or image—it is fastened concretely; limericks are indefinite, imprecise, and trivial—they are loose and partial. The one is serious even when humorous for it is human; the others are insipid even when droll for they are insidious. The one is less popular than populist—fit for mature and discriminating minds; the others are famously famished—tolerable for small children perhaps, but little more.[10]

"Like so much else in this poor fallen world," Lear continued, "limericks take the path of least resistance. They come cheaply and easily. Beware of all such things."[11]

James Q. Wilson, a professor of management and public policy, makes the same point—not about limericks, but about life. He says: "The best things in life invariably cost us something. We must sacrifice to attain them, to achieve them, to keep them, even to enjoy them."[12]

That is one of the most important lessons we can learn in life. It is the message that we know we ought to instill in our children: Patience, commitment, diligence, constancy, and discipline will ultimately pay off if we are willing to defer gratification long enough for the seeds we have sown to sprout and bear.

A flippant, shallow, and imprecise approach to anything—be it sports or academics, business or pleasure, friendship or marriage—is ultimately self-defeating. It is not likely to satisfy any appetite—at least, not for long.

The world is indeed full of seemingly harmless little distractions; humorous and silly things; banal and trivial things; things

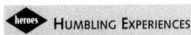 **HUMBLING EXPERIENCES**

He has shown you, O man, what is good and what the Lord requires of you: to do justice, to love mercy, and to walk humbly with your God (Micah 6:8).

Humble discipline has always been among the most highly appreciated characteristics of the heroes of the faith. Across the span of history those who have made the greatest impact for the greatest good have invariably been those who have walked in quiet obedience and holy fear of God. Examples abound:

Athanasius (300–373) was one of the giants of the church's Patristic Age. As a young deacon from Alexandria, he attended the First Ecumenical Council at Nicaea where he took a leading role in shaping the Nicene Creed. His bold defense of the doctrine of the Trinity against the Arian heresy demanded his attentions throughout his life and resulted in repeated exiles from his beloved home. He was also involved in various conflicts in the arena of politics, the arts, liturgical renewal, monastic development, New Testament canonisity, and judicial reform. He wrote several important works including biographies, commentaries, systematic theologies, and devotional treatises. His short classic, On the Incarnation, is still a staple of any solid theological education. Yet despite a life filled with furious activity and controversy it was for his personal piety and humble faith that he earned for himself the sobriquet Athanasius conta mundum, or "Athanasius against the world." Long seasons of prayer and fasting punctuated his life with an air of humility and faithfulness that his opponents simply were unable to match.

Henry Meldith (1544–1572) was a young Huguenot pastor in central Navarre renowned for his holiness and humility. During the early days of the Reformation—when passions were high and tempers were short—he taught his congregation discretion and long-suffering through an exercise of the basic Biblical disciplines of prayer and fasting. In a society riven by political and theological strife, they were able to build bridges of reconciliation. Meldith himself became a legate to Henry of Navarre, who eventually assumed the throne of France. He carried a message of humility, faithfulness, and quiet obedience to the great conferences of Poissy in 1561 and New Rochelle in 1571. Several accounts of those meetings note the powerful influence his prayerful attitude and life of discipline had upon the other attendees. That he was accidentally killed in the riotous St. Bartholomew Day Massacre in Paris the following year probably sealed the fate of the

Huguenot community more than any other single event. The still-wavering king lamented his death as "the loss of France's humblest Christian."[13]

In 1625, *Nicholas Ferrar* (1579–1637) retired from a promising parliamentary career in London and moved to a Christian community in Huntingdonshire. The community was marked by extreme Puritan piety: They fasted regularly—both publicly and privately; twice a day they all attended the liturgical offices in their tiny church; at every hour during the day some members joined in a little office of prayer so that the whole Psalter was recited daily; and at night, at least two members of the household maintained a "nightwatch of prayer" and the Psalter was again recited. They were marked by their charity and pro-life activism as well—so that their spiritual disciplines were not merely turned inward. Ferrar focused their practical and merciful concerns on abandoned boys that roamed the byways. Ultimately, the community developed one of the most effective alternatives to the humanism of the day through simple Christian service and unfaltering spiritual devotion.

Dozens of others could be cited throughout the wide span of history: Benedict of Nursia (d. 550), Gerald of Mayo (d. 732), Martin Bucer (d. 1551), Thomas Cranmer (d. 1556), Gemma Galgani (d. 1903), Lottie Moon (d. 1912), and E. M. Bounds (d. 1913). Each demonstrated a humbleness of life and faith through careful attention to the basic Christian disciplines: prayer and fasting. And as a result, they left their mark upon eternity as well as upon history.

that take the path of least resistance; things that come cheaply and easily. "Beware of all such things."[14]

Now, that is not to say that we cannot have fun; that we cannot ever let down our guard; that we are compelled to be continually intellectually vigilant. On the contrary, some of the most profound moments in life come when a dad and his kids have tickle fights in the middle of the living room floor; or when best friends wile away the hours together confiding their fondest hopes and dreams; or when brothers and sisters are stricken by a fit of giggles in the grocery store line; or when a grandmom hunkers down to a tiny table for a make-believe afternoon tea party.

But then, moments like these never come cheaply and easily—they are fruit from the carefully tended gardens of love and trust.

Lear explains:

> It is all a matter of proportion. There is nothing intrinsically wrong with limericks or any other form of silliness. It is when the shallow things completely supersede and supplant more serious things that we get into trouble. When what people want replaces what people *need*, then the truth is obscured.[15]

Sadly, that is a lesson very nearly lost on us in this odd to-whom-it-may-concern, instant-everything day of microwavable meals, prefab buildings, bottom-rung bureaucracy, fit-for-the-market education, knee-jerk public misinformation, and predigested formula entertainment. Thus temporary expediencies supersede permanent exigencies.

Even the church has fallen prey to this "spirit of the times." We don't want worship to be too terribly demanding. We don't want doctrine that challenges our pet notions. We want music that we're comfortable with. We want preaching that reassures us, that reinforces our peculiar preferences, that affords us a sense of serenity. We want cheap grace; positive thinking; easy faith. We want Christianity Lite.

It is almost as if we are attempting to reduce the profundities of the faith to a simple formula—to a kind of theological limerick:

> Jesus loves me, this I know,
> For the Bible tells me so.
> Little ones to Him belong.
> They are weak, but He is strong.
> Yes, He loves me, or, so I'm told.[16]

But a genuine holy and reverent fear of almighty God cannot be reduced to such shallow sentiments. Knowing God demands more than soppy feelings or maudlin emotions. Just as the virtues of justice and mercy are not realized in our lives haphazardly or lackadaisically, a commitment to spiritual humility requires a walk of determined discipleship. Humble faith is the fruit of a maturity in grace honed over time by unhurried fellowship and everyday obedience.

Sadly, that is not a message proclaimed too terribly often in our time. You only have to look at the modern church's approach to the Biblical disciplines of fasting and prayer to see just how true that is. These basic building blocks of discipleship were once the hallmarks of living in humility before God. But apparently, no longer.

Fasting and prayer are not easy. They are not terribly comfortable. They are unlikely to capture the fascinated attentions of popular fashion and fancy. So, we don't practice them. Plain and simple. We've relegated them to the long ago and far away.

We'd much rather attend to growth seminars, building programs, demographic surveys, and capital fundraising campaigns. Never mind the fact that the Scriptures never once mention growth seminars, building programs, demographic surveys, or capital fund raising campaigns, while fasting and prayer are not only mentioned, they are mandated.

But then, at a time when the disciplines of the Christian life are much more like limericks than sonnets—when humble faith is regarded as little more than a shallow sentiment—this is not all that surprising.

❖ THE DISCIPLINE OF FASTING

The Hebrew word for "fast" used throughout the Old Testament is *tsome*. The Greek word used throughout the New Testament is *nacetis*. Both literally mean "to cover over" or "to affix." The idea is not simply to cover over the mouth—and thus to refrain from eating—but to affix the attentions to other matters altogether. It is "to focus on" or "to fasten on" spiritual matters rather than merely temporal matters. It is "to hold fast" to

Christ—and nothing else. It is to abstain from one thing in order to attain to another.

It is only by a slow and patient walk in grace that we are able to fully comprehend that "man shall not live by bread alone" (Matthew 4:4). Fasting is a means that God has appointed to realize anew how it is that Christ has liberated us from the tyranny of the flesh and from the awful surrender of the spirit to the body and its appetite. It is a mighty provocation for us to "humble [ourselves] under the mighty hand of God" (1 Peter 5:6).

Whenever and wherever it is mentioned in the Bible, this gracious appointment of the mature Christian life—the discipline of fasting—has a conspicuously prominent role in humbling God's people so that they can concentrate on spiritual things:

- Joshua and the elders kept a solemn fast after their people were defeated by the men of Ai (Joshua 7:6).

- Jehoshaphat appointed a day of fasting and prayer throughout his kingdom when the confederated forces of Ammon and Moab came against him (2 Chronicles 20:3).

- When Queen Esther felt herself and her people to be in danger from the conspiracy of Haman, she set apart a season of solemn prayer and fasting (Esther 4:16).

- Ezra, when setting out on his mission to Jerusalem, assembled the returning captives at the river Ahava, and there proclaimed a fast (Ezra 8:21).

- David fasted and prayed in humiliation in the aftermath of the Bathsheba incident (2 Samuel 12:16).

- The inhabitants of Nineveh set apart a season of special prayer and fasting following the pronouncement of judgment by Jonah (Jonah 3:7–8).

- Even the hardened Ahab fasted and cried for mercy when the judgment of God was announced against him by Elijah (1 Kings 21:27).

- In the New Testament, we see the pious prophetess Anna

engaged in serving God day and night with fastings and prayers (Luke 2:37).

- Cornelius, the devout centurion, likewise was engaged in fasting and prayer when the Lord first appeared to him (Acts 10:30).

- The apostle Paul repeatedly speaks of his habit of waiting on God by fastings as well as by prayer (2 Corinthians 6:5; 11:27).

- And even our Lord Jesus entered on His public ministry only after a long season of preparatory fasting (Matthew 4:2).

Mentioned more than seventy-five times in the Bible—more than baptism, the Lord's Supper, witnessing, or even tithing—fasting is one of the most basic and essential of the disciplines of the Christian life.

Living as we do in these limericklike times, the very idea of fasting seems a bit arcane and esoteric. Perhaps a tad legalistic. Maybe even bordering on fanatical. But from a Biblical perspective it is just a normal aspect of humble faith.

In the Sermon on the Mount, Jesus drove home the importance of normal, regular fasting with a warning, a command, and a promise:

> When you fast, do not be like the hypocrites, with a sad countenance. For they disfigure their faces that they may appear to men to be fasting. Assuredly, I say to you, they have their reward. But you, when you fast, anoint your head and wash your face, so that you do not appear to men to be fasting, but to your Father who is in the secret place; and your Father who sees in secret will reward you openly. (Matthew 6:16–18)

First, notice that fasting is not an exercise of ritual correctness for those who must put on holier-than-thou airs. Jesus said that when we fast, we are not to look like it. None of that baptized-in-vinegar look. No woe-is-me-I'm-in-the-midst-of-a-spiritual-trial expression to wrinkle our nose or mar our visage. Fasting is supposed to evoke humility. If we fast for some outward, physiological, or social benefit; if we fast for whatever sympathy, empathy, or kudos we can muster, then we have already received our reward in full. "Do not be like the hypocrites, with a sad countenance," that is the warning.

Second, fasting is to be a part of our regular routine. It is to be seamlessly woven into our normal lifestyles. It is to be fully integrated into our walk with both God and man—with a minimum of disruption. We're to do good—but we're to look good while doing it. "Anoint your head and wash your face," that is the command.

Third, fasting is Godward in its orientation. Its only audience is Him. Its only intent is Him. Its only object is Him. It is wholly and completely subsumed in Him. "And your Father who sees in secret will reward you," that is the promise.

Inherent in all three—the warning, the command, and the promise—is the assumption that no matter what, one way or another, the disciples will fast. That much is understood. It is assumed. It is a given. "When you fast," Jesus says (v. 16). And again He says, "when you fast" (v. 17). No ifs, ands, or buts about it. "When."

Our fasting may be absolute (Deuteronomy 9:9) or partial (Daniel 10:3). It may be entirely private (Nehemiah 2:1) or demonstrably corporate (Jeremiah 36:6). It may be occasional (Acts 13:3) or seasonal (Zechariah 9:19). But one thing is certain: if we are followers of Christ; if we are genuine Christian disciples; if we are seriously seeking the will of God, obeying His Word, and walking in dependence on Him, we will fast (Matthew 9:14–15).

It is interesting to consider that Adam and Eve lost both their spiritual purity and their temporal paradise—all because they failed to fast at the appropriate time.

It is equally interesting to survey the annals of history to discover that virtually all the heroes of the faith through the ages have put a high priority on fasting. From Athanasius to

Augustine, from Polycarp to Patrick, from John Chrysostom to John Calvin, from Brother Andrew to Mother Teresa, and from Francis of Assisi to Francis Schaeffer, the saints of yore took advantage of every appointment of grace—not the least of which was fasting.[17] Not only that, but they encouraged their churches, their communities, and their nations to do likewise. It is nothing if not common to find references to whole congregations consecrating themselves to covenantal fasts and solemn assemblies. Calls by national leaders for days of prayer and fasting were regular occurrences throughout the West during the glory days of Christendom.[18] Washington, Adams, Jackson, Lee, Davis, Harding, Coolidge, and Eisenhower all stood foursquare in that tradition of "seeking first the kingdom" by establishing regular days of national repentance and fasting.[19]

It would have been inconceivable to any of them to neglect such an essential aspect of humble discipleship—as inconceivable as substituting recovery for repentance, serenity for sanctification, or limericks for creeds.

Otto Blumhardt, the great seventeenth-century Lutheran missionary, speculated that should the day ever come when such substitutions did actually occur, the minions of the "culture war" would be the least of our worries. He said:

> On the day the church abandons its care of the poor, its fervent ministry of supplication, and its intently chosen fast—for whatever good will or intentions—on that day we will undoubtedly see its clergy dragged off in wickedness and promiscuity, its parishes awhoring after greed and avarice, and its congregations awash in every vain imagination and unspeakable perversion. On that day, the church will cease to be the church. May it never be. May it never be. Stay that day with the hand of faithful diligence, I pray. Stay that day with the fastening of faith.[20]

❖ THE DISCIPLINE OF PRAYER

Prayer is the most common Christian expression of humble faith; but like fasting it may be among the least practiced Christian disciplines. It is said that prayer is the universal language of the soul; but it is actually the solitary province of the supplicating saint. Prayer, as the unconscious heart-cry in times of distress, is the currency of all humanity; but prayer, as the deep and committed soul-bond in communion with almighty God, is an exceptionally rare and precious jewel.

Certainly, regular seasons of prayer are essential to spiritual humility—which is why spiritual humility seems to be so terribly scarce. We take our time with God in snatches. We throw out petitions rapid-fire on the run. At best, we rush through our laundry lists of wants and needs. Even in the corporate life of the church prayer gets short shrift—only briefly imposed like talismans at predictable intervals in worship services, business meetings, and meals. And thus we prove the mettle of our woefully insubstantial and unresolved limericklike faith.

The great romantic poet Samuel Taylor Coleridge sadly observed:

> The act of praying is the very highest energy of which the human mind is capable; praying that is, with the total concentration of the faculties on God. The great mass of worldly men, learned men, and yea, even religious men are absolutely incapable of prayer.[21]

In contrast, the heroes of the faith through the ages have always been diligent, vigilant, and constant in prayer. They humbled themselves before God with prayers, petitions, and supplications, always acknowledging their utter dependency upon His mercy and grace. Athanasius prayed five hours each day.[22] Augustine once set aside eighteen months to do nothing but pray.[23] Bernard of Clairveaux would not begin his daily activities until he had spent at least three hours in prayer.

Charles Simeon devoted the hours from four till eight in the morning to God.[24] John Wesley spent two hours daily in prayer—beginning well before dawn.[25] John Fletcher regularly spent all night in prayer. His greeting to friends was always, "Do I meet you praying?"[26]

Martin Luther often commented, "I have so much business I cannot get on without spending three hours daily in prayer."[26] Francis Asbury rose each morning at four in order to spend two hours in prayer. Samuel Rutherford began praying at three. If ever Joseph Alleine heard other craftsmen plying their business before he was up, he would exclaim, "Oh how this shames me. Doth not my master deserve more than theirs?"

John Calvin, John Knox, and Theodore Beza vowed to one another to devote two hours daily to prayer. John Welch thought the day ill-spent if he did not spend eight or ten hours in prayer. "The story of prayer," E. M. Bounds once said, "is the story of great achievements." Indeed, it is.

Thus, he asserted:

There ought to be no adjustment of life or spirit for the closet hours. Without intermission, incessantly, assiduously; that ought to describe the opulence, and energy, and unabated ceaseless strength and fullness of effort in prayer; like the full and exhaustless and spontaneous flow of an artesian stream.[28]

Similarly, Homer W. Hodge argued:

Prayer should be the breath of our breathing, the thought of our thinking, the soul of our feeling, the life of our living, the sound of our hearing, and the growth of our growing. Prayer is length without end, width without bounds, height without top, and depth without bottom; illimitable in its breadth, exhaustless in height, fathomless in depths, and infinite in extension. Oh, for determined men and women who will rise early and really burn for God. Oh for a faith that will sweep into heaven with the early dawning of morning and have ships from a shoreless sea loaded in the soul's harbor ere the ordinary laborer has knocked the dew from the scythe or the lack-luster has turned from his pallet of straw to spread nature's treasures of fruit before the early buyers. Oh, for such.[29]

Not surprisingly, the Scriptures are brimming with exhortations to be such—to be constant in prayer:

- "Oh, give thanks to the Lord! Call upon His name; make known His deeds among the peoples! Sing to Him, sing psalms to Him; talk of all His wondrous works! Glory in His holy name; let the hearts of those rejoice who seek the Lord! Seek the Lord and His strength; seek His face evermore!" (1 Chronicles 16:8–11)

- "Ask, and it will be given to you; seek, and you will find; knock, and it will be opened to you" (Matthew 7:7).

- "Watch and pray, lest you enter into temptation. The spirit indeed is willing, but the flesh is weak" (Matthew 26:41).

- "Watch therefore, and pray always that you may be counted worthy to escape all these things that will come to pass, and to stand before the Son of Man" (Luke 21:36).

- "Praying always with all prayer and supplication in the Spirit, being watchful to this end with all perseverance and supplication for all the saints" (Ephesians 6:18).

We are to pray.

We are to pray with wholeheartedness (Jeremiah 29:13). We are to pray with contrition (2 Chronicles 7:14). We are to pray with all faith (Mark 11:24). We are to pray with righteous fervor (James 5:16). We are to pray out of obedience (1 John 3:22) and with full confidence (John 15:7). We are to pray in the morning (Mark 1:35), and in the evening (Mark 6:46), during the night watch (Luke 6:12), and at all other times (1 Thessalonians 5:17).

God has given us access to His throne (Hebrews 4:16) and fellowship with Christ (1 Corinthians 1:9). And He expects us to make use of that glorious privilege at every opportunity (1 Timothy 2:8).

Throughout the Scriptures the priority place of prayer is more than evident in the lives and ministries of God's chosen people:

- Abraham was a man of prayer. He was "the friend of God" and thus, enjoyed close and intimate relations with Him (Genesis 15:1–21).

- Joseph was a godly man who feared the Lord, seeking Him in prayer. He boldly and publicly declared his utter dependence upon the Lord when his long-lost brothers appeared before him in Egypt (Genesis 42:18).

- Moses, too, was constant in his fellowship with God. When the nation of Israel rebelled against the Lord and against His appointed leaders, Moses sought mercy and long-suffering on their behalf (Numbers 14:11–38).

- Likewise, Joshua was fervent in prayer. After the calamity at Ai, he tore his clothes, fell on his face before the ark, and cried out for understanding, mercy, and restoration (Joshua 7:6–15).

- Gideon prayed for wisdom, direction, and assurance just before his fateful confrontation with the armies of the Midianites and Amalekites in the Valley of Jezreel (Judges 6:36–40).

- Samuel prayed on the occasion of Saul's consecration and installation as king over the nation of Israel (1 Samuel 12:16–25).

- David prayed as he arose in the dawning of the day, yielding the very meditations of his heart to the scrutiny of the Lord (Psalm 5:1–3).

- Solomon prayed before the altar of the Lord in the presence of all the congregation. He interceded on behalf of the nation, for the renewal of the covenant, and for the blessings of providence (1 Kings 8:22–53).

- Elijah prayed during his dramatic confrontation with Ahab,

Jezebel, and the prophets of Baal on Mt. Carmel (1 Kings 18:36–37).

- Jeremiah prayed even as he prophesied of covenantal justice before the skeptical nation (Jeremiah 14:1–9).

- Daniel prayed in the face of persecution, opposition, and possible humiliation (Daniel 6:10).

- Though naked, beaten, imprisoned, and shackled, Paul and Silas were praying and singing hymns to God in the inner prison of Phillipi (Acts 16:25).

In the Sermon on the Mount, Jesus not only taught His disciples about fasting, He taught them about prayer:

> And when you pray, you shall not be like the hypocrites. For they love to pray standing in the synagogues and on the corners of the streets, that they may be seen by men. Assuredly, I say to you, they have their reward. But you, when you pray, go into your room, and when you have shut your door, pray to your Father who is in the secret place; and your Father who sees in secret will reward you openly. And when you pray, do not use vain repetitions as the heathen do. For they think they will be heard for their many words. Therefore do not be like them. For your Father knows the things you have need of before you ask Him. (Matthew 6:5–8)

Following these basic introductory instructions, He gave them His model for prayer—known as the Lord's Prayer:

> In this manner, therefore, pray: Our Father in heaven, hallowed be Your name. Your kingdom come. Your will be done on earth as it is in heaven. Give us this day our daily bread. And forgive us our debts, as we forgive our debtors. And do not lead us into temptation, but deliver us from the evil one. For Yours is the kingdom and the power and the glory forever. Amen. (Matthew 6:9–13).

As He did with fasting, Jesus emphasized the importance of consistent, committed prayer with a warning, a command, and a promise.

First, notice that prayer is not a means for self-promotion—either before men or before God. The throne room of the Most High is not some kind of cosmic vending machine for our every want, whim, or worry any more than it is a showcase for our eloquence or our reverence. It is instead a schoolhouse for humility. Others make a spectacle of themselves when they pray that way. "Do not be like them." That is the warning.

Second, prayer is to be habitual. It is the expression of our relationship with God. It is to be intimate. It is to be personal. It is to be as practical as our daily bread. It is to be as lofty as the outworkings of providence in heaven and on earth. It is to be as pointed as our trespasses and our trespassers. But above all, it is to be regular. "When you pray," Jesus said. "In this manner, therefore, pray." That is the command.

Third, prayer is objectively hedged by God's will. As the *Shorter Catechism* of the *Westminster Confession* says, "Prayer is an offering up of our desires unto God for things agreeable to His will."[30] We are not to pray simply in order to get something. We are to pray in order to be something (James 4:3). We pray in order to be conformed to God's will. And "He who sees in secret will reward openly," for He "knows the things we have need of before we ask Him." That is the promise.

And, oh what a promise!

> If My people who are called by My name will humble themselves, and pray and seek My face, and turn from their wicked ways, then I will hear from heaven, and will forgive their sin and heal their land. (2 Chronicles 7:14)

In accord with the good providence of God, prayer binds and it looses (Matthew 18:18). It casts down and it raises up (Mark 11:23–24). It ushers in peace (1 Timothy 2:1–2), forgiveness (Mark 11:25), healing (James 5:14–15), liberty (2 Corinthians 3:17), wisdom (1 Kings 3:3–14), and protection (Psalm 41:2). Clearly, "the effective, fervent prayer of a righteous man avails much" (James 5:16).

Samuel Chadwick, a Puritan of great renown, aptly wrote:

Satan dreads nothing but prayer. Activities are multiplied that
prayer may be ousted, and organizations are increased that
prayer may have no chance. The one concern of the devil is to
keep the saints from praying. He fears nothing from prayerless
studies, prayerless work, prayerless religion. He laughs at our
toil, mocks at our wisdom, but trembles when we pray.[31]

❖ THE NEHEMIAH MODEL

Nehemiah was undoubtedly a man of decisive action. He was
assuredly a man of vast influence. But in the time of crisis, instead
of immediately throwing his political weight around, exercising
his political clout, calling in his political favors, and organizing his
political resources, Nehemiah fasted and prayed. Instead of charg-
ing boldly before the throne of Artaxerxes, he humbled himself
before the throne of God:

So it was, when I heard these words, that I sat down and wept,
and mourned for many days; I was fasting and praying before
the God of heaven. And I said: "I pray, Lord God of heaven,
O great and awesome God, You who keep Your covenant and
mercy with those who love You and observe Your commandments, please let Your ear be attentive and Your eyes open,
that You may hear the prayer of Your servant which I pray
before You now, day and night, for the children of Israel Your
servants, and confess the sins of the children of Israel which
we have sinned against You. Both my father's house and I have
sinned. We have acted very corruptly against You, and have
not kept the commandments, the statutes, nor the ordinances
which You commanded Your servant Moses. Remember, I pray,
the word that You commanded Your servant Moses, saying, 'If
you are unfaithful, I will scatter you among the nations; but if
you return to Me, and keep My commandments and do them,
though some of you were cast out to the farthest part of the
heavens, yet I will gather them from there, and bring them to
the place which I have chosen as a dwelling for My name.'

Now these are Your servants and Your people, whom You have redeemed by Your great power, and by Your strong hand. O Lord, I pray, please let Your ear be attentive to the prayer of Your servant, and to the prayer of Your servants who desire to fear Your name; and let Your servant prosper this day, I pray, and grant him mercy in the sight of this man." For I was the king's cupbearer. (Nehemiah 1:4–11)

For an entire month he fasted and prayed (Nehemiah 1:1; 2:1).

His response to the crisis in Jerusalem speaks volumes for his character and for the character of his faith. He understood clearly the consequences of sin. He had a good grasp of the dynamics of history. He showed a thorough understanding of divine providence. He obviously understood the multigenerational nature of the kingdom task. His response gives testimony to his utter dependence upon God, and his confidence in Biblical problem solving. He wanted to do things God's way, in God's time, with God's help, in accord with God's will. He lived a life of undoubted spiritual humility.

So he fasted and prayed.

And not just this once. His humble commitment to these disciplines marked his life throughout his entire career. At every turn, Nehemiah demonstrated devotion to the Lord God on high. When he appeared before Artaxerxes to make petition to rebuild the walls of Jerusalem—fresh from a month of fasting and prayer—he once again breathed a prayer of supplication (Nehemiah 2:4). When he entered the ruined city to begin the task, he again resorted to petition (Nehemiah 2:12). When threats of violence and conspiracy jeopardized the fledgling reconstruction project, he sought the face of God (Nehemiah 4:2). When there were conflicts and crises among the people that required his judicious hand, first he prayed (Nehemiah 5:19). When an attempt on his life threatened the entire project, he didn't panic—he made petition to the Lord (Nehemiah 6:9). When his own brethren turned against him, he sought heavenly refuge (Nehemiah 6:14). When he led the people to undertake covenant renewal, he called them to a new season of fasting and prayer (Nehemiah 9:1–38). And when the work on the walls was complete, again he consecrated the time in the holy disciplines (Nehemiah 13:31).

Of course, fasting and praying weren't all that he did. But it was the foundation of all that he did. Like anyone called by God into the arena of the culture, he lived out the full dimensions of an integrated Biblical worldview. He invested himself in careful planning (Nehemiah 2:5–6). He laid the groundwork with cautious attention to detail (Nehemiah 2:7–8). He enlisted qualified help (Nehemiah 2:9). He encouraged his workers (Nehemiah 2:17–18). He motivated them (Nehemiah 4:14–20). He organized and delegated the various tasks (Nehemiah 3:1–32). He anticipated difficulty and made provision for it (Nehemiah 2:19–20; 6:1–14). He improvised when he had to (Nehemiah 4:21–23), and he worked (Nehemiah 4:23). He sacrificed (Nehemiah 5:14–19), led (Nehemiah 13:4–30), and governed (Nehemiah 7:1–7). But undergirding all these necessary activities was his constant reliance upon Almighty God. Undergirding them all was a humble faith marked by fasting and prayer.

Nehemiah was confident that God would give him success (Nehemiah 2:20). He was sure God would give him strength (Nehemiah 6:9), show him favor (Nehemiah 2:18), and see him through (Nehemiah 2:12). He was unwavering in his optimism because the work was conceived by God, not by him (Nehemiah 7:5). It was God's project, not his.

Thus, it is clear that Nehemiah didn't fast and pray in order to *get* something. He humbled himself before the Lord in order to *be* something (James 4:3). He wanted to be conformed to God's will. He wanted to be used in God's work. He wanted to be obedient.

And his humble devotional life was a gracious means to that end.

❖ How Should We Then Live?

Like Nehemiah, we live in a time of crisis. We live in a day of dis-integrating forces—when the very fabric of our civilization is in jeopardy. When lasciviousness and concupiscence are very nearly behavioral norms while righteousness and sanctification have become cultural laughingstocks. In such a time, at such a moment, how should we then live?

Instead of responding as Nehemiah did, all too often I am afraid we are a bit limericklike:

> There were three little birds in a wood
> Who always sang hymns when they could.
> What the words were about
> They could never make out.
> But they felt it was doing them good.[32]

Will that kind of limerick-level commitment, limerick-level disci-pleship, limerick-level faith suffice in these dire days? Hardly.

The Bible tells us that in the past when God's people sought to strengthen their devotional life—to sharpen their intercessions and give passion to their supplications—they fasted and prayed (Ezra 8:3). When they were intent on seeking God's guidance in difficult times, they fasted and prayed (Acts 14:23). When they were wont to express grief—whether over the consequences of their own sins or the sins of others—they fasted and prayed (2 Samuel 1:11–12). When they sought deliverance or protection in times of trouble, they fasted and prayed (2 Chronicles 20:3–4). When they desired to express repentance and a return to the fold of faith, they fasted and prayed (Joel 2:12). When they desired to demonstrate humility before the throne of God, they fasted and prayed (Psalm 35:13). When they expressed concern for the ongo-ing work of the ministry, they fasted and prayed (Daniel 9:3). When they wished to minister to the needs of others, they fasted and prayed (Isaiah 58:6–7). When they sought to overcome temp-tation and dedicate themselves to holiness, they fasted and prayed

(Matthew 4:1–11). When they desired to express their highest love, honor, worship, and praise to the Father, they fasted and prayed (Luke 2:37). They fasted and prayed as a mark of true discipleship and profound humility.

Long ago, the Byzantine theologian Adeimantos of Thesily wrote: "Upon these hang the whole of our outward expression of faith, of hope, and of love: prayer and fasting."[33]

Likewise, Cephalos of Chalcedon said: "The care of our Christian culture would surely disintegrate should we ever abandon our beatific disciplines: intercessions and fastings."[34]

For many—whose god seems to be their stomach—this is a kind of radical notion. But from the Biblical perspective, there is hardly a better way to "taste and see that the Lord He is good." There is hardly a more effective means of appropriating God's grace—thus "fastening faith" to more sure foundations than mere appetites and desires can allow.

Not that we really have a choice about the matter; this is the normal maturation of the Christian life in spiritual humility and divine grace.

While he still occupied the White House, Calvin Coolidge wrote:

> There are those who suppose that when it comes to matters of religion, we all have the prerogative to pick and choose what we will and will not believe or observe. But according to the Christian religion, it is God who does the picking and choosing. Our job is simply to submit. Of course, that's the problem, isn't it? It is never simple to simply submit.[35]

Therefore, we ought to heed the admonition of the prophet Isaiah:

> Seek the Lord while He may be found, call upon Him while He is near. Let the wicked forsake his way, and the unrighteous man his thoughts; let him return to the Lord, and He will have mercy on him; and to our God, for He will abundantly pardon. "For My thoughts are not your thoughts, nor are your

ways My ways," says the Lord. "For as the heavens are higher
than the earth, so are My ways higher than your ways, and My
thoughts than your thoughts. For as the rain comes down, and
the snow from heaven, and do not return there, but water the
earth, and make it bring forth and bud, that it may give seed
to the sower and bread to the eater, so shall My word be that
goes forth from My mouth; it shall not return to Me void, but
it shall accomplish what I please, and it shall prosper in the
thing for which I sent it. For you shall go out with joy, and be
led out with peace; the mountains and the hills shall break
forth into singing before you, and all the trees of the field shall
clap their hands. Instead of the thorn shall come up the
cypress tree, and instead of the brier shall come up the myrtle
tree; and it shall be to the Lord for a name, for an everlasting
sign that shall not be cut off" (Isaiah 55:6–13).

❖ RIGHT WHERE HE WANTS US

I don't know about you but I'm not good enough to live out the
full implications of the Micah Mandate. I'm not disciplined
enough. I get hungry and distracted. It is easier for me to live life
on the level of limericks. I'm just not a sonnet sort of guy. I'm not
personally qualified for holiness. But then, I'm not really qualified
for any of the important roles I find myself filling in this life,
either—as a father or a husband.

I remember only too well the sense of blinding panic I felt
course through my veins the very first time I held my firstborn in
my arms. I just kept thinking over and over again: *What on earth
have I gotten myself into?*

As I gazed down in wonder at his red little face, with tears
streaming down my cheeks, I was forced to realize that I was no
less helpless than he.

Which is right where God wanted me. And still does. And
you no less than me. Dependent upon His grace—utterly, completely, and entirely—both to do what God wants us to do and to
be what God wants us to be. That is humility.

According to Oswald Chambers: "We cannot save ourselves nor sanctify ourselves, God does that; but God will not give us good habits, He will not give us character, He will not make us walk aright."[36]

The prophet Micah told the people of his day that God did not desire their sacrifices, their gifts, or their very bodies (Micah 6:7). Instead, He desired another "good" altogether (Micah 6:8). He wanted them to "look to the Lord" for their all-in-all (Micah 7:7). He "required" them (Micah 6:8).

Our walk of holiness and humility—evidenced in our adherence to the devotional disciplines of the faith—is a sure sign that we have indeed offered ourselves up as living sacrifices, acceptable to God (Romans 12:1). And that is the essence of the Micah Mandate.

The Discipline of Humility

He has shown you, O man, what is good and what the Lord requires of you: to do justice, to love mercy, and to walk humbly with your God (Micah 6:8).

❖ Read the startlingly contemporary prophetic message of Isaiah 58. Notice how internal disciplines are directly correlated to external societal conditions. How does this correlation reinforce the message of Isaiah's colleague, Micah? What implications does it have for the church in our day?

❖ Biographies of Christian heroes offer revealing glimpses into the devotional lives and habits of those who have gone before us in faith. Make it a point, whenever you read about believers in the past, to take note of the central place of prayer and fasting in their everyday affairs. We really ought to pass on such stirring stories of faithfulness, diligence, and obedience in days gone by—so try to weave them into your conversations and tell them to your friends and family. Often the first step toward imitation is inspiration.

❖ Books on prayer and the various other disciplines of holiness abound. And certainly, it is a good thing to read them. But it is an even better thing to put them into practice. Make a commitment to get past Square One. You don't really need all the latest discipleship gizmos and gadgets, just resolve to walk in faith: Just do it.

❖ Discipline is hardest when attempted alone. We all need accountability. Why not ask a friend to help reinforce your conviction to avoid limericklike superficiality and to get serious about prayer and fasting? Or maybe you can start a small accountability group at your church so that there are several people who will bolster and strengthen one another.

❖ Though all too often encrusted by unthinking ritual and unexamined habit, the liturgical church calendar was originally designed to be an aid to our devotional lives—to give order and structure to our times of prayer and fasting. Why not revisit the calendar with an eye toward reigniting our comprehension of God's redemptive plan for the ages and through the ages?

PART FIVE:
The Right Balance

❖❖

He that acknowledges the obligations of morality, and
pleases his vanity with enforcing them to others, concludes
himself zealous in the cause of virtue, though he has no
longer any regard to her precepts, than they conform to his
own desires; and counts himself among her warmest
lovers, because he praises her beauty, though every rival
steals away his heart.

SAMUEL JOHNSON

Since the time of Bacon the world has been running away
from, rather than toward, first principles, so that, on the
verbal level, we see "fact" substituted for "truth."

RICHARD WEAVER

9

Having It All

A contempt of the monuments and the wisdom of the past, may be justly reckoned one of the reigning follies of these days, to which pride and idleness have equally contributed.

SAMUEL JOHNSON

Those who have no concern for their ancestors will, by simple application of the same rule, have none for their descendants.

RICHARD WEAVER

Vienna is the beautiful and historic hub of Central and Eastern Europe—just as it has been for more than a thousand years. Thus, it is an international city unlike any other. London, New York, and Paris all boast diverse and multicultural communities—the legacy of far-flung empires and financial interests. But Vienna's character is drawn from a kind of supranationalism unique to Hapsburg domains. Here Northern Europe meets the Balkans, Western Europe meets the Steppes, and the Alps tumble down toward the Adriatic. Like London's suburbanized *imperia*, New York's urbanized *ethnos*, and Paris's domesticated *outremer*, Vienna serves as a vast roiling mix of peoples and traditions. But instead of being a melting pot, it is more like a cauldron of its famed goulash—deliciously incongruous.

The airport, roads, and hotels are all high-tech German but the food, hospitality, and music are all Old World Hapsburg. It is a seductive place with its magnificent theaters, its resplendent palaces, and its broad, bustling boulevards. But the one place where all the strains of Vienna's wide-ranging heritage is most evident is at the Stephansdomplatz—the city's beautiful Gothic cathedral.

Consecrated as a Romanesque basilica in 1147, the church has endured the tumult of war, fire, plague, revolution, conquest, and imperial ambition. Over the years, vast Gothic towers, chapels, vaults, spires, and portals were added in a wild variety of architectural textures and scales. Yet in the end, they all seem to harmonize with one another beautifully. Though conceived quite separately, they appear to coalesce into an inconsonant unity.

Whenever I am able to visit the great church, I am reminded of the nature of the body of Christ—the eternal church, not made of bricks and mortar. The topsy-turvy adventure that the Gospel inevitably spawns among believers is as oddly paradoxical as that ancient structure—but not just because it is improbably diverse yet singularly unified. It is because the whole feat of beauty and balance was actually achieved by anonymous, ordinary people.

Certainly the imperial House of Hapsburg employed a few master craftsmen from time to time over the years to complete one fantastic project or another in the cathedral. But the vast majority of the construction was undertaken by the faithful members of the congregation. Like most of the other great Gothic architectural wonders throughout Europe, the Stephansdomplatz was built by the folks of the town. There were virtually no professional artisans. There were practically no renowned architects. There were no corporate contractors, no certified engineers, and no planning commissions. That feat of stupendous architectural beauty was accomplished by the simple men and women at hand. The extraordinary was achieved by the ordinary.

That is actually the great lesson of all of history. It has always been ordinary people who ultimately were the ones to shape the outcome of great human events—not kings and princes, not masters and tyrants. It has always been laborers and workmen, cousins and acquaintances who have upended the expectations of the brilliant and the glamorous, the expert and the meticulous. It has been plain folks, simple people, who have literally changed the course of history—because they are the stuff of which history is made. They are the ones who make the world go round.

Most of the grand-glorious headline-making events through the ages have been little more than backdrops to the real drama of green grocers, village cobblers, next-door neighbors, and grandfathers. Despite all the hype, hoopla, and hysteria of sensational turns-of-events, the ordinary people who tend their gardens and raise their children and perfect their trades and mind their businesses are the ones who make or break a culture. Just as they always have. Just as they always will.

G. K. Chesterton said: "The most extraordinary thing in the world is an ordinary man and an ordinary woman and their ordinary children. For indeed, the first shall be last and the last shall be first."[1]

Whether building cathedrals like the Stephansdomplatz, toppling evil empires like the Soviet Union, or establishing justice, mercy, and humble faith in this poor fallen world, all of history's most significant developments have been wrought by babushkas and bourgeoisie, shopkeepers and students, dads and daughters, peasants and populists.

Intellectuals and elitists are loathe to admit it, but the accomplishments of the quiet and the unsung actually outstrip the loudly publicized deeds of the rich and the regarded. Those who write the histories and steer the cultural apparatus are wont to regard the gifts of ordinary people with scorn, but they are in the end overwhelmed by the torrent of truth evident in God's good providence in the coursing of time.

That is precisely why the Christian worldview stands out so brilliantly against the gray dullness of modern thought—it is bril-

GUARDING BALANCE

He has shown you, O man, what is good and what the Lord requires
of you: to do justice, to love mercy, and to walk humbly with your
God (Micah 6:8).

An integrated balance of justice, mercy, and humble faith has always
been a hallmark of the church's heroes. Never yielding to the easy
temptations of one extreme or another, they were ordinary men and
women who simply served those around them as priests and servants—
thus guarding the land with their righteousness. Examples abound:

Late in the third century, *Afra of Augsburg* (277–304) developed a
ministry to the abandoned children of prisoners, thieves, smugglers,
pirates, runaway slaves, and brigands. Herself a former prostitute, she
cared for the despised and the rejected with a special fervor, taking
them into her home, creating an adoption network, and sacrificing all
she had that out of her lack they might be satisfied. Her faith and
piety were renowned. Her struggle for justice was unparalleled. And
her ministry of mercy was an inspiration to thousands. Ultimately, her
well-integrated balanced approach to the work of the Gospel in the
world came under the scrutiny of the authorities. Considered a grave
danger to state security because of her influence, she was martyred
during the great persecution of Diocletian.

John of Amathus (551–620) was born in Cyprus, though he is best
known for his work in Egypt. The greater part of his life was spent
engaged in public service and civil affairs. He married young and faithfully raised his children in the nurture and admonition of the Lord.
Despite the fact that he was entirely untrained in theology, his unflagging personal piety and evident wisdom encouraged the people of
Alexandria to call him to be their patriarch and pastor at the age of
fifty. He threw himself into his new responsibilities with characteristic
zeal. He injected new life into that old church by establishing innumerable ministries to the needy. He endowed several health care institutions—including the very first maternity hospital. He founded several
homes for the aged and infirm. He opened hospices and lodges for
travelers. He tore down the remnants of the old infanticide walls outside the city with his own hands and called on his parishioners to join
him in defending the sanctity of human life in the future. So prolific
were his deeds of justice and mercy that he eventually became known
as John the Almsgiver.

Born to a poor but pious Scottish family, *David Livingstone* (1813–
1873) committed his life early on to the work of the priesthood of

believers. Driven by the dictates of the Great Commission, he went to Africa in 1841 as a missionary-explorer. Going where no white man had ever gone before, Livingstone penetrated the deepest reaches of the continent proclaiming the Good News of Christ. He understood only too well though, that the purpose of missions extended far beyond merely the proffer of heaven to the hapless and hopeless. In his widely influential book, *Missionary Travels and Researches in Southern Africa,* he wrote, "The indirect benefits, which to the casual observer lie beneath the surface and are inappreciable, in reference to the wide diffusion of Christianity at some future time, are worth all the money and labor that have been extended to produce them." Among those "indirect benefits" in Livingstone's work were the dramatic curtailment of both the native abortion and slave trades. A legend in his own time and a paradigm of missionary efficacy ever since, Livingstone demonstrated the power of the authentic church in the face of the horrors of heathenism.

Dozens of others could be cited throughout the wide span of history: Thecla of Iconium (d. 70), Tartian of Lorrai (d. 189), Adamnan of Iona (d. 697), Blaise Pascal (d.1662), William Wilberforce (d. 1833), B.B. Warfield (d. 1921), Maximilian Kolbe (d. 1941). Each demonstrated a balance in life and faith through a careful integration of justice, mercy, and humility before God. And as a result, they became model "priests" for all who have come after.

liant because it is mundane. The Christian faith has always acknowledged that a community's strength is not in its leaders— it is in its followers. It recognizes that the real decision makers in any culture are the anonymous plodders who are secretly the heroes of history by virtue of their consistent attention to the details that actually matter—enjoying their wives, loving their children, helping their neighbors, worshiping in Spirit and in truth, seeking righteousness, and applying their unique gifts to the affairs of everyday life. Thus, the masters of the universe are not musclebound Greek gods come down from Olympus. They are ordinary folks—believers like you and me.

The Micah Mandate appears at first glance to be a part of the repertoire of the especially skilled, the uniquely prepared, and the remarkably qualified. It looks and sounds hard—like an unscalable summit of spiritual heights. It appears to be attainable for the select few, the elite, and the privileged. Like some kind of spiritual juggling act or devotional gymnastics, it seems to be an ideal for the fit, the ambitious, and the talented.

But nothing could be farther from the truth. Like the building of cathedrals, the Micah Mandate is peculiarly the domain of the ordinary. The simplest people doing the simplest things has always been the profoundest course to achieve the profoundest things.

When we understand that, we will be able to actually do it.

❖ PRIESTLY SERVICE

"Church architecture," according to the great Medieval builder and designer Michel di Goivanni, "ought to be an earthly and temporal fulfillment of the Savior's own prophesy that though the voices of men be still, the rocks and stones themselves will cry out with the laud and praise and honor due unto the King of kings and the Lord of lords."[2]

We don't have to fabricate buttresses and bells, transepts and chancels, or ambulatories and sacristies to transform the most mundane things into the most glorious though. The fact is, God has dispersed among His people a rich treasury of spiritual gifts that equip and enable even the most plain among us to contribute magnificently to the work of the Gospel in the world (1 Corinthians 12:4–12). Every single member of the body of Christ, however humble, however obscure, however feeble, and however despised by the minions of this world, is vital to the overall work of the ministry (1 Peter 4:10).

This notion was the cornerstone of the Reformation—often called the doctrine of the priesthood of believers. It was at the crux of the struggle over justification, ecclesiastical authority, and even mysticism in worship that pitted Martin Luther against Erasmus, Eck, and ultimately the pope himself. Later, it was at issue when John Calvin came into conflict with the City Council of Geneva and when John Knox confronted Mary Queen of Scots. According to historian Philip Schaff, "The doctrine of the priesthood of believers was at the very heart of the principle of Protestantism."[3]

But the doctrine was no sixteenth-century innovation. In fact, the notion that every believer is responsible to do "the work of ministry" (Ephesians 4:12) and to exercise their gifts (Romans 12:6) is as ancient as revelation itself. Even the earliest stories of God's redemptive work make this plain.

For example, the tragic record of Sodom and Gomorrah can be best understood through the lens of this important doctrine.

The two cities were obviously consumed with vile and detestable sin early on in their recorded history. The people there were perverse (Genesis 19:5). They were violent (Genesis 19:9). They were arrogant, careless, and selfish (Ezekiel 16:49). They were haughty, self-destructive, and abominable (Ezekiel 16:50). They were utterly wicked (Genesis 18:20).

But that is not why God ultimately judged and destroyed them.

Despite all the debauchery, lasciviousness, and blasphemy, the Bible makes it clear that God was more than willing to spare the cities—even after He had pronounced His intended judgment:

> Abraham came near [to the Lord] and said, "Would You also destroy the righteous with the wicked? Suppose there were fifty righteous within the city; would You also destroy the place and not spare it for the fifty righteous that were in it? Far be it from You to do such a thing as this, to slay the righteous with the wicked, so that the righteous should be as the wicked; far be it from You! Shall not the Judge of all the earth do right?" So the Lord said, "If I find in Sodom fifty righteous within the city, then I will spare all the place for their sakes." (Genesis 18:23–26)

Abraham appealed to the Lord just before the intended destruction of Sodom and Gomorrah. God responded that if fifty men could be found who were, in effect, guarding the city with their righteousness, then He would relent.

So, Abraham decided to bargain some more:

> Abraham answered and said, "Indeed now, I who am but dust and ashes have taken it upon myself to speak to the Lord: Suppose there were five less than the fifty righteous; would You destroy all of the city for lack of five?" So He said, "If I find there forty-five, I will not destroy it." (Genesis 18:27–28)

Again, God told Abraham He would spare the cities if only there were forty-five good men guarding the people with their righteousness. "And he spoke to Him yet again and said, 'Suppose there should be forty found there?' So He said, 'I will not do it for the sake of forty'" (Genesis 18:29).

Once again, God said that He would acknowledge the preserving power of just forty righteous men. "Then he said, 'Let not the Lord be angry, and I will speak: Suppose thirty should be found there?' So He said, 'I will not do it if I find thirty there'" (Genesis 18:30).

Even " a little leaven leavens the whole lump" (1 Corinthians 5:6). God told Abraham that He would not judge the city on account of the protection afforded by just thirty righteous men. "And he said, 'Now behold, I have ventured to speak to the Lord; suppose twenty are found there?' And He said, 'I will not destroy it on account of the twenty'" (Genesis 18:31).

Even twenty guardians were enough to stay the hand of execution.

> Then he said, "Let not the Lord be angry, and I will speak but once more: Suppose ten should be found there?" And He said, "I will not destroy it for the sake of the ten." So the Lord went His way as soon as He had finished speaking with Abraham; and Abraham returned to his place. (Genesis 18:32–33)

The moral of this seemingly tedious lesson is abundantly clear: God will spare the wicked for the sake of the righteous. If good men will guard the cities, they are safe. But, if there are no such guardians, disaster is inevitable.

God has always called His people to be priests. The Israelites were chosen out of all the peoples of the earth to be "a nation of priests" (Exodus 19:6). And since the Day of Pentecost, when the church was grafted into the kingdom inheriting the promises, privileges, and place of Israel (Romans 2:28–29), God has called us to be a "kingdom of priests" as well (1 Peter 2:5; Revelation 1:6; 5:10).

The Hebrew word often used for "priest" in the Old Testament is *kohen*. It literally means "to serve," "to minister," or "to guard." The Greek word often used in the New Testament is *hierateuo*. It also literally means "to serve as a guardian" or "to minister." Thus a priest is someone who protects. He preserves. He ministers mercy and stays the hand of destruction and defilement. He serves those around him as a kind of spiritual watchman or guard.

Throughout the Bible those who were called to the priestly office were given the responsibility to mercifully protect the people through holy service:

- Adam was called to serve as a priest. He was to "tend and keep" the garden (Genesis 2:15). But he failed to do his duty and the calamity of the Fall resulted (Genesis 3:1–20).

- Aaron was called to serve as a priest. He was to guard the people from sin and shame (Exodus 32:25). But he failed to do his duty and the people began straightaway to worship and revel before a golden calf (Exodus 32:1–6).

- The Levites were called to serve as priests. Why? Because they guarded the integrity of God when all the rest of Israel was consumed with idolatry (Exodus 32:26–29). It was not until the Levites failed to the uttermost that God brought condemnation and judgment upon Israel (Jeremiah 6:13–15).

Man was made to be a priest before God. He was made to guard against evil. He was made to serve. Thus, the inclination to priesthood is inescapable. Even if he ultimately fails—as Adam, Aaron, and the Levites ultimately did—man's impulse to some kind of service remains. If man fails to be a true priest guarding the true sanctuary, he will become a false priest, guarding a false sanctuary. He will turn from selfless service to self-aggrandizing service:

- When Cain was cast out from the presence of the Lord (Genesis 4:12), he settled in the land of wandering (Genesis 4:16). There in a wilderness of vagrancy and nomadism, he established a false city—after all, what kind of city can be built on the foundations of dispossession? He became a false priest—taking upon himself the "guarding" power of "naming." And he propagated a false people for himself and his posterity (Genesis 4:17).

- After the flood, Nimrod, grandson of the accursed Ham, founded the false kingdom of Babel (Genesis 10:8–10). His people, bent on rebellion, "named" themselves priests (Genesis 11:4), and built false sanctuary (Genesis 11:1–4).

- When Jeroboam split Israel in half, taking the ten northern tribes with him, it was inevitable that he, too, would establish a false kingdom (1 Kings 12:20) and a false sanctuary (1 Kings 12:25–29), served by false priests (1 Kings 12:30–31).

Of course, each of these forays into self-serving priesthood ended in the judgment of God. Only a true priesthood serving in a true sanctuary can offer true protection. When man fails to do his duty, destruction occurs.

Thus, the whole reason that Sodom and Gomorrah were destroyed was that the men in the city refused to guard it with their righteousness. They refused to serve as true priests. Adam was evicted from Eden because he failed as a priest. Lot had to abandon what was in a sense a new Eden, because he, too, failed as a priest (Genesis 13:10).

In each case, they lost everything they had because they

refused to serve; they refused to live lives of merciful selflessness; they succumbed to sins of omission.

It is not surprising to discover then that Jesus commissioned His disciples to be priests, serving and nurturing the nations (Matthew 28:18–20; Acts 1:8). He told them that they had inherited the mantle of Israel's priesthood, and thus were to be the caretakers of the waters of life (Revelation 22:17), the bread of life (John 6:31; 1 Corinthians 11:24) and the Word of Life (1 John 1:1). They were to preserve and guard the earth. He said to them: "You are the salt of the earth; but if the salt loses its flavor, how shall it be seasoned? It is then good for nothing but to be thrown out and trampled underfoot by men" (Matthew 5:13).

In the ancient world, salt was highly valued for a number of reasons. It was used to season the food of man (Job 6:6) and of beast (Isaiah 30:24). It was used as a medicine (Ezekiel 16:4) and as a preservative (Exodus 30:35). It was symbolic of loyalty (Numbers 18:19), discretion (Colossians 4:6), purity (Mark 9:49), and perpetuity (2 Chronicles 13:5).

Interestingly, salt was also the mandatory accompaniment of some of the priestly sacrifices in the Old Testamental period, including the cereal (Leviticus 2:13) and burnt offerings (Ezekiel 43:24).

When Jesus told His disciples that they were to be " the salt of the earth" (Matthew 5:13), the immediate priestly implications would have been obvious to them. They were to serve by guarding the nations with their covenantal loyalty in discretion, purity, and perpetuity. They were to be the medicine of hope; they were to be a merciful preserving agent, restraining sin; they were to be living sacrifices:

> You also, as living stones, are being built up a spiritual house, a
> holy priesthood, to offer up spiritual sacrifices acceptable to
> God through Jesus Christ. Therefore it is also contained in the
> Scripture, "Behold, I lay in Zion a chief cornerstone, elect,
> precious, and he who believes on Him will by no means be put

to shame." Therefore, to you who believe, He is precious; but to those who are disobedient, "The stone which the builders rejected has become the chief cornerstone," and "a stone of stumbling and a rock of offense." They stumble, being disobedient to the word, to which they also were appointed. But you are a chosen generation, a royal priesthood, a holy nation, His own special people, that you may proclaim the praises of Him who called you out of darkness into His marvelous light; who once were not a people but are now the people of God, who had not obtained mercy but now have obtained mercy. (1 Peter 2:5–10)

The survival of any nation depends on the fulfillment of the priestly servanthood duties. If the people of God fail to be salt, then even the most providentially privileged nation cannot be preserved from putrefaction; it will fall into judgment.

Notice that when God describes the priestly task of His people throughout the Bible, He invariably uses civil or cultural terminology: We are to be ambassadors (2 Corinthians 5:20), judges (1 Corinthians 6:3), rulers (Ephesians 1:11), and witnesses (Acts 1:8). Notice, too, that this language is not simply symbolic. Whenever God engages His people in the work of guarding a culture or a land, He establishes them in ministries marked by a passion for justice, concern for mercy, and a heart of humble faithfulness.

But notice, too, that the call to be priests guarding the land goes out to every believer, regardless of background, preparation, or status. Every Christian is uniquely equipped by the power of the Holy Spirit to serve those whom God has placed around us. The doctrine of the priesthood of believers is not selective, it is universal.

The Micah Mandate's triad of virtues—justice, mercy, and humble faith—is particularly relevant to our call to serve as priests. Justice is the pursuit of righteous standards in our communities and our relationships. Eschewing the extremes of left or right, of liberal or conservative, of antinomian or legalistic, of

Herodian or Pharisaical, it holds up the Scriptures as the plumb line and bottom line for every human endeavor. Mercy is the personal touch of the Gospel. Where justice is cut and dried, mercy is personal and compassionate. Where justice is no respecter of persons, mercy extends its respect to all men everywhere. Humble faith is simply the recognition of who God is and what He has done. It is the awestruck and fearful response of the redeemed in the face of grace. A true priest cannot possibly carry out his or her servant responsibilities as salt, light, and guard without a careful inculcation of each of these virtues.

In a very real sense, the Micah Mandate is a call to fulfill this priesthood role. It is a challenge for each of us to move beyond the immobilized spectator church of our day into the fullness of the Reformation—and indeed the Biblical—vision of true spirituality and effectual ministry. It is a word of faith, hope, and love for a needy world on the very brink of disaster. It is the common man's manifesto.

❖ Patron Saint

Birmingham, Alabama, was a wild and untamed mining town in the heart of the reconstructed South when James Alexander Bryan came to pastor the Third Presbyterian Church there in 1888. When he died in 1941, Birmingham had become a vibrant industrial center. In the years between, Brother Bryan—as he was affectionately called—won the hearts of generation after generation of her citizens.

He was an unlikely hero for the bustling town though. For one thing, he was noticeably inept as a pulpiteer. His sermons were often halting, rambling, and inarticulate. Though entirely committed to the authority of the Scriptures and the centrality of preaching, he simply was not a skilled orator.

He was also a poor administrator. He was notoriously disorganized. When it came to the niggling details of management, he was often absent-minded and forgetful. He never seemed to lose sight of the "big picture," but all the necessary increments just got lost in the shuffle. Though perpetually busy, he was easily distracted and rarely kept up with his workload.

He didn't even maintain a particularly winsome appearance. He was more often than not disheveled, shabbily dressed, and hastily groomed. He was shy, soft-spoken, and had a slight stutter. In a day and time when manliness and an imposing presence were especially esteemed, he was merely slight and retiring.

Not surprisingly, during his long tenure as pastor, his church never really grew. When he died, membership stood at just under a hundred—right where it was shortly after he arrived in Birmingham a half-century earlier.

Nevertheless, he was practically a cultural icon in the city. Near the end of his life of service, he was honored by local leaders and dignitaries in a citywide celebration. The president of the City Commission said: "No man in Birmingham is better known or better loved than Brother Bryan. There is one man in this city about whom we are all agreed, and he is Brother Bryan."[4]

The editor of the city newspaper agreed: "Brother Bryan is the only man, whom we have ever known, whose motives have never been questioned. He is the one man for whom we are all unanimous."[5]

The city erected a statue of the humble pastor at one of its busiest intersections near downtown. It portrayed him in a posture of prayer and proclaimed him "the patron saint of Birmingham."[6] On the occasion of its unveiling, Hugo Black, the Supreme Court justice, asserted:

> This dedication raises our community to its loftiest heights, just as Brother Bryan has all these long years of his faithful and selfless service. The statue, let us hope, will inspire those here today, those who know Brother Bryan, and all those who come after, to love our neighbors as ourselves, even as he has.[7]

When Brother Bryan died, the entire city mourned his passing. Thousands of men, women, and children from every walk of life crowded around the tiny sanctuary and followed the solemn cortege at his funeral. Flags were lowered to half-mast and the mayor proclaimed an official day of prayer and fasting.

How had this seemingly inept pastor won over an entire city so completely? How had this painfully ordinary man accomplished a feat so extraordinary as this?

Very simply, Brother Bryan was a common man who proved to be an uncommon example of the Micah Mandate. Though he violated all the rules of success, church growth, worldly acclaim, and effectiveness, he seemed to incarnate the essence of the faith once and for all delivered unto the saints. He was, as many called him, "religion in shoes."[8]

He made it a habit to make a circuit every morning just before dawn to all the factories, shops, fire and police stations, schools, and offices downtown to pray with as many common working men and women as he could. He would simply announce himself, drop to his knees wherever he was, and begin to intercede for each of them. Over time, his obvious piety became a cherished emblem of personal concern in a harshly impersonal industrial world. He was the unofficial chaplain to the entire community—it was often said that the words most often on his lips were, "Let us pray."

Brother Bryan also distinguished himself with his selfless service to the poor, the needy, the brokenhearted, and the sick. His indefatigable efforts to encourage the distressed led him to establish several city outreaches to the homeless, to orphans and widows, and to the victims of war and pestilence overseas. More than any rich philanthropist, more than any well-endowed foundation, more than any charitable institution, he demonstrated the power and effect of merciful service on the fabric of a community.

He was a faithful pro-life stalwart as well. When a Planned Parenthood representative came to Birmingham in 1937, he was a vocal critic—calling on Christians to uphold their legacy of concern and care and thus make the vast organization's services unnecessary and unwanted. Though a confirmed nonpartisan politically, he often lobbied magistrates when issues of justice arose—he was, for instance, an early champion of civil rights and racial reconciliation. His unassailable character, his pure motives, and his holy demeanor enabled him to take such controversial stands without polarizing or alienating his beloved fellow citizens. Somehow they understood that his commitment to justice was a natural outgrowth of his humble faith and merciful service—one could not be had without the others.

Like so many heroes of the faith who had gone before him, Brother Bryan put into practice the Reformation doctrine of the priesthood of all believers—he thoroughly integrated the virtues of justice, mercy, and humility before God, conscientiously guarding the land with his righteousness. Like the cathedral builders of ages gone by, he was a terribly ordinary man who nevertheless accomplished extraordinary feats.

On the day following his funeral, the newspaper in Birmingham commented:

> We have had set before us the clearest example of what it
> must mean to be a follower of Christ. There can be little
> doubt to anyone familiar with Brother Bryan's life and work
> that the high ideals of the faith may actually be manifested.
> And that poses a tremendously prophetic challenge to us all.[9]

Indeed, it does.

The Changing of the Guard

> He has shown you, O man, what is good and what the Lord
> requires of you: to do justice, to love mercy, and to walk humbly
> with your God (Micah 6:8).

❖ Can just one person really make a difference? We know that in the political realm, it is axiomatic that the involvement of every person does indeed count: In 1645, Oliver Cromwell gained control of England by one vote; in 1776, one vote determined that English, not German, would be the official American language; in 1845, one vote brought Texas into the Union; in 1860, one vote determined that the radical Unitarians would gain control of the Republican Party, thus sparking the War between the States; in 1923, one vote gave Adolf Hitler control of the Nazi Party; in 1960, John F. Kennedy defeated Richard Nixon for the presidency by less than one vote per precinct. Again and again this theme resounds. Survey the Scriptures to underscore this theme in your own mind—focus particularly on the books of Judges and Acts.

❖ Now, examine your own life experience: How many times has a single person, acting faithfully, dramatically influenced you for good? Make a list of those instances of God's good providence through the priestly ministry of others.

❖ What are your gifts? What are you called to do? How should the principles and precepts of the priesthood of believers be manifested in your own life and work? Why not keep a ministry journal documenting the opportunities and challenges God poses for you each day in these arenas?

10

Where the Action Is

*The hidden origin of all power, all suasion, and all purpose, is
the assemblage of the covenant people: the church.*

SAMUEL JOHNSON

*It is always surprising to the uninitiated, the power that lies in
essential and primordial things—discredited though they may be
by the concourse of modernity.*

RICHARD WEAVER

As I travel around the country and speak to different groups, I am
often asked what I think is the greatest threat to the integrity and
security of American life and culture. I suppose that they expect
me to name one of the many humanistic juggernauts that seem to
be forever laying siege to justice, mercy, and humble faith.

Perhaps they expect me to name the American Civil Liberties
Union. And for good reason. There can be little doubt that the
ACLU has subverted justice in this land to an extraordinary
degree.[1] With more than six thousand cases in the courts each
year and with a blatantly political agenda, the vast reach of the
organization has tragically affected virtually every community and
every family in America. But I don't think that it actually poses
the gravest threat to our culture today.

Perhaps they expect me to name Planned Parenthood. And
for good reason. There can be little doubt that that organization
has subverted mercy in this land to an extraordinary degree.[2] With

nearly two hundred affiliates and more than eight hundred clinics nationwide, the multibillion-dollar abortion and sex education conglomerate has defiled the minds of the children, exploited the predicaments of the needy, and appropriated the resources of the taxpayer in horrifyingly unprecedented ways. But I don't think that it actually poses the gravest threat to our culture today.

Perhaps they expect me to name the National Education Association. Again, for good reason. There can be little doubt that the NEA has subverted humble faith in this land to an extraordinary degree.[3] Now controlling more than 90 percent of the government schools in America, the organization and its army of lobbyists, bureaucrats, and activists are responsible for the profound failure of public education today—its ideological extremism, its lack of academic achievement, its brutal administrative centralization, and its insensitivity to the unique integrity of families, schools, or communities. But I don't think that it actually poses the gravest threat to our culture today.

Perhaps they expect me to name some homosexual activist group like Act Up, an environmentalist group like Greenpeace, a globalist group like the United Nations, or a New Age group like Tikkun. And certainly each of these organizations ought to raise alarms and cause us great concern. But I don't think that any of them actually pose the gravest threat to our culture today.

In fact, all of these groups taken together still do not seriously threaten justice, mercy, and humble faith. They are merely symptoms of a deeper miasma. Even with their access to billions of corporate philanthropy dollars and tax revenues, their huge professional staffs, their monolithic control over the major media outlets, and their stranglehold on the apparatus of cultural power, they do not have the wherewithal to wreak havoc on the essential fabric of our society.

Only one earthly institution has that kind of deleterious power: the church.

It is only when the church fails to fulfill its calling in this poor fallen world that we have to really worry. It is only when the church fails to uphold the standards of justice, mercy, and humble faith that the onslaughts of the enemies of truth can possibly have their intended ill-effects. It is only when the church creates a vacuum by its own inactivity and impiety that the minions of this world have the opportunity to exploit the innocent, the foolish, or the inattentive.

That is one of the reasons why this book has not been filled with war stories, horror stories, or heart-tugging, tear-jerking, and soul-searching stories. I didn't want to leave the impression that the ACLU is to blame for the obvious deterioration of justice today, or Planned Parenthood for the absence of mercy, or the NEA for the subversion of humble faith. Because they're not.

The only reason these groups have been able to make headway with their vile plans is that the church has not been all that God has called us to be or done all that God has called us to do.

G. K. Chesterton once quipped that any new book of modern social inquiry is bound to be all too predictable in both its form and function:

> It begins as a rule with an analysis, with statistics, with tables
> of population, decrease of crime among Congregationalists,
> growth of hysteria among policemen, and similar ascertained
> facts; it ends with a chapter that is generally called *The*
> *Remedy*. It is almost wholly due to this careful, solid, and sci-
> entific method that the remedy is never found. For this
> scheme of medical question and answer is a blunder; the first
> great blunder of sociology. It is always called stating the dis-
> ease before we find the cure. But it is the whole definition and
> dignity of man that in social matters we must actually find the
> cure before we find the disease.[4]

This book is obviously born of a concern for the disease of moral and social disintegration in our time. But as Chesterton has said, we need not approach our subject medically—which might lead us to put our trust in mere institutional or political remedies.

Thus, I have taken the tack of essentially announcing the cure rather than offering yet another diagnosis or description of the malady.

And the cure is simply the church adhering to its essential calling. It is found when the elect of God yield to their divine mandate in every aspect and in every detail of their lives.

❖ A CULTURE WAR MAELSTROM

One of the greatest men and most brilliant minds Africa ever produced—standing shoulder to shoulder with such greats as Athanasius, Origen, and Tertullian—was Augustine of Hippo. He was born in 354 at Tagaste—in present-day Algeria—of a pagan father and a Christian mother. He was brought up as a Christian but not baptized.

He studied rhetoric at the great University of Carthage in order to become a lawyer, but later gave up his plan for a career in teaching. His study of philosophy—with an emphasis on Platonism and Manichaenism—resulted in a complete renunciation of Christianity. He lived a self-confessedly debauched life—including keeping a mistress for fifteen years by whom he had a son.

In pursuit of opportunities to improve his academic standing he took teaching posts—first in Rome and later in Milan. It was in this latter city that he fell under the sway of the great bishop and rhetorician Ambrose. After a long and tortured battle of the soul—described in his classic work *Confessions*—Augustine was converted under Ambrose's ministry and was baptized in 386.

After some two years of intensive discipling and catechizing, he returned to Africa and established a quasi-monastic community in Hippo. There he founded his famous *Classicum Academae*—devoted to study, writing, and the work of cultural transformation. The school was famed for its emphasis on art, music, politics, and ideas.

FIGHTING THE GOOD FIGHT

He has shown you, O man, what is good and what the Lord requires of you: to do justice, to love mercy, and to walk humbly with your God (Micah 6:8).

It has never been an easy task to keep the church on its proper course. The twin temptations of this poor fallen world—to compromise with the fleshly passions on the one hand and to flee from earthly passions on the other—have always posed great perils to orthodoxy and orthopraxy. Nevertheless, God in His good providence has supplied the church with champions of balanced integrity who have forged for it a great legacy of truth. Examples abound:

Nicholas of Myra (287–340), the fourth-century pastor who inspired the tradition of Santa Claus, may not have lived at the North Pole or traveled by reindeer and sleigh but he certainly was a paradigm of graciousness, generosity, and Christian charity. His great love and concern for children drew him into a crusade that ultimately resulted in imperial pro-life statutes that remained in place in Byzantium for more than a thousand years. His tender pastoral care saw his flock through the fierce conflagrations of persecution and heresy. In the end, orthodoxy owed its survival to his evident compassion as much as it did to the theological formulations of his Nicean peers.

Born in Northern Ireland to a wealthy Presbyterian family, *Amy Carmichael* (1867–1951) became one of the best-known missionaries of the first half of the twentieth century. Her ministry took her first to Japan, then to Ceylon, and finally to the Dohnavur province of India. Although sarti and immolation had been legally banned, to her horror she discovered that ritual abortion and female infanticide were still quite common. In addition, many of the young girls that she had come to work with were still being systematically sold off as slaves to the nearby pagan temples to be raised as cult prostitutes. She immediately established a ministry to protect and shelter the girls. Although she had to suffer the persecution of various Hindu sects and the bureaucratic resistance of the British colonial government, Carmichael built an effective and dynamic ministry renowned for its courage and compassion. Sadly, many of her fellow missionaries in India—having partially accepted the presuppositions of Malthusian thought—believed that her effort to build an orphanage and school was actually a "worldly activity" that distracted her from the "saving of souls." To such accusations she simply replied, "Souls are more or less firmly attached to bodies." Since her death in 1951, her Dohnavur

Fellowship has continued to carry on ministries of evangelism, education, and medical aid among the poor and helpless.

Corrie ten Boom (1893–1983) lived with her father and sister in Haarlem, Holland, where she assisted in the family watchmaking business and ministered to a number of mentally retarded children. Early in 1940, the nation fell to the invading Germans. Though at first the occupation seemed bearable enough to Corrie and her family, gradually her Christian conscience was pained as she saw more and more evidence of anti-Semitic persecution. When Jews began to disappear, together the ten Booms began plotting ways to subvert the Nazi's murderous designs. Eventually, their home became the hub of the Dutch underground in Haarlam. A secret room was put in one of the bedrooms so that they could hide Jews. In 1944, Corrie was arrested—along with her sister and her father who both eventually died in German concentration camps—for their illicit pro-life rescue efforts. Providentially, Corrie was released from prison just a week before her cell block was to be exterminated. For the rest of her life, Corrie traveled around the world sharing the consolation and the power of life in Christ and became a living symbol of the church's persistence of vision.

Dozens of others could be cited throughout the wide span of history: Cyprian of Carthage (d. 258), Antony of Egypt (d. 356), Hilary of Poitiers (d. 367), Bede (d. 735), Alcuin (d. 804), John Owen (d. 1683), and Oswald Chambers (d. 1917). Each demonstrated the reality that the church is a perpetually defeated thing that always survives its conquerers—as long as it remains faithful to its call to do justice, love mercy, and walk humbly with almighty God.

In 391 the steadfastness, holiness, and giftedness of Augustine were recognized and he was ordained against his own objections. In 394 he was elevated as coadjutor in the diocese. And in 396 he was elevated to the bishopric of the city.

Most of his quite brilliant writings have endured the test of time—I have eight thick volumes that sit on my desk—and are widely read to this day. His commentaries—on Genesis and Psalms particularly—are of inestimable value. His apologetics—like his *Contra Manichae* or *Contra Pelagae*—continue to set the standard for orthodoxy. And his didactae—such as his *Sanctus Dei* or *De Trinitate*—formed the first, and arguably the best, systematic theologies the church has ever produced.

But he is perhaps best known for—and made his greatest contribution with—his analysis of the culture war here on earth and its relation to the war in the heavenlies. Entitled *De Civitate Dei*—or *The City of God*—the book continues to define the terms of the debate better than any other work written before or since.

According to Augustine, culture is not a reflection of a people's race, ethnicity, folklore, politics, language, or heritage. Rather it is an outworking of a people's creed. In other words, culture is the temporal manifestation of a people's faith. If a culture begins to change, it is not because of fads, fashions, or the passing of time, it is because of a shift in worldview—it is because of a change of faith. Thus, race, ethnicity, folklore, politics, language, or heritage is simply an expression of a deeper paradigm rooted in the covenantal and spiritual matrix of a community's church and the integrity of its witness.

The reason that he spent so much of his life and ministry critiquing the pagan philosophies of the world and exposing the aberrant theologies of the church was that Augustine understood only too well that those things matter not only in the realm of eternity determining the spiritual destiny of masses of humanity but also in the realm of the here and now determining the temporal destiny of whole civilizations.

Unlike Tertullian who decried the cultural applicability of the church, asking, "What hath Athens to do with Jerusalem?" Augustine recognized that a people's dominant worldview inevitably shapes the world they have in view. And he also recognized that the church is the genesis point for the development of that worldview as it faithfully fulfills its calling to do justice, love mercy, and walk humbly with almighty God.

❖ TINY PUSHES

Bridging the gap between activism and devotion, the Micah Mandate describes a comprehensive and integrated worldview of vital faith and meaningful activity for the church. It presents what C. S. Lewis called "Mere Christianity,"[5] what John Stott called "Basic Christianity,"[6] and what William Wilberforce called "Real Christianity."[7] It delineates the ingredients of a balanced Christian life. It provides us with an incentive to walk in the footsteps of those uncommonly common heroes who have gone before us—to get our priorities straight, to put first things first, and to emphasize what really matters most. It outlines a strategic plan for us to begin to do what God wants us to do and to be what God wants us to be.

It offers the church a model not only of fealty and faithfulness but of anticipation and hopefulness as well.

After all, the future of our culture does not depend upon the machinations of political messiahs or the manipulations of institutional solutions. Neither does it depend on the emergence of some new brilliant spokesman or inspiring leader who has the strength or ability to overcome the forces of darkness. Instead, the future of our culture depends upon ordinary men and women in the church who are willing to live lives of justice, mercy, and humility before God. It depends on people like you and me who determine to live balanced lives in accord with the good providence of God before a watching world.

Writing to one of her many literary friends, the remarkable Helen Keller said:

> I long to accomplish a great and noble task, but it is my chief duty to accomplish humble tasks as though they were great and noble. The world is moved along not by the mighty shoves of its heroes, but by the aggregate of the tiny pushes of each honest worker.[8]

Now it is time for all of us who comprise the aggregate to

begin to live out the prophetic implications of that kind of faith ourselves by accomplishing the humble tasks of the church's ministry to the world—as though they were great and noble. It is time for us to change the world with our tiny pushes of justice, mercy, and humble faith.

In the end, we must say along with Titus and the apostle Paul, "These things are good and profitable for all men" (Titus 3:8).

Against All Odds

He has shown you, O man, what is good and what the Lord requires of you: to do justice, to love mercy, and to walk humbly with your God (Micah 6:8).

* Review the "impossible" situations of the Bible: from the stories of Abraham, Moses, David, and Elijah to the predicaments of Gideon, Daniel, Lazarus, and Paul. Then reread the paean to faith in Hebrews 11–12. When we walk by faith and not by sight, the odds look significantly better, don't they?

* Make a list of all the "impossible" situations the church faces in our own day: from cultural disarray and social disintegration to legalized abortion and a profligate media. Begin to pray specifically that God would raise up new champions in each of these areas to confound the rebellious in the world and the recalcitrant in the church.

* Now, make a list of all the "impossible" situations in your own life. Select a passage of Scripture to memorize that outlines some aspect of God's "exceedingly great and precious promises" (2 Peter 1:4) relating to each.

* Finally, go to work. Face the odds. Do what God has called you to do. Be what God has called you to be. And always remember: The church is "Plan A" in God's great scheme of things—and there is no "Plan B."

Notes

Quotes from Samuel Johnson are taken from *An Omnibus of Wit and Wisdom* (London: Carrel Brothers, 1966); quotes from Richard Weaver are taken from *Ideas Have Consequences* (Chicago: University of Chicago, 1948).

Acknowledgments

1. G. K. Chesterton, *Orthodoxy* (London: Minerva, 1908), p. 11.
2. Ibid.

Introduction

1. Hilaire Belloc, *Charles the First* (Philadelphia: Lippincott, 1933), p. 22.
2. William J. Bennett, *The Index of Leading Cultural Indicators* (New York: Simon and Schuster, 1994), p. 8.
3. Ibid.
4. Arthur Schlessinger, *The Disuniting of America* (New York: Simon and Schuster, 1993).
5. Daniel Patrick Moynihan, *Pandaemonium* (New York: Oxford, 1993).
6. *Forbes,* 14 September 1992.
7. Bennett, p. 10.
8. Os Guinness, *The American Hour* (New York: Free Press, 1992), p. 4.
9. Zbigniew Brzezinski, *Out of Control* (New York: Scribners, 1993).
10. *Forbes,* 14 September 1992.
11. Charles Colson, *Against the Night* (Ann Arbor, MI: Servant, 1989), p. 19.
12. George Grant, *The Family Under Siege* (Minneapolis, MN: Bethany House, 1994).
13. George Grant and Mark Horne, *Legislating Immorality* (Chicago, IL: Moody Press, 1993).
14. George Grant, *The 57% Solution* (Franklin, TN: Adroit Press, 1993).
15. George Barna, *Absolute Confusion* (Ventura, CA: Regal, 1993).
16. David Wells, *No Place for Truth* (Grand Rapids, MI: Eerdmans, 1993), p. 4.
17. Jerram Barrs et al., *What in the World Is Real?* (Champaign, IL: Communication Institute, 1982).
18. Francis A. Schaeffer, *How Should We Then Live?* (Old Tappan, NJ: Revell, 1976).
19. Umberto Eco, *The Name of the Rose* (New York: Harcourt Brace, 1983), p. 73.
20. Henry Van Til, *The Calvinistic Concept of Culture* (Philadelphia: Presbyterian and Reformed, 1959).
21. Phillip Schaff, *The Principle of Protestantism* (Philadelphia: United Church Press, 1964).
22. Charles Hodge, *Commentary on Romans* (Wheaton, IL: Crossway, 1994).
23. Gardiner Spring, *The Obligations of the Bible to the World* (New York: Taylor and Dodd, 1839).
24. J. C. Ryle, *The Old Paths* (London: James Clarke, 1959), p. vii.

Chapter 1

1. Charles Swindoll, *Living Beyond the Daily Grind* (New York: Inspiration Press, 1994), p. 408.

NOTES

2. Ibid.
3. James L. Brewster, *Philosophical Themes in Everyday Life* (New York: Scribner, Welford, and Co., 1870), pp. 43–58.
4. Ibid., p. 44.
5. Ibid., p. 46.
6. Ibid., pp. 56–58.
7. *The European Standard*, 19 April 1994.
8. Brewster, p. 44.
9. Theodore Roosevelt, *Foes of Our Own Household* (New York: Scribners, 1926), p. 132.
10. Ibid.
11. Ibid.
12. Ibid., pp. 132–133.
13. Evan Davis, *Our Greatest President: The Life and Letters of George Washington* (New York: Bedford, 1891), p. 366.
14. John Gilliam, *I Do Solemnly Swear: The Place of Public Oaths in American Life and Culture* (Cleveland, OH: Carter-Hone Theological Institute, 1951), p. 67.
15. Jimmy Carter, *Keeping Faith* (New York: Bantam, 1982), p. 20.
16. Gilliam, pp. 114–121.
17. *Litteratae* XLI:449; *Homilies* XI:420; *Marcion Agnostes* IV:410; *De Principis* III:305; *Commentaries* XIV:343; *Letters* IV:48; *Communio Viatorum* 12:4.
18. *Metropolitan Tabernacle Pulpit* 1557:505–16.
19. C. E. B. Cranfield, *Commenting on the Commentators* (Edinburgh: University Press, 1955), p. 239.
20. James Carter Braxton, *Gouverneur Morris* (Charleston, SC: Braden-Lowell Press, 1911), p. 101.
21. Hans Bruchner, *The Dawning of Darkness: An Eyewitness Account of the Soviet Debacle* (Los Angeles: Freedom's Light, 1959), p. 97.
22. Ibid., p. 99.
23. Charles Spurgeon, *The Quotable Spurgeon* (London: Gwenndel, 1966), p. 56.
24. Fernanda Eberstadt, *Isaac and His Devils* (New York: Viking, 1990), p. 89.
25. John W. Whitehead, *The Separation Illusion* (Milford, MI: Mott Media, 1977), p. 21.
26. Shorter Catechism, 1:1.
27. George Washington, *Programs and Papers* (Washington, DC: Washington Bicentennial Committee, 1932), p. 33.
28. Daniel Wise, *Vanquished Victors* (New York: Nelson and Phillips, 1876), p. 78.
29. J. C. Ryle, *Christian Leaders of the Eighteenth Century* (Edinburgh, UK: Banner of Truth Trust, 1978), p. 15.
30. Ibid., p. 18.
31. Ibid., p. 15.
32. Ibid.
33. Albert Collins, *The Foundations of Romanticism in English Letters* (London: Green and Tottenham, 1926), p. 77.

Chapter 2

1. Francis Schaeffer, *A Christian Manifesto* (Wheaton, IL: Crossway, 1981), p. 17.

2. Ibid.

3. Ibid.

4. E. F. Schumacher, *Small Is Beautiful* (New York: Harper and Row, 1975), p. 52.

5. Alvin Toffler, *Future Shock* (New York: Bantam, 1971), p. 158.

6. Schumacher, p. 52.

7. James Sire, *How to Read Slowly* (Wheaton, IL: Harold Shaw, 1978), pp. 14–15.

8. Oswald Chambers, *Biblical Ethics* (Ft. Washington, PA: Christian Literature Crusade, 1964), p. 35.

9. John Calvin, *Golden Booklet of the True Christian Life* (Grand Rapids, MI: Baker, 1952), p. 26.

10. Harold Latternic, *Spurgeon and Society* (London: New Baptist Union, 1981), p. 33.

11. Fred Lybrand, *Heavenly Citizenship* (Shippensburg, PA: Treasure House, 1993), p. 130.

12. Ibid., p. 129.

13. Francis Schaeffer, *The Great Evangelical Disaster* (Wheaton, IL: Crossway, 1983), p. 11.

14. Ibid., p. 39.

15. Harold G. Lee, *Henrico Parish* (Richmond, VA: Landmark, 1978), p. 11.

16. Ibid.

17. Ibid., p. 12.

18. Ibid.

19. Michael Scott Horton, *Beyond Culture Wars* (Chicago, IL: Moody Press, 1994), p. 263.

Chapter 3

1. George Grant, *The 57% Solution* (Franklin, TN: Adroit Press, 1993), p. 60.

2. G. K. Chesterton, *G. F. Watts* (New York: E.P. Dutton, 1901), p. 110.

3. Eric Vogelin, *Omnibus* (Jackson, MS: The Southern Company, 1969), p. 23.

4. Ibid., p. 45.

5. Michael Franz, *Eric Voegelin and the Politics of Spiritual Revolt* (Baton Rouge, LA: Louisana State University Press, 1992), pp. 5–6.

6. Horton Kael and William Loomis, *A Documentary History of Liberal Thought* (New York: M. H. Cushman, 1956), p. 246.

7. Ibid.

8. Ibid, p. 228.

9. Ibid.

10. Ibid, p. 331.

11. Francis Schaeffer, *Reclaiming the World* (Mechanicsburg, MI: Gospel Films, 1982), p. 133.

12. Bernard Laslo, *A Christian's Holiness* (London: Gospel Colporterage Society, 1929), p. 19.

13. Ibid.

14. Ibid.

15. John MacArthur, *The Gospel According to Jesus* (Grand Rapids, MI: Zondervan, 1988), p. 21.

16. Ibid.

17. J. C. Ryle, *Holiness* (Grand Rapids, MI: Baker, 1979), p. 57.

18. George Whitefield, The Journals (Carlyle, PA: Banner of Truth Trust, 1977), p. 324.

19. Jonathan Edwards, *Works* (Edinburgh, UK: Banner of Truth, 1979), p. 237.

20. William Dougherty, *Animosity Toward the Future* (New York: Carson and Lowe, 1981), p. 246.

21. Ibid.

22. Thomas Paine, *Common Sense* (New York: Bartlet and Caine, 1991), p. 14.

23. Karl Temple, ed., *Documentary History of America* (New York: Thompson and Evans, 1977), p. 33.

24. Ibid.

25. Ibid.

26. Ibid.

27. *Christian History*, XII: 2.

28. *Christian History*, XII: 2.

29. John Cullen Morrison, *The Great Evangelists of the Eighteenth Century* (London: Gambel and Price, 1958), p. 153.

30. James Allen Grant, *George Whitefield in Scotland* (Edinburgh, UK: MacDonald, Kleeve, and Furrows: 1979), p. 88.

31. Ibid.

32. *Christian History*, XII: 2.

33. Undoubtedly there were a great many innovative evangelists both before and after Whitefield who contributed to modern evangelistic methodology and practice, but Whitefield stands out in innumerable ways. See J. C. Ryle, *Christian Leaders of the Eighteenth Century* (Edinburgh, UK: Banner of Truth Trust, 1978).

34. Again, a great number of notables contributed to the flowering of the Great Awakening. But none more significantly than Whitefield. See John Pollock, *George Whitefield and the Great Awakening* (Tring, UK: Lion, 1972).

35. Though John and Charles Wesley are today known as the founders of Methodism, it was Whitefield who actually enticed them to join his fledgling movement. See Arnold Dallimore, *George Whitefield* (Wheaton, IL: Crossway Books, 1990).

36. The connection between the ideas of Christian liberty exposited by Whitefield and the ideas of political liberty expounded by the Founding Fathers has been ably explored in numerous scholarly works. See Ellis Sandoz, *Political Sermons of the American Founding Era* (Indianapolis, IN: Liberty, 1991).

37. Carl Vrestead, *Whitefield* (London: Empire Bible Association, 1936), p. 44.

38. Ibid.

39. Ibid.

40. Ibid., p. 45.

41. Ibid.

42. Ibid.

43. Ibid., p. 90.

44. Ibid.

45. Dallimore, *George Whitefield*, p. 136.

46. Vrestead, *Whitefield*, p. 91.
47. Christian History, XII: 2.
48. Ibid.
49. Ibid.
50. Ibid.
51. Ibid.
52. Oxford Archaeological Society, LXXX: 44.

Chapter 4

1. Martyn Lloyd-Jones, *The Heart of the Gospel* (Wheaton, IL: Crossway, 1991), p. 62.
2. *The Journal of Invective*, Spring 1992.
3. Ibid., p. 63.
4. Oswald Chambers, *The Best from All His Works* (Nashville, TN: Oliver Nelson, 1989), II:213.
5. John Callio, *Pluralism* (New York: Academia, 1990), p. 6.
6. Ibid.
7. Ibid.
8. Ibid.
9. Os Guinness, *The American Hour* (New York: Free Press, 1993), p. 148.
10. Ibid.
11. Ibid.
12. James Q. Wilson, *The Moral Sense* (New York: Free Press, 1993).
13. William Bennett, *The De-Valuing of America* (New York: Summit, 1992).
14. James Dobson and Gary Bauer, *Children at Risk* (Dallas, TX: Word, 1990).
15. James Davison Hunter, *Culture Wars* (New York: Basic Books, 1991).
16. Carlton Davis, *The American Covenant* (Portsmouth, NH: Heritage, 1978), p. 3.
17. Alexis de Tocqueville, *Democracy in America* (New York: Vintage, 1945), II: 9.
18. Lewis, *Surprised By Joy* (New York: Macmillan, 1970), p. 14.
19. Jerry Kirk, *The Mind Polluters* (Nashville, TN: Thomas Nelson, 1985), pp. 34–35.
20. Reid Carpenter, *Pittsburgh Leadership Foundation* (Pittsburgh, PA: PLF, 1988), p. 19.
21. *Report of the Attorney General* (Nashville, TN: Rutledge Hill, 1986).
22. Walter Evans, *The Bordellos of Nevada* (Reno, NV: Desert Visitor, 1979).
23. *Coral Ridge Impact*, May 1990.
24. Cal Thomas, *Things That Matter Most* (Grand Rapids, MI: Zondervan, 1994).
25. William Bennett, *Index of Leading Cultural Indicators* (New York: Simon and Schuster, 1994).
26. *New York Newsday*, 2 February 1988.
27. Ibid.
28. Ibid.
29. Ibid.
30. George Grant and Mark Horne, *Legislating Immorality* (Chicago, IL: Moody, 1993), pp. 21–47.
31. Ibid., pp. 109–141.
32. Carrington Boggin, *The Rights of Gay People* (New York: Bantam, 1983).
33. *Fort Lauderdale Sun Sentinel*, 14 May 1989.
34. Ibid.

NOTES

35. Norman Dorsen, ed., *Our Endangered Rights* (New York: Pantheon, 1984), p. x.
36. *Christian Observer*, Spring 1988.
37. Robert Goguet, *The Origin of Laws* (New York: John Taylor, 1821), p. 302.
38. Ibid., p. 99.
39. Nathan Villard, *The Founding Era* (New York: Baker, Harbridge, and Wilson, 1958), p. 47.
40. Gardiner Spring, *The Obligations of the World to the Bible* (New York: Taylor and Dodd, 1821), pp. 101–102.
41. Aleksandr Solzhenitsyn, *A Warning to the West* (New York: Harper and Row, 1978), p. 64.
42. Wilson, p. ix.
43. James Carlyle, *Jonathan Edwards* (Edinburgh, UK: Light and Life, 1962), p. 21.
44. Ibid.
45. Ibid.
46. Ibid.
47. Ibid., p. 22.
48. Ibid., p. 23.
49. Ibid.
50. John Gerstner, *The Rational Biblical Theology of Jonathan Edwards* (Powhatan, VA: Berea, 1991), I:20.
51. Ibid.
52. Ibid.
53. Ibid., p. 7.
54. Arthur Eastman, Caesar Blake, et al., eds., *The Norton Reader: An Anthology of Expository Prose* (New York: Norton, 1965), p. 1108.
55. Garland Ferry, *Basic Hermeneutics* (Philadelphia: American Reformed Convention, 1929), p. 162.
56. Jonathan Edwards, *Sinners in the Hands of an Angry God* (Phillipsburg, NJ: Presbyterian and Reformed, 1992), p. 3.
57. Gerstner, *The Rational Biblical Theology of Johathan Edwards*, p. 6.
58. Ibid., p. 14.
59. Ibid., p. 4.
60. Ibid.
61. Ibid., p. 5.
62. Ferry, p. 162–163.
63. John Gerstner, *Repent Or Perish* (Ligonier, PA: Soli Deo Gloria, 1990), pp. 27–29.
64. Ibid.
65. Ibid.
66. Ibid., p. 11.
67. Carlyle, p. 14.
68. Ibid.
69. Ibid.
70. Perry Miller, *The New England Polity* (Boston: O'Roarke and Fellis, 1966), p. 88.
71. *Eklesia* XV: 231.
72. Jonathan Edwards, *Sinners in the Hands of an Angry God* (Phillipsburg, NJ: Presbyterian and Reformed, 1993), p. 5.

73. J. I. Packer, *God Has Spoken* (Downers Grove, IL: IVP, 1979).

74. A. W. Tozer, *The Old Cross and the New* (Gary, IN: Alliance, 1961), p. 4.

75. Ibid.

76. Ibid.

77. G. K. Chesterton, *Omnibus* (Sheed and Ward, 1938), p. 149.

Chapter 5

1. *Houston Chronicle*, 18 May 1986; *Forbes*, 14 September 1992; *Forbes*, 9 September 1993; *Wall Street Journal*, 16 April 1992; Harvey Mackay, *Swim with the Sharks* (William Morrow, 1988), p. 1.

2. Chuck Colson and Jack Eckerd, *Why America Doesn't Work* (Dallas, TX: Word, 1991), p. 168.

3. George Gilder, *The Spirit of Enterprise* (New York: Simon and Schuster, 1984); Michael Gerber, *Power Point* (New York: HarperCollins, 1991); Tom Peters, *Thriving on Chaos* (New York: Knopf, 1987); Stephen Covey, Roger Merrill, and Rebecca Merrill, *First Things First* (New York: Simon and Schuster, 1994).

4. Bill Clinton and Al Gore, *Putting People First* (New York: Times, 1992); Ross Perot, *United We Stand* (New York: Hyperion, 1992); Bill Clinton, *The President's Health Security Plan* (New York: Times, 1993).

5. Faith in God is personal and objective. Faith in faith is impersonal and subjective. Faith in God transcends self-interest and self-fulfillment. Faith in faith descends into self-reliance and self-assurance. Faith in God is a belief in Someone who has revealed Himself to man "at many times and in various ways" (Hebrews 1:1). Faith in faith is simply "a belief" in something or anything (James 2:19).

6. James 1:1; 2 Peter 1:1; Colossians 4:12; 2 Timothy 2:24; Psalm 105:42; Nehemiah 9:14; Psalm 89:3; Romans 6:20.

7. George Grant, *Bringing in the Sheaves: Transforming Poverty into Productivity* (Brentwood, TN: Wolgemuth and Hyatt, 1985).

8. George Grant, *Third Time Around* (Brentwood, TN: Wolgemuth and Hyatt, 1990).

9. John Dillenberger, ed., *Martin Luther* (New York: Doubleday, 1961), p. 18.

10. *Confessions* XVIII:2.

11. Terra Ecalivat, VI: 82

12. George H. Neville, *Good Works* (Edinburgh, UK: McGavock, 1956), p. 202.

13. Ibid.

14. Henry Cabot Lodge and Theodore Roosevelt, *Hero Tales from American History* (New York: Century, 1895), p. 5.

15. Ibid.

16. Ibid., p. 6.

17. Henry Lee, *Memoirs* (Richmond, VA: Norfolk Isle, 1852), p. 124.

18. Lodge, p. 9.

19. B. L. Cartwright, *Washington* (Boston: Little, Brown, 1924), p. 166.

20. Ibid.

21. Ibid.

22. Ibid.

23. Edward Hickman, ed., *Works* (Edinburgh, UK: Banner of Truth, 1979), II: 237.

NOTES

24. The following list is by no means comprehensive, but it may provide you with a good starting place for personal study:

Exodus 22:25	Leviticus 19:10	Leviticus 23:22
Leviticus 25:35–37	Numbers 18:24	Deuteronomy 14:29
Deuteronomy 15:1–2	Deuteronomy 24:19–21	Ruth 2:1–23
Ruth 4:1–12	Psalm 41:1–3	Proverbs 11:25
Proverbs 14:21	Proverbs 14:31	Proverbs 17:5
Proverbs 21:13	Proverbs 22:9	Proverbs 28:27
Proverbs 29:7	Proverbs 31:8–9	Isaiah 1:10–17
Isaiah 10:1–2	Isaiah 32:6–8	Isaiah 58:1–12
Amos 5:1–27	Matthew 5:16	Matthew 7:12
Matthew 10:8	Matthew 25:31–46	Mark 12:44
Luke 3:11	Luke 6:38	Luke 9:48
Luke 10:30–37	Luke 11:41	Luke 12:33–34
Acts 20:35	Romans 12:8–20	2 Corinthians 1:3–4
2 Corinthians 8:1–24	2 Corinthians 9:7	Galatians 5:6
Galatians 6:2	Galatians 6:9–10	Ephesians 5:2
Ephesians 2:8–10	2 Thessalonians 3:6–10	1 Timothy 5:8
1 Timothy 6:18–19	Titus 2:11–14	Titus 3:1
Titus 3:8	Titus 3:14	Hebrews 13:16
James 2:14–26	1 John 3:17	

Chapter 6

1. E. M. Bounds, *Prayer for the Day* (Atlanta: Lockerbie and Laudin, 1936), p. xiii.
2. James Blackburn, *Persecution Today* (New York: The National Bible Society, 1990), p. 18.
3. Ibid.
4. Ibid.
5. Ibid.
6. Bounds, *Prayer for the Day*, p. xiv.
7. Ibid.
8. Ibid.
9. Ibid.
10. *Walt Kelley's Pogo Letter*, Spring 1994.
11. Kenneth Meyers, *All God's Children Wear Blue Suede Shoes* (Wheaton, IL: Crossway, 1989), p.xi.
12. Neil Postman, *Amusing Ourselves to Death* (New York: Penguin, 1985), p. 115.
13. *World*, 14 May 1992.
14. Eugene Peterson, *A Long Obedience in the Same Direction* (Downers Grove, IL: IVP, 1986).
15. David Wells, *No Place for Truth* (Grand Rapids, MI: Eerdmans, 1993).
16. *Breakpoint*, May 1994.
17. John Gerstner, *Wrongly Dividing the Word of Truth* (Brentwood, TN: Wolgemuth and Hyatt, 1991), p. ix.
18. Dave Hunt and T. A. McMahon, *The Seduction of Christianity* (Eugene, OR: Harvest, 1985), p. 20.
19. George Barna, *The Frog in the Kettle* (Ventura, CA: Regal, 1990), p. 7.

20. John White, *Flirting with the World* (Wheaton, IL: Harold Shaw, 1982).
21. Gerstner, p. 263.
22. *The Horse's Mouth*, April 1994.
23. Hunt and McMahon, p. 11.
24. Gary DeMar and Peter Leithart, *The Reduction of Christianity* (Atlanta, GA: American Vision, 1988).
25. John MacArthur, *Ashamed of the Gospel* (Wheaton, IL: Crossway, 1993).
26. White, p. 9.
27. Peter Kreeft, *Back to Virtue* (San Francisco: Ignatius, 1986), p. 19.
28. *World*, 7 May 1994.
29. Hugh Latimer, *Sermons Before King Edward VI* (Philadelphia, PA: North Valley, 1897), p. 184.
30. Richard Steele, *The Tradesman's Calling* (Hartford, CT: Mills, 1903), pp. 14–15.
31. Martin Luther, *The Estate of Marriage* (St. Louis, MO: Lutheran Educational Foundation, 1969), p. 84.
32. Hyksos Pappas, *Cotton Mather* (New York: Athena, 1926), p. 67.
33. William Tyndale, *Parable of the Wicked Mammon* (Toronto: Knox, 1961, p. 140.
34. John Calvin, *New Testament Commentaries* (Grand Rapids, MI: Eerdmans, 1972), III: 88
35. Benjamin Tatar, *Luther and the Work Ethic* (Glasgow, UK: St. Anthony's, 1949), p. 34.
36. Gleanings, March 1986.
37. Langdon Lowe, *The Work of God in the South* (London: Murray, Stockbrough, and Wilson, 1896), p. 38.
38. John Bunyan, *Pilgrim's Progress* (New York: Penguin, 1965), p. 51.
39. Ibid., p. 27.
40. Francis Schaeffer, *The Great Evangelical Disaster* (Wheaton, IL: Crossway, 1983), p. 37.
41. Ibid., p. 51.
42. *Tennessee Education Review*, July 1993.

Chapter 7

1. *Eklesia* XX:43.
2. *Christian History*, XIII:1.
3. Ibid.
4. Ibid.
5. Barrett Wendell, *Cotton Mather* (New York: Barnes and Noble, 1992), pp. 154–163.
6. Garland Beecher Ford, *The Early Puritan Synthesis* (Boston: Holliman and Hertz, 1949), p. 34.
7. Ibid.
8. Ibid., p. 196.
9. *Confessions* II:1–2.
10. Ibid.
11. Ibid.

12. Thomas Johnson, *The Life and Letters of Benjamin Palmer* (Edinburgh, UK: Banner of Truth, 1987), p. 207.

13. Paul Vitz, *Texas Education Review*, March 1990, vol. 7, no. 3.

14. J. C. Ryle, *Discussions* (London: H. and H. Jones, 1928), p. 177.

15. Joseph Aulen, *Sermons* (New York: Trammel, 1956), p. 243.

16. *Eklesia* XX:43.

17. Ibid.

18. Ibid.

19. J. I. Packer, *Knowing God* (Downers Grove, IL: IVP, 1973), p. 29.

20. *Westminster Shorter Catechism*, 1:1.

21. Brendan de Prinster, *The Fear of God* (Johannesburg, South Africa: Kuyperian Tract Society, 1978), p. 34.

22. Ibid., p. 91.

23. Peter Leithart, *The Kingdom and the Power: Recovering the Centrality of the Church* (Phillipsburg, NJ: P&R, 1993), pp. 142–143.

24. Ibid., p. iii.

25. Ford, p. 48.

26. C. S. Lewis, Christian Behavior (New York: Macmillan, 1943), pp. 44–45.

27. Maria L. H. Blumhardt, *Pioneer to Africa* (St. Louis, MO: Wittenburg, 1949), p. 6.

Chapter 8

1. Karen Gascony, *An Anthology of Limericks* (London: Frontline, 1990), p. 34.

2. Ibid., p. 71.

3. Louis Untermeyer, ed., *Lots of Limericks* (New York: Bell, 1961), p. 27.

4. Ibid., p. 23.

5. Nye, p. 88.

6. Russell Thom Nye, *Edward Lear* (Brighton, UK: Alfaeric Mews, 1988), p. 90.

7. Gascony, p. 112.

8. Gascony, p. 64.

9. Ibid., p. 40.

10. Nye, p. 89.

11. Ibid.

12. *The Spectator*, March 5, 1994.

13. Gerard Hellenique, *The Huguenots* (New York: Ypres Press, 1975), p. 177.

14. Nye, p. 89.

15. Ibid., p. 90.

16. Trystram Gylberd, *Collected Verse* (Humble, TX: Vorthos, 1986), p. 45.

17. Basil Konaric, *Synaxarion: Fasting and Liturgy* (Toronto: Orthodox Troparion, 1981), p. 128; Steven Huntington, *Puritan Discipline* (Tulsa, OK: Reformed Baptist, 1973), p. xi; Gordon Darby, *Fasting* (Hargrave, UK: Lightway, 1987), 3; and Arthur Wallis, *God's Chosen Fast* (Eastbourne, UK: Victory, 1969).

18. Darby, pp. 5–9.

19. Ibid.

20. Maria L. H. Blumhardt, *Pioneer to Africa* (St. Louis, MO: Wittenburg, 1949), p. 6.

21. Ken Leighton, *The High Call of Prayer* (Kensington, UK: Victory, 1970), p. 56.

22. Konaric, p. 129.

23. Ibid.

24. E. M. Bounds, *Power Through Prayer* (Grand Rapids, MI: Zondervan, 1962), p. 36.

25. Ibid.

26. Ibid., p. 37.

27. Ibid.

28. E. M. Bounds, *The Possibilities of Prayer* (Old Tappan, NJ: Flemming Revell, 1923), p. 13.

29. Homer W. Hodge, *Anthology* (Atlanta, GA: Gospel Press, 1927), p. 34–35.

30. *The Confession of Faith* (Richmond, VA: John Knox, 1944).

31. David Bullock, *Puritan Piety* (Edinburgh, UK: Kirk House, 1956), p. 103.

32. Gascony, p. 64.

33. Konaric, p. 131.

34. Ibid.

35. Elmer Jansen, *Faith in the White House* (New York: Harlen, 1966), p. 34.

36. Oswald Chambers, *Devotional Notes* (Phoenix: Forthright Productions, 1982) pp. 145–46.

Chapter 9

1. G. K. Chesterton, *Omnibus* (Sheed and Ward, 1938), p. 122.

2. Harvey Colpepper, *Light Unto the Darkness* (London: Bilthieus Publications, 1981), p. 22.

3. Arnold Duffy, *The Reformation* (London: Longworth Press, 1977), p. 97.

4. Hunter Blakely, *Religion in Shoes* (Birmingham, AL: Southern University Press, 1989), p. 146.

5. Ibid.

6. Ibid., p. 190.

7. Ibid., p. 191.

8. Ibid., p. 198.

9. Ibid., p. 88.

Chapter 10

1. George Grant, *Trial and Error: The American Civil Liberties Union and Its Impact on Your Family* (Franklin, TN: Adroit Press, 1993).

2. George Grant, *Grand Illusions: The Legacy of Planned Parenthood* (Franklin, TN: Adroit Press, 1992).

3. George Grant, *The Family Under Siege: What the New Social Engineers Have in Mind for You and Your Children* (Minneapolis, MN: Bethany, 1994).

4. G. K. Chesterton, *What's Wrong With the World* (New York: Dodd Mead, 1910), p. 1.

5. C. S. Lewis, *Mere Christianity* (New York: Macmillan, 1952).

6. John Stott, *Basic Christianity* (Downers Grove, IL: IVP, 1971).

7. William Wilberforce, *Real Christianity* (Portland, OR: Multnomah, 1982).

8. H. Lyndon Kilmer, *Helen Keller* (New York: Skillen and Fortas, 1964), p. 164.

Printed in the USA
CPSIA information can be obtained
at www.ICGtesting.com
JSHW012022140824
68134JS00033B/2823